THE EVERYTHING.
GUIDE TO
CUSTOMER ENGAGEMENT

D1540996

Dear Reader,

I'm so glad you picked up a copy of this book. I am honored to be able to share my observations, perspectives, and tips with you about how to effectively engage with your customers.

Customer service and marketing have been personal passions of mine for a number of years. I grew up in a family-owned business, so I had my introduction to customer relations at a very young age. Since that time, I've worked with organizations in a wide range of industries, large and small. One thing I have noticed, though: regardless of industry, size, or geography, there is one constant desire—the need to effectively connect, engage, and retain customers.

Unfortunately, many businesses make missteps in their interactions with customers, most of the time unintentionally. While it can take time and effort to continually engage and delight customers, it's not a difficult or expensive process. It's something that we can and should be doing all of the time.

I hope you'll find some useful tips within these pages and that you'll be able to put them to good use in your business. A happy customer is the best kind of customer!

Linda Pophal

Welcome to the EVERYTHING® Series!

These handy, accessible books give you all you need to tackle a difficult project, gain a new hobby, comprehend a fascinating topic, prepare for an exam, or even brush up on something you learned back in school but have since forgotten.

You can choose to read an Everything® book from cover to cover or just pick out the information you want from our four useful boxes: e-questions, e-facts, e-alerts, and e-ssentials.

We give you everything you need to know on the subject, but throw in a lot of fun stuff along the way, too.

We now have more than 400 Everything® books in print, spanning such wide-ranging categories as weddings, pregnancy, cooking, music instruction, foreign language, crafts, pets, New Age, and so much more. When you're done reading them all, you can finally say you know Everything®!

QUESTION

Answers to common questions

FACT

Important snippets of information

ALERT

Urgent warnings

ESSENTIAL

Quick handy tips

PUBLISHER Karen Cooper

MANAGING EDITOR, EVERYTHING® SERIES Lisa Laing

COPY CHIEF Casey Ebert

ASSISTANT PRODUCTION EDITOR Alex Guarco

ACQUISITIONS EDITOR Lisa Laing

ASSOCIATE DEVELOPMENT EDITOR Eileen Mullan

EVERYTHING® SERIES COVER DESIGNER Erin Alexander

Visit the entire Everything® series at *www.everything.com*

THE EVERYTHING®

GUIDE TO CUSTOMER ENGAGEMENT

Connect with customers to:
Build trust · Foster loyalty · Grow a successful business

Linda Pophal

Avon, Massachusetts

This book is dedicated to all those business owners out there who are committed to making positive and effective connections with their customers. The fact that you're reading this book suggests that you're already doing a great job!

An Everything® Series Book.
Everything® and everything.com® are registered trademarks of F+W Media, Inc.

Published by
Adams Media, a division of F+W Media, Inc.
57 Littlefield Street, Avon, MA 02322. U.S.A.
www.adamsmedia.com

ISBN 10: 1-4405-8055-3
ISBN 13: 978-1-4405-8055-0
eISBN 10: 1-4405-8056-1
eISBN 13: 978-1-4405-8056-7

Printed in the United States of America.

10   9   8   7   6   5   4   3   2   1

Library of Congress Cataloging-in-Publication Data

Pophal, Linda.
   The everything guide to customer engagement / Linda Pophal.
      pages cm. -- (An everything series book)
   Includes index.
   ISBN-13: 978-1-4405-8055-0 (pb)
   ISBN-10: 1-4405-8055-3 (pb)
   ISBN-13: 978-1-4405-8056-7 (ebook)
   ISBN-10: 1-4405-8056-1 (ebook)
   1. Customer relations. 2. Customer services. I. Title.
   HF5415.5.P67 2014
   658.8'12--dc23

                    2014014158

Cover images © vanatchanan/123RF; iStockphoto.com/Alex Belomlinsky/browndogstudios.

This book is available at quantity discounts for bulk purchases.
For information, please call 1-800-289-0963.

Contents

Acknowledgments

No work effort is ever done alone, and that was certainly the case with this book. I want to thank my agent, Bob Diforio, for making this project possible, and Adams Media managing editor Lisa Laing for choosing me to write this book. I also want to thank Adams Media development editor Eileen Mullan and copyeditor Kate Petrella for their attention to detail and helpful advice.

Special thanks to Rachel Vick, mass communication, PR, and mulitmedia student at the University of Wisconsin–Eau Claire. Rachel helped draft content, conduct interviews and research, and format the book for publication. I literally could not have done this without her help!

Thanks also to my son, Justin Grensing, who helps me often with projects like this. His research and writing skills are exceptional, but most of all I appreciate the opportunity to stay connected with him now that he's an adult and off pursuing his own interests.

And, of course, thanks to my husband, Dave, who has become very adept at online search, is a good sounding board, and is never too busy to bring food and beverages to keep me going!

This was a fun project, but wouldn't have been possible without a group effort. Thank you!

Top Ten Ways to Connect with Your Customers in the Twenty-First Century

1. Websites. Your website is an important tool whether you're a traditional brick-and-mortar business or you conduct business online. In fact, in many cases, if you don't have a website, you virtually don't exist (pun intended).

2. Blogs. A blog can provide you with an opportunity to stay engaged with your customers while providing them useful information.

3. Video and visual images. Video and visual images are hot in the twenty-first century. Tools like YouTube, Pinterest, Instagram, and others have taken the world by storm. And, as we all know, a picture truly is worth a thousand words.

4. Social media. Regardless of the demographics of your audience, chances are there's at least one social media tool that can help you connect with them.

5. Online communities. Whether interacting through social media communities on platforms like LinkedIn or Google+, gathering a group of like-minded people with shared interests in online forums can be a great way to stay engaged.

6. Research. Ongoing research through a variety of channels can help you stay on top of the things that matter most to your customers so that you can continually make improvements to keep them engaged and loyal.

7. The media. Don't overlook the media as an important way to keep your name in front of your key audiences.

8. Service recovery. When you mess up, as you will, service recovery can help turn a dissatisfied customer into a loyal fan. But you need to respond quickly, sincerely, and effectively.

9. Follow-up. When customers interact with you, take the time to follow up with them. A thank-you means a lot in any century.

10. Face-to-face interaction! Despite the proliferation of technology and online means of communication, nothing beats good old face-to-face connections with your customers.

Introduction

IN THE TWENTY-FIRST CENTURY, customers rule! This isn't to say that customers haven't always been important. Of course they have. But as the world has morphed from a focus on farming to a focus on manufacturing, and then to service, and now to an emerging focus on technology as a product and service enabler, the ability to successfully engage with customers is more important than ever before.

While customers in the nineteenth and even twentieth centuries might have been limited in their product and service choices, today they have the ability to purchase goods and services from around the world. Still, though, they are increasingly fickle. Customers today won't be slowed down. If you don't have what they're looking for, they'll look somewhere else. If you don't provide high-quality products or services, they'll consider other options. If you don't provide exceptional service, they'll find another company that will. And if you don't demonstrate that their continued business and goodwill matters to you, they'll turn to the many other suppliers they have to choose from.

This book explores the importance of, and opportunities in, customer engagement for companies in any industry, whether focused on product or service, B2B or B2C. You will learn why customers matter, and how to consider your customer base strategically. You'll learn how to analyze and understand customers and how to position goods or services alongside competitive offerings.

You will also gain insights into both traditional and new media forms of communication, helping you understand this world of ever-expanding communication offerings. In addition, you'll learn how marketers can gather useful insights and inputs from various audiences and how these insights can be incorporated into your marketing planning and business practices.

From traditional business development to social media engagement, this book will offer best practice insights, tips, and examples to help business owners better connect with their audiences.

It will help you explore the opportunities and options in online technology and communication forums, and look at practical implications as well as strategic imperatives. Businesses no longer need to expend significant amounts of time and money to effectively engage with their audiences. Today's wide array of communication channels means that businesses, however small, can effectively position themselves in the minds of their customers against even the largest players.

Today's business owners may be both excited and overwhelmed by the vast array of opportunities to engage with their customers. This book will help you wade through the options, identify those most likely to resonate with your audiences, and learn methods of engagement that have proven to be effective in both traditional and new media environments.

Ultimately, for any business, it always has been and always will be about the customer. While the tools for reaching customers may change, the basic principles remain the same. Those businesses that take the time to thoroughly understand their customers, engage in authentic two-way conversations fueled by input from various channels, and act on those inputs to deliver increasingly higher levels of satisfaction will be the businesses that excel in the twenty-first-century marketplace.

What are you waiting for? It's time to engage!

CHAPTER 1

The Basics of Customer Engagement

Good companies know that the ability to engage customers is one of the most important aspects of running a successful business. Customer engagement is the process of connecting with customers in meaningful ways. Decades ago these interactions took place most frequently face-to-face, across counters in corner stores. Today they still take place face-to-face, but technology has expanded the opportunities for connecting significantly. Every company, whether it provides goods or services, is for-profit or not-for-profit, and regardless of the industry or geography it serves, benefits from the ability to attract and retain customers.

Small Businesses and Customer Engagement

Research about the percentage of new businesses that fail each year, or within a certain period of time after the business launches, is widespread. The Small Business Administration, for instance, indicates that more than half of all new businesses fail in their first five years.

Why? The reasons are many, but generally boil down to a company's failure to effectively engage with consumers. Engaging with customers is, after all, what business is all about. Some of the "big rocks," or most important issues, in this area are:

- **Going into business for you, rather than for them.** The bottom line is that regardless of what type of business you're going into, you have to have a market—you have to have a clearly defined group of people who are likely to want what it is you have to sell.
- **Not knowing what it is your customers are buying.** You may know what you're selling, but you may not know what your potential customers are buying. These two things are not always the same. As entrepreneur Victor Kiam, president and CEO of Remington Products, famously understood, he may have been selling a razor, but his customers were buying a smooth shave.
- **Failing to read the tea leaves.** Many businesspeople who ultimately fail in their efforts will shake their heads and lament that they "just don't know what happened." Other, more insightful businesspeople will admit that they ignored a number of warning signs along the way, like new competition, a decline in number of customers, indications of customer dissatisfaction, etc.
- **Undercapitalizing.** As the old saying goes, "you have to spend money to make money." Often undercapitalization is exhibited through lack of focus on two key areas—employees and marketing. Your employees have a direct impact on how your business is perceived; if you underpay or make quick decisions here, you'll likely regret it later. Even small businesses need to be competitive, especially businesses in service industries where employees *are* the product. These interactions matter. Hiring the most skilled and capable staff members you can afford reflects, ultimately, on you. Similarly, your marketing efforts need to be designed to make your target audiences aware of what

you have to offer and informed about the reasons why what you have to offer is better than other alternatives.

- **Ignoring the competition.** You will have competition. In fact, the better your product or idea, the more likely you will have competition—and quickly. Ignore the competition at your own peril. To succeed long-term you need to be continually updating, upgrading, and reinventing what you have to offer.
- **Cutting corners.** Particularly during tough economic times it can be tempting to "cut back." Many businesses feel that they're cutting back on the little things, but sometimes those little things can make a big difference. It can be difficult to see the value that customers place on some of the value-added attributes they enjoy as they interact with the businesses they frequent—the exceptional service, the no-questions-asked guarantee, the free shipping. Difficult, that is, until those little things are taken away. Then it becomes quickly apparent.

Ask ten people to define "small business" and you'll likely receive ten different answers. The U.S. Government's Small Business Administration (SBA) defines a small business as any business that is "independently owned and operated, is organized for profit, and is not dominant in its field."

- **Losing interest.** You've probably interacted with businesses that seem to lose their energy and enthusiasm over time. Their products become stale and outdated. Their service becomes ho-hum. Their marketing materials become irrelevant. Their employees—even their owners—become complacent and out of touch.
- **Losing touch.** Does anybody use a typewriter anymore? Who owns a VHS machine? And whatever happened to Borders? There are examples all around us, stemming back for decades, of successful businesses that failed to identify and respond to disruptive innovation that threatened their livelihood. On the other hand, there are also examples of businesses that have been around for hundreds of years: CIGNA (insurance company) since 1792, Old Farmer's Almanac since

1792, Jim Beam since 1795, DuPont since 1802. The fact that these companies are still in business suggests that they've found a way to remain relevant, to defy the competition and, importantly, to continue to meet the always changing needs of the markets they're serving.

These are just the tip of the iceberg when it comes to the issues that large and small companies face as they attempt to remain relevant and valued by the markets they serve. When you think about the "best of the best" and the "worst of the worst," which names come to mind? And, if you were to arrange these companies or products along a continuum, where would yours fall?

The Evolution of the Customer

Customers are the basis of success for pretty much every business, of every kind, everywhere in the world. Without them businesses literally could not exist. The exchange of goods and services for something of value has fueled the economy for centuries. According to Etymonline.com, the term "customer" originated in the late Middle Ages from the term "customs official," and originally broadly referred to "a person with whom one has dealings." Therefore, in a sense, both a buyer and a seller could be seen as a "customer" based on this early definition.

Going back throughout history, there have always been "customers." For example, food, raw materials, and other basic items were often traded for prized luxury items, such as obsidian (volcanic glass) in the Ancient Near East, according to ArchAtlas.org. In this sense, ancient peoples trading basic goods were essentially both proprietor and customer. Possessors of obsidian were customers for other goods, but also proprietors who "sold" obsidian to their customers.

Trade was a natural progression from a time of self-sufficiency, when humans barely hunted or produced enough food to survive, to a time when agriculture allowed for a surplus of goods that could be bartered with other humans. Currency has also evolved, yet its remnants remain part of our business culture. For instance, salt was used as an early form of currency, given its relatively limited availability. In fact, according to SaltWorks.us, the word "salary" has its origins in the Roman word for salt rations given to Roman soldiers—*salarium argentum*.

As the economy in the United States has changed from agrarian, or farming-centric, to manufacturing, then to service, and now to technology-driven, or e-commerce, one thing has remained constant: the critical role that the customer plays.

QUESTION

What are business touchpoints and why are they important?
A touchpoint is basically any place or situation in which you have direct interaction with customers. This could be the cashier who rings up customers' purchases or the customer service rep who works the phones at a call center. It could also be the spokesperson in your Internet, TV, or radio ads. Touchpoints should be the primary focus of customer service. Every interaction you have with a customer, or they have with you, matters.

Yet some companies *do* ignore customers or, at a minimum, take them for granted. As a consumer yourself, you can probably think of any number of businesses you have interacted with that did not pay enough attention to you or your needs. What have you done when you've encountered those companies? If faced with readily available and comparable alternatives to what they had to offer, chances are you decided to take your business elsewhere.

That's what customers do. That's what *your* customers will do if you fail to engage them.

Big Business Icons

Fortunately, small businesses can take many cues from big business icons that have become known for exceptional customer service and effective customer engagement. Names like Zappos, Southwest Airlines, and Nordstrom come to mind. What are their customer engagement philosophies? Here are some examples of what they say about themselves:

- **Nordstrom:** "An unerring eye for what's next in fashion. A relentless drive to exceed expectations. For more than 100 years, Nordstrom has worked to deliver the best possible shopping experience, helping customers possess style—not just buy fashion . . . Since 1901, we've been committed to providing our customers with the best possible service—and to improving it every day."
- **Zappos:** "We've been asked by a lot of people how we've grown so quickly, and the answer is actually really simple . . . We've aligned the entire organization around one mission: to provide the best customer service possible. Internally, we call this our WOW philosophy."
- **Southwest Airlines:** "The mission of Southwest Airlines is dedication to the highest quality of Customer Service delivered with a sense of warmth, friendliness, individual price and Company Spirit."

What do all of these statements have in common? A strong focus on customers and how they are valued by the organization. Yet, look at any company's self-declarations and you're likely to see the same commitment to the customer.

ESSENTIAL

Learning from business failures can be just as instructive as learning from success stories, if not more so. In recent years some top companies like Borders, Compaq, Woolworth's, General Foods, and TWA—among others—simply went away. There's much to be learned about what they did, or didn't do, that led to their demise. The failures of others can help you cement your own future success. There are ample opportunities these days to connect with others or learn about their experiences through online chat rooms or forums, trade journals, social media sites, etc. Being attuned to what's happening both in your own industry and in the overall business environment can help you spot both potential barriers and new opportunities.

In 2013, *Business Insider* published a piece about the fifteen worst companies for customer service. Let's take a look at how some of these companies speak about their commitment to customers:

- **Long Island Power Authority** is first on the list, having come under criticism for its performance during Hurricane Sandy. What does the company say about its commitment to customers? Well, nothing anymore—as of January 1, 2014, Long Island has a new electric company managed by Public Service Electric and Gas Company (PSE&G).
- **Northeast Utilities** is second on the list (power companies seem to be taking a beating!). That company also was impacted by outages created by a hurricane—Hurricane Irene—some of which lasted for two weeks. While the utility still exists, the CEO of its subsidiary Connecticut Light and Power was replaced. Its stated mission: "One company, focused on delivering reliable energy and superior customer service."
- **Charter Communications**, another utility company, but in the communication realm, shows up third on this list. In fact, it's been on the list for more than a decade! The president and CEO's statement on the company website's "About Us" page may be particularly telling: "We, at our core, are a service organization. And every product we sell has a huge service component."

The rest of the list includes Comcast, Facebook, United Airlines, Time Warner Cable, LinkedIn, Cox Communications, American Airlines, Twitter, US Airways, Delta, CenturyLink, and Bank of America. So, despite the fact that many of these organizations espouse a strong commitment to customers and customer service, their customers seem to have a different perspective.

ALERT

Don't be too quick to change your business model. Small business owners can be understandably impatient to generate the results that will ensure their success. But don't be in a hurry to give up on what might be a good thing just because you don't see results materialize immediately. Consider that many companies have taken years to find the "sweet spot" in terms of effectively connecting with customers. Listen, learn, and make modifications—but don't give up too early!

What does that suggest? It suggests that effective customer engagement is about more than simply *saying* customers matter. It doesn't really matter if you say that you are "focused on delivering exceptional customer service." It's about *proving* through words and actions that you can *actually deliver* on these promises.

What Engagement Means

What does engagement mean? The answer is not as straightforward as you might think. It can be instructive to start with what engagement does *not* mean. Do thousands of Facebook fans signify engagement? Do hundreds of Twitter retweets reflect engagement? Does a high Google ranking mean that your audience is highly engaged with you?

No. While each of these metrics can be useful, they do not in and of themselves reflect engagement. What does? Really, two things: continued business and positive word of mouth.

Engagement and the Small Business

In many ways, small businesses have an advantage when it comes to customer engagement. Their size means that there are fewer "moving parts" to manage. Consider the complexity that Zappos faces in continuing to maintain its positive image among customers and noncustomers. The more employees you have, the more interactions (or "touchpoints") you have, the more communications you have, the more challenging it is to ensure excellence in every interaction.

Small businesses have the advantage of more readily being able to monitor the actions and interactions that their employees have. They are more readily able to provide immediate feedback and course correction, as necessary, when these actions don't live up to expectations. They often (but not always) have a smaller number of customers with whom they need to interact, which means they can get to know their customers more personally—and have more personal interactions with them.

Small businesses have challenges when it comes to engaging customers too, of course.

You have fewer resources at your disposal, and often tighter budgets, so it can be difficult to provide the incentives, perks, and exceptional experiences that larger organizations can provide. Those limited resources may also mean that it will be a challenge to get your name out there so that potential customers can become aware of you and the great things that you are doing.

FACT

It certainly comes as no surprise that not every new business achieves success. But just how many of these start-ups fail? According to Bloomberg, eight out of ten are unsuccessful. That's a significant percentage, and you certainly don't want to be one of those eight! The biggest reason for failure is not being close enough to customers, or potential customers, to fully understand their needs.

Perhaps most challenging for many small businesses is the ability to attract and retain exceptional employees. Employees have a very dramatic impact on customer experiences and perceptions. Small businesses that are not able to compete with the wages and benefits offered by larger organizations are certainly at a disadvantage here.

Still, despite these drawbacks, there are some small businesses that have made a name for themselves by effectively engaging with customers and providing the kind of service and experience that leads to repeat business, positive word of mouth, and a healthy bottom line.

Why Engagement Matters

Why does customer engagement matter? The simple answer, of course, is that without customers businesses literally would not exist. But many businesses, despite poor service that is either ongoing (as is the case with Charter) or situational (Northeast Utilities), continue to slug along. For those—and, in fact, all—businesses, lack of customer engagement can have a number of impacts, some significant, some subtle.

Customer engagement matters to shareholders. PeopleMetrics' "2013 Most Engaging Customer Experiences" study found that retailers who were able to increase customer engagement by just five points saw an increase in share price of 56 percent! Small businesses may not have shareholders—yet—but as your small business grows and potentially may become a large, publicly held organization, the impact of customer engagement on share price should certainly drive continued focus on the customer.

Customer engagement matters to customers. That should be obvious, but all too often it is not. Customers, given comparable alternatives, will not continue to do business with a company that is not effectively meeting their needs. Equally important, if not more so, they will share their negative experiences with others.

Consequently, customer engagement matters to your target market at large. These are potential customers who have never engaged with you and may have never yet heard of you! Why does customer engagement matter to customers you don't even have yet? Because when they do hear of you, do you want it to be from one of your customers who has great things to say or one who has been consistently underwhelmed? The answer is obvious.

Customer engagement matters to your employees. Do you think employees like working for a company that has disgruntled customers? How many of your employees come to work every day thinking, "Gee, I hope I encounter some crabby customers today!"? Not many. No, employees like to work for companies that are well respected. Consider the droves of applicants that Google receives on an ongoing basis. In fact, even interns clamor to work at Google (and a movie—*The Internship*—was made in 2013 to illustrate this). If you think your employees don't care about the service you provide and how effectively you engage your customers, think again.

ESSENTIAL

Hiring employees who are interested in your products or services is a great way to bolster customer service without having to shell out the kinds of wages and benefits that employees might find in larger businesses. Employees who are interested in their work are more likely to engage with customers and may find nonfinancial value in working for you.

Finally, customer engagement matters to you (or it should). There is so much that you can learn from engaged customers that can help you improve or introduce new products or services. Their input and interactions can be instructive and can lead to innovation and continuous improvement—resulting in a continuous, positive cycle that drives business and a positive bottom line.

Small Business Engagement Rock Stars

One good clue as to which small businesses are rocking it when it comes to providing exceptional customer experiences is the list of small businesses recognized through *Fortune*'s annual Best Small Workplaces awards. In 2013, twenty-five small businesses made the list. Some are little known; others, like Radio Flyer, are iconic:

- Based in Chicago, **Radio Flyer** is a toy company that has been around for almost 100 years (since 1917). A sense of fun permeates the company, from the top down. In fact, the CEO is referred to as "the Chief Wagon Officer." With just sixty employees, the company generates $85 million in revenue annually.
- **Kahler Slater** is an architecture/design firm based in Milwaukee, Wisconsin, where employees are often entertained by leaders dressed in costumes that run the gamut from *Star Trek*–themed to World Wrestling Foundation characters. A pontoon boat—"The Experience"—is available to employees to donate to their favorite charities or nonprofits for use in fundraising events. Or, employees can use the boat for cruises themselves, as long as one of the company's trained "captains" is at the helm.
- With 119 employees, **Ruby Receptionists** is a virtual receptionist service firm dedicated to "WOW-ing" clients. That starts with ensuring that employees are happy and engaged. The company takes part in a wide range of activities—from dress-up days to providing $100 bonuses just for showing up. Known as "Rubys," the receptionists celebrate when they receive client accolades, which is often, and they're encouraged to keep these items of recognition in a "Smile File."

Forbes' definition of "small business" may be a bit lofty for some: its award criteria indicates that the publication considers companies with annual sales under $1 billion to fall into this category. The Small Business

Administration's definition casts a broader brush and includes any business that is "independently owned and operated, is organized for profit, and is not dominant in its field."

ALERT

Don't be fooled by the success of the big-name companies in the *Business Insider* list of the fifteen worst customer service companies. Looking at that list may make you think that it's not that difficult to succeed despite poor customer service. The fact is that most of the companies on the list are essentially monopolies, leaving consumers little to no alternatives. Most businesses aren't in that situation, and fed up customers can easily turn to competitors.

There are both opportunities and challenges in today's business market. Not every business will succeed. Those that do have a good understanding of what it takes to "wow" their customers every time, all of the time.

CHAPTER 2

Who Is Your Customer?

One fundamental question any business should be able to answer is, "Who do you serve?" Everyone you serve is a customer. One misstep that some businesses make (even very large ones) is not thoroughly and specifically identifying those they serve. They cast a wide net and hope to benefit from "anything that sticks." In fact, many new business owners often simply wish to attract whatever customers they can. While that may seem logical, the reality is that the more clearly and specifically you can identify a target group of those you wish to serve, the more successful you will be in connecting with them and compelling them to some desired end result.

Understanding Who You Serve

The basis of success for any business is identifying a target audience that could benefit from what you have to offer them. In some respects, this can be a bit of a chicken-and-egg dilemma. While marketing experts traditionally have suggested that to be successful you must identify a need in the market and then take steps to address that need through a particular product or service, there are plenty of examples of products and services that have achieved success by creating a need that consumers didn't know they had! The personal computer is a primary example of this. Consumers didn't create demand for a personal computer. Instead, the development of this new tool generated demand because of the product's ability to provide value in ways that resonated with the market. The frequent emergence of other new products and services suggests that small businesses can succeed both by identifying and meeting existing needs *and* by creating demand for an innovative new product or service that consumers didn't even realize would benefit them. The Sony Walkman and today's smartphones are great examples of this.

FACT

Just as you may have secondary audiences for your products or services, you need to be constantly on the watch for companies that may see your primary audience as their secondary audience. These are your indirect competitors. For example, eco-friendly cars might appeal to the customer base of a bicycle shop, even though those products and businesses are not in direct competition.

The key to being able to effectively create new, and desired, options for consumers is a thorough understanding of who you serve and what they value, as well as the identification or anticipation of problems that your product or service solution might help to solve. As the old proverb goes, "Necessity is the mother of invention."

For the past few years, Nielsen has been evaluating a wide range of consumer products and selecting the "breakthrough innovation winners" for the year. In 2013 the products on the list included:

- Allegra Allergy
- Colgate Optic White
- Dannon Oikos Greek Yogurt
- Downy UNSTOPABLES in Wash Scent Booster
- Fiber One 90 Calorie Brownies
- Magnum Ice Cream
- Milo's Kitchen Home-Style Dog Treats
- MiO Liquid Water Enhancer
- Monster Rehab Energy Drink
- Reese's Minis
- Skinny Cow Candy
- Sparkling ICE
- Special K Cracker Chips

In some cases, these represent enhanced or improved versions of existing products, known as product extensions. Not all product extensions are successful, of course. Those that are, though, are generally driven by a close understanding of customers' needs, ongoing efforts to engage with and listen to customers to determine what new interests, tastes, or preferences they may have, and the ability to move to market quickly with new product innovations.

Primary and Secondary Audiences

Any company will have both primary and secondary audiences. Primary audiences represent the most obvious, or logical, target for a particular product or service. For instance, a company selling baking supplies might identify a primary market as bakers. But that isn't the only option. A baking supplies firm might also identify its target audience as retailers, or cafeterias, or schools that offer food services programs. There are any number of options and no "right or wrong" answers. It's important to note, though, that the choices you make will drive your future actions.

This illustrates that effective marketing can be both science and art. For instance, you would use very different channels and methods to engage bakers than you would to engage school administrators. Clearly the decisions you make here are very important.

In addition to primary audiences, you will also have secondary audiences. Using the original example in the previous paragraphs, a company offering baking supplies might prioritize the list, resulting in primary targets and secondary audiences that may also hold value. So, in this case, the primary markets might be bakers and retailers; the secondary audiences might be school systems and educators.

In addition to considering the primary and secondary audiences you hope to sell your products and services to, you will also want to consider any intermediaries that might impact your ability to reach the end-user consumer.

The Role of Intermediaries

Intermediaries play a very important role in reaching end-user consumers. A simple example is the intermediary role of parents for the toy industry. While children are technically the primary audience, they may not be the actual decision-maker (although they certainly can exert a lot of influence!). So, while toy companies will want to be very aware of the preferences of their target audience of children, they also need to be aware of the preferences, concerns, and desires of the intervening audience of parents.

Many types of businesses have intermediaries that must be influenced in order to lead to a final purchase decision. Healthcare is an industry that illustrates this well. While patients are the obvious end users, they are influenced by a variety of intermediaries that might include parents (if the patients are minors), insurance providers, employers (who often select insurance coverage that drives patients to specific providers), and physicians, who may make referrals to other physicians.

These intermediaries must also be considered as a very important "customer" group who must be engaged just as much as or, in some cases, to a greater degree than the end-user customer.

New vs. Returning Customers

Customers are the "coin of the realm" for any business. Yet, despite the obvious nature of this statement, it is not uncommon for businesses to seemingly overlook or minimize the importance of their existing customers in favor of going out to seek new customers. New customers are certainly important, and that pipeline of new customers to your business must be continually managed, but ignoring your current customers can be very risky.

Here's an all-too-common example: new-customer incentives. In your quest to build your customer base you offer special discounts or incentives to new customers coming on board. That can be a great strategy and may certainly result in new customers, but what message does this practice send to loyal, existing customers?

For instance, one DISH Network customer posted this in an online forum: "We have been a dish network customer for about 10 years and there are no special perks for us. New customers get a discount in their monthly service and receive a free Hopper or other device. Current customers do not get these incentives. We are currently looking at other options since we are not appreciated when it comes to trying to keep current customers with DISH Network."

This individual is likely not alone in this view. And that's a problem. While offering incentives to drive new customers to your business can work, it must be done thoughtfully to ensure that these efforts don't create a negative impact on existing, loyal customers.

The Lifetime Value of a Customer

Your customers represent obvious value to your business, and it pays to know what that value is. Clearly some customers are more valuable than others—those who spend more with your business, those who require less "time and attention," and those who are strong proponents of what you have to offer. Knowing who they are can help you think strategically about how you will connect with them. This does not mean to suggest that you should not treat *all* of your customers well; obviously you should. However, the amount of effort, time, and money you expend to engage with a customer that represents $100,000 in revenue per year should certainly be more than you would invest in a customer who represents revenue of $100 per year.

Do you currently know what the lifetime value of your customers is? Do you know who your most valuable customers are? Consider a simple example based on a very small business, a management consultancy. The business is owned by an individual proprietor who has been in business for about five years. The business owner currently has twenty clients. Two of these clients bring in about $100,000 each, annually. Five bring in about $20,000 each; the remaining clients are each at about $1,000.

QUESTION

How can you identify potential new markets?
Think about the "pain points" existing consumers face, or that you face yourself. Think about the sources of minor, but widely experienced inconveniences, as well as major societal needs. How much would consumers pay to avoid these headaches? Is there a way your business can address their pain points?

Certainly it is clear that you should do everything you can to retain those top two customers and that some of those customers at the low end of your annual revenue may not provide much value to you—and may keep you from serving the higher-revenue clients. Eyeballing the data may not provide you with the extent of information you need, but there is an actual calculation that you can—and should!—do to specifically determine the lifetime value of each of your customers. It is:

(Average Sale) × (Expected Monthly or Annual Transactions) × (Average Monthly or Annual Retention Time)

To do this calculation you will need to determine the average length of time that most of your customers stay with you, calculate an average sale, and, based on the data you have on current customers, determine the expected annual transactions a typical customer would have with you.

There's a certain amount of guesswork involved here. But doing this calculation can give you some valuable information to help you determine how much effort to put into attracting and retaining a customer and, in some cases, when to let a customer go. Hopefully, it is now apparent to you, if it wasn't already, that your current customers represent significant value to you and that you should be expending as much, if not more, time and effort in attempting to keep them on board as you do in attempting to bring in new customers.

However, the dollar value of a customer only tells part of the picture. Customers represent other costs of providing service, and sometimes those costs may be deemed too significant to maintain.

When to Turn Away Potential New Customers

It may be hard to believe, but not every customer will be a good fit for you. In fact, there may be some potential customers whom you simply choose not to serve. Why? Generally, it's either because you do not have the right product or service to effectively meet their needs or you feel that it might require more time and effort to serve their needs than you are able to, or wish to, provide.

Consider, for example, the $1,000/year clients of the management consultancy firm discussed earlier. Some of those clients may actually consume a great deal of time and energy, which would likely be worth it if you could boost their annual sales volume. So, for instance, if a client is generating $1,000 in revenue, but they are consuming $2,000 worth of time required to serve their needs, you are experiencing a net loss on that account. You might determine that you cannot afford to continue serving these customers.

Tough decisions, yes, but decisions that companies often need to make. In fact, in addition to choosing not to take on a new customer or client, there may also be times when you decide, for very good reason, to "fire" a customer.

When to "Fire" Existing Customers

Sometimes a customer is simply not a good fit. Whether or not a customer is a good fit for your organization generally reflects your ability to serve their needs effectively at a cost you are willing to bear. A customer who is extremely demanding, for instance, and who causes stress or frustration for your staff, or causes you to incur costs above and beyond the value the customer provides to your organization, is a customer you likely cannot afford to retain.

For instance, suppose you operate a PR firm with much of your work focused on attaining media placements for clients, often through interviews with various journalists, reporters, and freelancers. Your contract with one client is based on payment for placement, with premiums applied to big media outlets like the *Wall Street Journal*. Yet, despite your best efforts to get reporters to interview this client, for various reasons the placements never materialize—the client fails to be available at the scheduled time, fails to provide follow-up information, or fails to provide information that these reporters value. To date: no placements, despite quite a bit of effort on your part. Is it time to part ways? Possibly.

ALERT

Sometimes there may be conflicts between the needs of your intermediate audience and the end user. For example, parents might not want their children to eat the sugary foods they crave; insurance companies might not want to offer the expensive but comprehensive healthcare their customers desire. Whether to focus your message on the intermediary or the end user will ultimately depend on the specific dynamic of the relationship.

At a minimum, such a situation would require a "critical conversation" with the client in which you outline the issues that you have been facing and how those issues are impacting your shared objectives of gaining appropriate placements. At this point (and actually at the beginning of any client relationship), you should also determine the amount you can afford to "spend" on retaining a client or customer when the ratio between your costs and the resultant revenue received goes out of balance.

In this case, suppose that placement in a top-tier publication would net you $5,000. Your hourly agency rate is $125. If you've spent more than forty hours attempting to serve this client, you're at a break-even point. Obviously, no business can stay in business if it's not making a profit, so you would have to determine how much margin you need to make on each client to cover your overhead expenses and provide a desired level of profit. Customers or clients not consistently meeting this level of performance are those whom it may be time to "fire."

There may be other "costs" to consider as well. For instance:

- The customer is difficult or abusive to staff or other customers. "Psychic costs" can be a factor as well and may contribute to other costs—for example, the cost of increased turnover among employees who decide to seek employment elsewhere. Such customers may also result in the loss of other customers.
- The customer has a negative impact on your brand. Perhaps you're in the B2B market and you do business with a wide range of businesses, one of which has developed a reputation for unsavory dealings with its own customers. Is this a business that you wish to be associated with?

It's a simple formula really. When should you fire a customer? When the cost of serving that customer becomes greater than the value received. A good best practice is to regularly review your customer list to determine whether the value you are receiving is worth the effort. That can be relatively straightforward if you have a small number of customers whom you know well.

ALERT

When it comes to lost customers, be sure you're making a distinction between gross customers lost and net customers lost. For example, if a new business model causes 50,000 customers to leave your business but brings in 75,000, that's a gross loss of 50,000, but a net *gain* of 25,000. Lost customers need to be thought of in the overall context of the business's changing consumer base.

However, even businesses with large databases can go through this process using technology solutions or applications like customer management systems or Microsoft Excel, among others. For example, you might assign a simple rating system to customers in your database of 1, 2, and 3. Customers with a 1 are great customers and require little attention; customers with a 2 require a moderate amount of attention and so may be assigned a cost of +20 percent. Customers with a 3 are your "challenging customers" and may be assigned a cost of +50 percent. If you've calculated an average cost to serve an average customer, you can apply this add-on percentage, compare the cost to revenue, and determine whether the difference meets your desired margin. If not, it may be time to part ways.

Keep in mind, though, that when "firing" a customer, it is important to distinguish between firing a specific customer and firing a segment of customers. The former is obviously much less costly than the latter. There will always be difficult customers for any business; however, before deciding to fire that customer, think about whether there are specific characteristics about that customer that are the root cause. Are these characteristics shared by other customers? Is there a way to accommodate them?

Learning from "Lost" Customers

Whether you have chosen to part ways or they have left of their own accord, there also is much to be learned from your "lost" customers—those who, for whatever reason, have chosen not to continue doing business with you.

How do you know when a customer is lost? It's not always as easy as you might think! Some organizations, of course, can tell when a customer is no longer a customer. A subscription-based service, for instance, readily knows when people don't renew their subscription or choose to unsubscribe. Other types of businesses, though, can't know that easily when they've lost a customer.

For instance, suppose you own a women's fashion boutique. You've been in business for three years. Your CMS (customer management system) gives you very good information about the sales you've made over these three years, and you can tell when the last purchase was made for any given customer. How, though, do you know when a customer is lost?

If a customer came into your boutique and made a purchase during the first week of business, but has not been back, is that customer lost? If the person came in two years ago but hasn't been back, is that customer lost?

As you see, it can be difficult to determine whether a customer truly is lost. Furthermore, the level of difficulty varies based on the type of product or service you provide. For example:

- How often should you expect a customer to need plumbing services?
- How often should you expect a customer to come into your very upscale restaurant?
- How often will you sell a customer a used car?

The answers to these questions will vary, not only by product or service, but also for each individual business. While you may not be able to tell with 100 percent certainty that a customer is lost, you can put a stake in the ground to establish a time frame of inactivity that might suggest to you that a customer is not coming back.

You may also use the data you have on your customers to help you mathematically define a point at which a customer may be lost. The first step is determining your "active" customers. Do this by looking at the list of customers who have made at least one purchase. Then calculate the greatest length of time between purchases made by a desired percentage of your customers—perhaps 90 percent. If 90 percent of your customers make their next purchase within one year, then one year would be your cutoff point. If that percentage of customers made their next purchase within two years, then that would be your cutoff point.

Those customers who have not made a purchase during the identified time frame are said to have "churned." Calculating a churn rate can help you track the extent to which you are losing customers over time. For instance, if you start the beginning of the month with 100 customers and, at the end of the month, you determine that three are lost (they have not made a purchase in more than one year, or whatever your time frame is), your churn rate would be 3 percent. You may determine that this is an acceptable rate for your business, or you may set a goal of reducing this percentage over time.

Once you've identified these customers you may have an opportunity to learn from them about why they left and what you might be able to do to either lure them back or avoid losing other customers in the future. Businesses seek this information in a variety of ways, from simple postcard mailings to focus groups and surveys. The results can be extremely useful in terms of identifying areas of opportunity to improve customer interactions and may also help you better define the time frame for identifying a "lost" customer.

Keep in mind that for some lost customers you have not necessarily done something wrong, or have somehow failed to engage them.

QUESTION

What is the average churn rate (the measure of the rate at which customers are leaving your organization) for most small businesses? The rate will vary, but data from Accenture (*www.accenture.com*) indicates that, among mature markets, about 18 percent of retail customers will switch their business due to poor service, and about 15 percent of bank customers will make a switch. On the low end are airlines (at about 6 percent) and utility companies (at about 9 percent). What is the level of risk your company has for seeing customers leave?

For instance, a healthcare provider was interested in developing a method for identifying lost patients. Because the provider's services are not subscription-based and because even charts that are transferred to other providers do not necessarily mean a patient has been lost (the person may simply have sought a second opinion, for example), the provider decided to come up with a "proxy" for determining when a patient was truly lost: three years without a visit. The staff then created a simple postcard mailing that was sent to patients who had not been seen by a provider for the past three years that said, "We miss you! We haven't seen you for a while and are hoping that you will provide us with some information to help us better serve you, and our other patients, in the future."

They asked some very basic questions on the postcard about why the patient had not been in for the past three years. They discovered some very useful bits of information. The provider found that the reason why a great majority of "lost" patients hadn't been in was not that they had decided to never come back, but that they had either not had a need for an appointment or were concerned about the rising costs of care, or changes in insurance coverage were keeping them away. Of those who had transferred their care elsewhere, the vast majority had done so because they had moved to another city.

That was great news for this provider. But the staff didn't simply leave it at that. They continued to monitor these "losses" on an ongoing basis as a means of helping to identify any early indications of a shift in the responses they were receiving.

The survey actually had a two-part benefit for the organization. They learned more about the actual level of "lost" patients they were experiencing, *and* the act of sending out these postcards actually served as a positive customer service touchpoint; many patients provided positive feedback about their experiences with the organization and expressed gratitude for the concern that the effort showed.

Not all was rosy, however! There were some patients who *had* left to seek care with another provider because they had been unhappy with either the care or the level of service they had received. This was important information too. It allowed the organization to review and investigate its practices, making improvements as necessary in an attempt to minimize these losses in the future.

Any type of organization can take this same type of approach when it isn't clear whether customers are really lost. Others know the exact moment when a customer chooses to leave. When that happens, consider it an opportunity to seek important feedback that can help the business do a better job in the future. In some cases, doing so may even result in the ability to get that customer back on board.

You may choose to be even more proactive in your approach to identifying lost customers. You might invite everyone on your customer list or in your database to let you know at any time if they have been dissatisfied with your products and services to the point that they considered leaving your organization, or actually did leave.

Whatever way you can use to gather and act on this information will serve you well!

CHAPTER 3

Defining Your Target Audience

By now you've seen the importance of having a very clear idea of who it is you wish to target in terms of primary and secondary markets and intermediary audiences. Defining your target audience involves a number of considerations and variables, each of which will influence the way you move forward in your attempts to effectively engage those you are attempting to serve.

B2C vs. B2B

Two acronyms that have become widely used, particularly as the world of e-commerce has emerged and grown, are B2C and B2B. B2C stands for "business to consumer" and means a business is reaching out to consumers or individuals. B2B stands for "business to business" and means a business is reaching out to sell its products or services to other business organizations.

For various reasons, B2B marketing can be significantly more complex than B2C marketing. Why? Because rather than reaching out to individuals who can be clearly identified (more about that later), you are attempting to reach out to a "business"—a somewhat intangible amalgam of individuals. As engagement really suggests contact between *people*, B2B engagement poses some challenges. Let's consider an example.

Suppose you are an HR consultant and you specialize in providing training that helps employees communicate more effectively with each other. You'd like to engage with *Fortune* 500 companies, but these are big companies with a lot of employees. To whom, specifically, should you reach out? And should you reach out to more than one individual in each organization? Clearly, that's not an easy question to answer.

ALERT

Don't bite off more than you can chew. Some companies want to have a broad overall market with a handful of sub-niches. This might work if you have the resources to market to and serve several different groups of customers, but if you can only muster a bare-bones effort to cater to several groups, you may be better off doing a great job with one or two.

Contrast that with a B2C company that sells hunting gear to deer hunters in the Midwest. They know who they need to engage—deer hunters.

In most cases, B2C marketing is less complex than B2B marketing. Another B2B consideration is the size of organization you will target.

Big vs. Small

By definition there are 500 companies on the *Fortune* 500 list. They are the largest companies in the country. There is also a *Fortune* Global 500 list representing the largest companies in the world. Walmart tops the *Fortune* 500 list and is number two on the global list (Royal Dutch Shell is number one).

The SBA defines a small business as one with less than 500 employees. There are about 28 million small businesses in the United States. Of these, more than 22 million are sole proprietorships, with no employees other than the owner. Since 1995 small businesses have generated more than 65 percent of all of the net new jobs in this country.

For-Profit vs. Not-for-Profit

Some businesses are for-profit. Some are not-for-profit. *All* are concerned about "making money," a point that is often misunderstood. The term "non-profit" has been widely used to refer to businesses that do not exist to generate profits for shareholders. A better term is "not-for-profit," which more specifically indicates that these businesses do not exist to make a profit. They exist to serve some constituency and, therefore, need to generate revenue to do so.

The American Humane Association is not-for-profit, but obviously needs to generate funding to provide shelter for animals and to pay the people who care for these animals (and the administrative staff required to keep the business running). The same is true of organizations as diverse as the Boy Scouts and Girl Scouts, Rotary, Goodwill, the Make-A-Wish Foundation, the Chambers of Commerce, and, in most cases, your local hospital. These organizations generate revenue through membership fees, donations, and special events. The revenue generated is channeled back into the organization to continue to support the organization's mission.

In contrast, for-profit organizations generate profits that go to their owners or shareholders. The owners or boards of directors may—and generally do—decide to channel some funds back into the business, but also elect to keep a portion of the profits for themselves.

That is the primary distinction between for-profit and not-for-profit organizations.

ESSENTIAL

When your customer is a business, try to "pierce the veil" of the business and figure out who the decision-makers are. Then try to discern what their needs, wants, and motivations are. Is there an internal drive to cut costs? Is the marketing department making a push for the company to be seen as environmentally friendly? Is the top management wary of a new competitor?

Both types of organizations, though, are very concerned with engaging with their customers and other target audiences. Not-for-profit organizations often rely heavily on volunteers. They also depend on donors to help fund their activities. Some, as is the case with healthcare-related organizations, may depend on patients and other types of clients. For-profit organizations have customers or clients rather than a constituency.

The primary point to recognize here is that, regardless of whether or not they exist to generate profit for members of the organization, both for-profit and not-for-profit organizations should be focused on customer engagement.

Finding Focus

You have to home in on your own individual market. Take for example this question from a small business owner: "What's the best way to communicate with the under-35-year-old market?" It's a legitimate question. Certainly marketers need to think carefully about how they will communicate with their market, recognizing that markets are different. The only problem with this question (and it's one that many marketers ask in one form or another) is that it doesn't go far enough to identify a specific market focus. The group of individuals who are under 35 is a very, very broad group, after all. What is the likelihood that there would be a single, "best" communication strategy for them?

The lesson here: the more you can focus on a specific target market segment, the more effectively you will be able to communicate with, and engage, that segment. Unfortunately, finding focus is a challenge for many organizations and frequently is particularly so for entrepreneurs. Very often those starting a new business believe that "everyone" could benefit from their product or service. While that may be true, it is generally a misguided notion to attempt to serve everyone. There are a couple of common reasons why businesses head in this direction:

- Failure to understand the value of being specific
- The fear of "missing opportunities" by not casting a wide net
- Jumping to tactics before spending sufficient time in analysis

In the case of the small business owner who asked this question, those under age thirty-five is still a pretty broad demographic. To be most effective, this owner would want to define additional attributes of the target audience, which might include such things as geography, income levels, profession/occupation, hobbies, purchase behaviors and habits, and so on. Those specific attributes will help the business owner to both select appropriate communication tools and create compelling messages.

QUESTION

When should a company attempt to reposition itself?
When Walmart started to attract higher-income customers by flirting with a slightly more upscale image, it alienated its base customers while failing to convince its new target. Ultimately the company returned to its low-price roots. Changing your company's market positioning is a pretty drastic move and shouldn't be undertaken on a whim. It can be very hard if not impossible to "take it back."

Lifestyle/family issues and profession likely come into play for any audience. In this case, for instance, an under-thirty-five audience may include many young parents. Consider, for example, the meeting industry. Those in the thirty-five-and-under category may have young families and so may be drawn to facilities that offer family-friendly activities. On the flip side, however, again because they may have young families, they may yearn for an adult getaway. Effective meeting planner companies would need to determine what these consumers want based on the audience and what they know about that audience and its preferences. Understanding the needs and preferences of your audience involves a combination of ongoing primary and secondary research.

At the outset, companies need to carefully determine who they wish to serve based on demographics including geography, age, sex, income, industry, etc., as well as psychographics (e.g., interests and hobbies). Their goal should be to identify the potential market segments that may hold promise based on these attributes and then to prioritize the markets to focus on those with the most promise of achieving the best results with the least effort (time and money).

Even though a small company selling widgets online *could* conceivably define its market as global doesn't mean that it should. Segmentation is all about prioritizing and maximizing resources. It is important to note that the decisions you make today do not mean that you are stuck with them and cannot review and, potentially, expand your market at some point later. In fact, you should undergo such a review at least annually.

A careful analysis of potential target market segments will allow you to identify the best communication tools to reach those segments and to create the most impactful messages to move those audiences toward some desired action (again, based on what you learn and know about these audiences).

The most successful organizations, small and large, do not attempt to be everything to everyone. They recognize the importance of segmenting and targeting specific market groups and, ultimately, positioning their products/ services against competitive offerings.

ALERT

Some consumers are savvier than others, and they do not like to be "classified" and "targeted." Different demographics may need a more subtle approach to marketing. If your niche market is independent, trendsetting young adults, they will probably balk at the thought of your categorizing them. It is critically important that you understand each of your customer segments and their preferences.

Creating a Mission Statement

A mission statement can be a very important tool for even small businesses to gain clarity around whom they exist to serve. A mission statement indicates the products and/or services a company provides and to whom it provides them. It is a statement of the current reality of the organization (unlike the vision statement, which is forward-looking). From a strategic planning perspective, mission statements drive the creation of strategies and tactics that will be relevant for a business. If the mission statement doesn't reflect reality, the choices made will be misinformed and, potentially, detrimental to the business.

Here's how the process works (in abbreviated form):

- Suppose a Wisconsin restaurant's mission statement is, "We provide locally grown and sourced menu items to residents of XYZ county."
- The restaurant is working on its strategic plan. Someone recommends adding tuna to the menu because it has become a very popular item for consumers. Given the mission statement, though, this strategy should be dismissed. Why? Because tuna would not be locally grown or sourced in Wisconsin.
- Now, the restaurant *could* decide to revisit its mission statement and modify it—that happens frequently enough, and it's often appropriate because the environment we operate in is continually changing. The key, though, is ensuring that all strategies are aligned with the current, stated mission.

All too often, businesses—especially small businesses—feel that they can successfully serve the masses. Rarely is this the case. In fact, very often finding a specific niche to serve can help a business successfully compete with other businesses and gain brand awareness among a select group. Serving more to fewer people is a better strategy than serving less to a lot of people. How can you find focus? Some important considerations come into play:

- Which audiences may currently be overlooked or underserved? For instance, a lot of attention is focused on new mothers; new fathers may represent an underserved segment for some product or service designed to meet their unique needs.

- Which audiences may be emerging? For instance, as Baby Boomers age, a variety of businesses are becoming laser-focused on their needs, ranging from retirement planning consultants to crematoriums!
- Which audiences may have changing needs? Some reports are indicating that Gen Y is becoming somewhat disillusioned with technology and yearning for more high-touch than high-tech. What might this suggest for businesses that sell board games or vinyl records?
- Which audiences may be growing or changing within your identified market area? Perhaps the population within your market is growing, and much of that growth is reflected by young business professionals; perhaps your geographic area is seeing an influx of retirees. What opportunities might these shifts represent for you?
- What issues, concerns, or problems might be emerging within your target population? For instance, as competition for jobs is on the upswing there may be a developing need for skills training in certain areas, or for job coaching or specialty placement services.

Regardless of whether your product or service *could* be used by virtually anyone, it pays to find focus.

Understanding Demographics

For both B2B and B2C businesses, one of the methods used to define target audiences is demographics. Demographics are quantifiable attributes of a population and include things like gender, age, income, education level, location, and ethnicity. Any objective attribute that can be used to define a consumer and can be literally "counted" may be considered a demographic. In any given population, for instance, you could count the number of males and females, you could identify the ages of these individuals, you could determine their incomes, etc.

Demographic information is important because it helps you to specifically focus on certain elements of a population that may be more interested in what you have to offer than others may be. Demographics are the focus of market segmentation. A variety of criteria can be applied to break down a large market into smaller segments.

QUESTION

How focused is too focused?
Obviously, if the market you've defined includes only a handful of identifiable individuals, you need to invite more people to the party. Don't make the mistake of adding demographic traits that do more harm in terms of leaving out consumers than they do good in terms of identifying the "perfect" customer.

In B2C markets, some commonly used demographic segmentation criteria include:

- Age
- Gender
- Geographic location
- Income
- Education
- Occupation
- Ethnicity
- Religion

In B2B markets, segmentation might involve:

- Industry
- Geographic location
- Company size
- Type of position

Demographic criteria are specific and based on objective, measurable characteristics. Psychographics are a bit "fuzzier."

Understanding Psychographics

The concept of psychographics is a little less objective, but no less important, than the concept of demographics. Psychographics are indications of attitudes, values, and interests. Psychographic attributes may be related to family orientation, interest in specific hobbies, political opinions, or any of a wide range of other classifications simply designed to help marketers gain a better, and more specific, understanding of those they hope to serve.

There are various tools available to help businesses focus on psychographic attributes. VALS is one of them. VALS (Values, Attitudes, and Lifestyles) is a proprietary methodology used to identify consumers based on a wide range of psychographic attributes tied to their geography. The system was developed in the 1970s at SRI International, a nonprofit research institute. The framework separates consumers into segments that include:

- Innovators
- Thinkers
- Believers
- Achievers
- Strivers
- Experiencers
- Makers
- Survivors

Both demographic and psychographic attributes should be considered when attempting to clearly define a target market.

Segmenting, Targeting, and Positioning

Some important marketing concepts that businesses should consider as they identify their potential target audiences are segmenting, targeting, and positioning (STP).

Segmenting

Segmenting involves breaking down the consumer universe into manageable market segments. The goal is to reach the most highly responsive consumers at the least cost. There is an infinite number of segments that an organization might choose for its marketing efforts, and various ways in which segmentation may be approached.

Demographic segmentation, for example, breaks down the market in terms of various characteristics like age, gender, race, marital status, income, education, or occupation.

ESSENTIAL

Taking a top-down approach to defining your market can help add some structure to your market definition. In addition to picking a set of traits and seeing how many consumers fit the mold, consider selecting a rough estimate of how large a customer base you can effectively serve and filter the overall market until you've reached that range.

Psychographic segmentation, by contrast, breaks down the market in terms of activities, interests, and opinions (AIO). An example of psychographic segmentation would be a sports retailer appealing to individuals who enjoy rock climbing.

Charles Schewe and Alexander Hiam, marketing experts and the authors of a number of books including *The Portable MBA in Marketing*, have indicated that certain criteria must be met to achieve marketing success:

- The market must be able to be identified and measured. For instance, you could identify an audience of people interested in country music; it would be more difficult—perhaps impossible—to identify people who had a fear of teddy bears.
- The segment must be large enough to be profitable. Even if you identified the group of people who feared teddy bears, their number would likely be too small to represent much value to you—unless you were selling an *extremely* expensive product or service!
- The market must be reachable. Marketers can reach females between the ages of twenty-five and forty without much trouble, but attempting to reach fifteen-year-old redheaded boys, or mothers who enjoy cooking and have lactose-intolerant children, would likely be more challenging.

- The segment must be responsive. Young women in their early twenties might be a promising segment for a high-end hair product, but not if they're in college and struggling to pay rent and tuition.

Segmentation may also be based on internal information that you have gathered about your customers. For instance, you may have data to suggest that a certain segment of your customer base is a heavy user of a particular product.

There are infinite possibilities involved in identifying market segments, as segments may be comprised of psychographic, demographic, and usage criteria in various combinations. Once you identify these possibilities, the next step is to determine which segments to target.

An important caveat: the segment that offers the most in terms of numbers of potential customers is not necessarily the segment you should select. These obvious segments most likely have already been targeted by your competitors. Your best opportunities may be in smaller segments that have not yet been targeted by others; even though the numbers may be smaller, the potential for positive impact may be greater.

Targeting

Once you select your segments, you must prioritize them so you can focus on those that are likely to be most responsive. Competition is an important factor in considering which segments to focus on. If a major competitor has already chosen a particular market segment, that segment might not be as promising to you as another segment that has not yet been selected by the competition.

Once you have a clear idea of the segment you wish to reach, the next step is to determine how you can most effectively reach—or target—them. The more information you've gathered about the attributes and attitudes that define the segment, the better you will be able to do this.

If you know, for instance, that these are working adults who drive to work every morning and listen to sports talk programming on the radio, an advertisement during this "drive time" might be a great way to reach your audience.

Or, if you're attempting to connect with young gamers who download free games on their mobile devices (which are offered free because of the online advertising that supports them), running a mobile ad might be a great way to reach your audience.

When considering which specific market segments to target it is important to consider the activities of the competition—both direct and indirect. Then you will seek ways of positioning what you have to offer in relation to what competitors have to offer.

Positioning

The American Marketing Association says that "positioning refers to the customer's perceptions of the place a product or brand occupies in a market segment." In some markets, a position is achieved by associating the benefits of a brand with the needs or lifestyle of the segments. More often, positioning involves the differentiation of the company's offering from the competition by making or implying a comparison in terms of specific attributes.

FACT

Thoroughly understanding the competition for your products and services—direct *and* indirect—can help you to be more precise in targeting specific segments that are most likely to respond to what you have to offer. The underlying question in this process is, "Where can you have the most impact?"

For example, Walmart has positioned itself as the low price leader. Its positioning statement, prominently displayed on its website and in communication materials, includes the statement "Always low prices. Always." Contrast this position with the position of Nordstrom, which states, "The company's philosophy has remained unchanged for more than 100 years since its establishment by John W. Nordstrom in 1901: offer the customer the best possible service, selection, quality and value." Nordstrom has selected a position based on service, selection, quality, and value—not price. Subtly different, yet clearly apparent to consumers who have experienced both stores.

Direct competitors are fairly obvious. Burger King is a direct competitor for McDonald's. Sears is a direct competitor for J.C. Penney. Indirect competition can be more difficult to identify and is sometimes overlooked as a consideration. Indirect competitors represent alternatives to your product. Indirect competition for Hardee's, therefore, could be Pizza Hut. It could also be the corner grocery store.

Research is critical for marketing success in any industry and for organizations of any size. It is very important to spend time understanding the target audience and their needs from both a demographic (e.g., age, sex, location, income level) and psychographic (values and beliefs) perspective. It is also important to understand what other competing priorities the audience may have and what barriers may exist that might limit their interest or ability to engage with your services.

Maybe your product or service is less expensive, maybe it includes a lifetime guarantee, maybe it has features that the audience values that your competitors are not offering. The key is to take the time to figure this out. There's little value in using "me too" offers; when you're "the same as" somebody else, you don't really present any unique value, and it will be difficult to move the market over to your product, especially when you're dealing with a loyal market segment.

Segmenting, targeting, and positioning are important tools to use in laying the groundwork for identifying—and building effective relationships with—those you seek to serve. The process of segmenting, targeting, and positioning allows you to develop a clear idea of your target audiences to boost the odds that you will be better able to connect with, and engage, them.

Having a detailed and clear definition of the *specific* market you wish to reach will ensure that you are focusing your efforts and are not using your resources unwisely. The more clearly you can identify that segment of the overall marketplace that will be most likely to be responsive to your product or service, the more expertly you will be able to identify those specific promotional tools that will achieve results.

Here are a few questions to ask yourself when considering targeting, segmenting, and positioning your audience:

1. Are you attempting to reach individuals? Businesses? Government agencies?
2. What are the demographic characteristics of your target market? If your audience is mostly individuals, what is their age, sex, income, education

level, profession, geography, and so on? If your audience is primarily business, what is the industry's size, location, and employee makeup?

3. What is the size of your target market?

4. What is the growth potential of your target market? (Increasing, decreasing, stagnant?)

5. What do you know about your target market that can help you identify specific communication tools that will be most effective?

- If your audience is composed primarily of individuals, ask yourself:

❑ Do they watch television? Which programs?
❑ Do they listen to the radio? Which stations? When?
❑ Do they read the newspaper? Which sections?
❑ What magazines do they read?
❑ What social activities do they participate in? Where do they spend their free time? (Health clubs? Golf courses? The mall?)
❑ What are their hobbies?
❑ Do they commute to work? Over what routes?

- If your audience is primarily businesses, ask yourself:

❑ What is the organizational structure?
❑ Who are the key decision-makers relative to your product/service?
❑ What are the characteristics and interests of these decision-makers? (Which trade associations do they belong to? Which journals do they read? What do they do in their free time?)

CHAPTER 4

Understanding Your Target Audience

The more you know about your target audience segments, the better you will be able to effectively connect and engage with them. Even when target audiences are very large, there are many tools and techniques that can help you learn more about them. Ongoing research should be a key part of your customer engagement activities.

The Role of Research

If you're like most businesspeople, when you think about marketing research, you think about some kind of long-range, very intensive, data-gathering exercise that involves a lot of time, money, and data analysis. And, yes, sometimes research can be like that. In reality, however, you are engaged in research almost all of the time, whether you know it or not. Research doesn't have to involve full-blown, statistically significant and often expensive initiatives that require extensive quantitative research and analysis. Sometimes, yes—but often, no.

All information and input can be valuable to a small business as it attempts to learn more about the markets it currently serves, and also those it would like to serve. The trick is determining when you need to gather more information, and when you have enough. Those decisions generally come down to two important considerations:

- The level of risk or reward involved in the decision you're attempting to make
- What it is you need to know to make a well-informed decision

The general process of gathering research involves two preliminary steps. The first is identifying your "researchable question," or what it is you need to know and what impact that will have on your business (the bigger the impact, the more extensive your research process is likely to be). For instance: "Why are our sales declining?," "What impact will an increase in price have on our sales volumes?," "How does our market perceive us in relation to our competitors?" Then you can begin the second step, which is the process of gathering information intended to help you answer the question(s) you have. Doing this involves another series of steps. After each step, you will ask yourself whether you have enough information to answer your question(s). Those inputs generally include, in this order:

1. Gathering internal information: sales data, customer satisfaction data, etc.
2. Gathering secondary information: information you might attain online by searching, by reviewing social media inputs, or by reviewing research or reports that others have generated

3. Conducting qualitative research: interviews, observation, focus groups
4. Conducting quantitative research: surveys, experiments

Once all of the inputs have been gathered, you can synthesize all of the information and convey it through findings, conclusions, and recommendations. All of these should be framed around the original researchable question(s) and should provide the data and information necessary to make a decision, again, based on the importance of that decision and the potential risk to the organization of making a poor decision.

ESSENTIAL

Sometimes your internal data will give you the answer(s) you need. For instance, you may have a POS (point of sale) system that allows you to gather a great deal of quantitative information about the interactions that your customers have with you. That's a rich source of data that can help you learn more about your customers and what's important to them based on what they buy, when they buy, and, of course, how much they spend. For instance, one small publishing firm found out through its sales analysis that customers who had purchased previous editions of a book were purchasing the updated editions. Based on this knowledge they began promoting new editions to prior purchasers through direct mail and were able to boost sales significantly in this manner.

Very often, you don't need to embark on an extensive—or expensive— research project to gather this information. However, much depends on the relative importance of the questions you have. For instance, one potentially risky question is whether or not you should move from a brick-and-mortar environment to an entirely online environment.

To answer this question you will likely need a combination of a wide range of inputs to help you make a good decision. Or maybe not. Maybe after you've evaluated your internal data, you find some information from another source (articles or studies done by others in your industry or field) that provide you with a pretty reliable indication that you would be better served by moving to a virtual delivery method.

The bottom line: when it comes to effective marketing research, it's really all about asking, and effectively answering, the right questions.

Primary Research

Primary research is simply research, or information, that you have gathered yourself. You don't always need to develop an elaborate survey to conduct research. Many companies choose to make use of existing information that is readily available, for obvious reasons. It's less expensive and it sharply cuts down on the time between asking the question and obtaining the answer.

You may not realize it, but you may already have a great deal of information available to you. For example, your sales records can provide you with valuable information about which products have a high sales volume and which don't. Call reports filled out by salespeople can provide you with information about customer responses to new products. This is primary research because the information is collected directly.

ALERT

A pitfall faced by many businesses is that they don't know what they don't know. You can't start targeting a market that you don't know exists; you can't avoid risks you can't see. The risk of being in the dark often far outweighs the cost of a little extra research. Fortunately, there are many sources of information available today, often at little or no cost. It pays to do your research!

In addition to the information you already have on hand, primary research may involve seeking additional inputs through a variety of sources. Focus groups and surveys are two commonly used methods.

Focus Groups

Focus groups are a qualitative form of research that can be very useful to marketers. Gathering groups of customers or potential customers together to explore issues can be a valuable first step in identifying issues and opportunities for marketing improvements in areas related to all elements of the marketing mix: product, price, place, and promotion.

The concept is simple. Focus groups simply bring together a group of people (generally ten to twelve per group) whose discussion is moderated by a focus group leader. Sessions are often audio- or videotaped for future study.

The selection of a facilitator is an important consideration. An outside facilitator offers a nonbiased, third-party view and may be less intimidating to participants. In addition, trained facilitators are experts in directing conversations among groups to ensure the proper focus and response to the issues the organization wishes to have addressed.

In addition to the selection of a facilitator, there are other logistical issues to consider. These include location for the sessions, length (sixty to ninety minutes is typical), refreshments, whether the session will be observed (often through a one-way mirror), whether to record the session on audio, video, or both, and whether payment will be offered to participants (this is most common in marketing or product research settings with consumers; not as common in employee focus group settings).

The first challenge in conducting a focus group occurs long before the participants are assembled. That challenge is gaining a consensus on what, exactly, you're looking for. The purpose or intent of the focus groups will direct selection of participants. After a general set of characteristics is established, a list of people who meet those criteria will be identified and randomly contacted, generally by phone or e-mail, to invite participation.

Typically a discussion guide is used to help direct the flow of the session and to ensure that key points are covered. In developing the discussion guide care should be taken to frame questions and discussion topics so they elicit more than "yes" or "no" answers. The objective is to get the participants talking.

Having more than one way to participate can be helpful. Some participants will be more than happy to talk in a group; others less so. Alternatives to discussion could include asking participants to make lists, rank priorities, and so on. A combination of these types of exercises in addition to discussing issues with the group can help generate participation from all and provide opportunities for transitions between topics.

It's important to understand that focus groups are not designed to provide definitive answers to your marketing questions. Focus groups, by their very nature, are qualitative interactions. Focus groups should be considered as one of a set of tools for doing market research. Their value lies in their ability to complement other forms of research, but they are not a replacement for those other devices. Focus groups don't provide quantitative information—you're not taking a large amount of random data and finding trends in it; you're getting a few in-depth opinions.

ALERT

While facilitating group discussions may seem easy, avoid the temptation to do it yourself. Expert facilitators make the process appear simple and unplanned. Nothing could be further from the truth. Focus groups are conversations with purpose. Skilled facilitators are best able to strategically interact with the group and to probe, follow up, and push for in-depth observations when appropriate.

Here are some additional points to ensure a positive outcome:

- Clarify your objectives up front. Know what you want and communicate those objectives to the professionals with whom you work.
- Use a professional moderator. Skilled in interpersonal interaction, professional moderators can ensure that all participants share their viewpoints and that the group isn't dominated by one outspoken member.
- Don't assume an outcome. The value of focus groups is their ability to surprise. You never know what the public thinks until you get members of the public together in a room, and they tell you, explicitly.
- Don't stop with just one. The more focus groups you hold, the wider the range of opinions you'll gather. While you still won't approach the validity of true quantitative research, you will have a better basis from which to determine your future direction.
- Don't "kill the messenger." The results you obtain may not be what you expected to hear. Keep an open mind and try to overcome your own biases and preconceived ideas.

Surveys or Questionnaires

Surveys or questionnaires, while often considered to be quantitative research tools (and sometimes they are), must be conducted appropriately to generate truly statistically reliable information. In many cases, especially with the advent of the Internet and the ability to conduct surveys and polls online, this information is not statistically sound. Still, the information gathered can be valuable and may provide good insights of a qualitative nature. Again, it's important to exercise caution when making any decisions of significant impact—either from a risk or reward standpoint—based on qualitative information.

QUESTION

Are online surveys valid?
They can be. The Internet has created many opportunities to conduct research more quickly and cost-effectively than in the past. If you're looking for reliable data, though, it's important to identify your population of interest and generate a representative sample that will yield the high-quality results you need to make a good decision.

Questionnaires can be delivered by mail, by phone, via in-person interviews, or online. The advantage of surveying by means of a questionnaire is that it can provide a timely measure of information and can be relatively cost-effective. The disadvantage can be a lower level of response, particularly with mail-in questionnaires.

Researchers use a number of ways to increase response to surveys, including:

- Sending out a pre-survey notice and a post-survey reminder to encourage response
- Mailing the survey first-class
- Offering the opportunity to complete the survey online
- Offering an incentive for completing the survey (i.e., product discounts, premium items, etc.)

There are a number of considerations to keep in mind when designing a survey:

- Keep the survey as short as possible. Consumers' time is precious and they resent long interviews or questionnaires.
- Identify your sample group and be sure the size is appropriate to ensure a valid response. If you only survey twenty individuals and receive a 20 percent response, you'll be dealing with only four completed surveys—not enough to give you a valid "reading" of the marketplace.
- Set goals. Define what you want your survey to accomplish and select the sample group based on these goals.
- Make sure the questions are clear and unbiased. You don't want to "lead" respondents to an answer—you want their honest opinions. Eliminate any questions in which the answer you're looking for is obvious.
- Break up long or complicated questions into two or more parts.
- Use simple check-offs or multiple-choice questions as much as possible. This makes it easier for respondents to reply and easier for you to tabulate the results.
- Make your survey stand out, but keep it professional-looking.
- Set a deadline for return of surveys.
- Include a cover letter with the survey that encourages people to respond.
- Pretest your survey on a small segment of your sample to uncover potential "bugs."

When is research not recommended? When you can obtain the information more quickly and less expensively through other means. Here's an example. Suppose you sell gift items through direct mail. You're wondering if a new product will interest customers. You could do a survey of a sample from your database or you could simply do some "test marketing." Choose the same sample of respondents and actually send them the offer for the new product. The results will be more accurate. You'll learn what people actually do, not what they say they will do. The information will be more immediate and the cost will be the same or less than what you'd spend on a formal survey.

Or, suppose you want to know the geographic location and purchasing history of your customers. If you've been collecting that data with every order you take and every invoice you send, you should already have that information in your database.

While surveys seem simple enough—consider the many you've completed over your lifetime—you need to put careful thought into designing a survey to ensure that the information obtained will be useful. Before deciding to conduct a survey, ask yourself a number of questions:

- What do you want to know? Be as specific as possible and try to quantify the information you seek. For instance, you might want to know what percentage of your customers would be interested in purchasing the XYZ product and in what price range you would stand to make the most profit. As you're preparing the survey, determine what responses you will want afterward and how the data will be used. Don't ask questions if you really don't need to know—or don't care about—the answers.

- Why do you need to know? There are thousands of surveys done each year that yield worthless information simply because the people conducting the survey didn't *really* need to know the information in the first place. Make sure that you have a solid business reason for gathering this information before you even begin the survey process.

- How much do you want to know? Again, don't waste your time or the time of your respondents by asking irrelevant questions. Determine how much you want to know in light of how much you *need* to know.

- When do you need the information? This is perhaps the most important question. Market research takes time. If you need an answer quickly, a survey may not be the vehicle for you.

- How much is the information worth to you? Surveys can be expensive to conduct. Sometimes the most cost-effective market research may simply be the introduction of a new product combined with monitoring customer response to it. If you determine that a survey is the only way to go, however, you also need to quantify how much the information you hope to gather is worth to you. Then you can establish the financial parameters under which you'll proceed.

- Can you afford to make an uninformed decision? The flip side of determining how much you can afford to spend is determining how much you stand to lose if you don't spend the time and money on the survey. Can you afford to proceed without hard evidence that you're headed in the right direction? Many businesspeople decide they cannot; that's why they take the time and spend the money to develop surveys.

A customer survey is a systematic and objective process of gathering, recording, and analyzing data to aid you in making marketing decisions. The responses you receive will not make the decisions for you—they may simply point you in the direction of any further information you need to gather. The actual preparation of the survey instrument is the most challenging part of conducting a survey.

- Copy must be simple and easy to understand. Remember, in a mail survey, you will not have a sales representative present to explain ambiguous points. Your copy must be understandable and easy to read.
- Frame questions so they can be answered straightforwardly. Avoid open-ended questions as much as possible. Such questions as, "What do you think about the XYZ product?" are open-ended and result in a wide variety of responses that can be difficult to categorize and quantify. Instead, frame your questions in the following way: "How would you rank the XYZ product?" Then give a series of responses that provide brief, descriptive phrases so that respondents can simply check their choices. When using this system, always remember to include an "Other" category to leave room for respondents to clarify what they mean.
- Don't ask leading questions. "You'd like to purchase the XYZ product for less than $100, wouldn't you?" is a leading question and not appropriate for a survey. Leading questions are those that imply the answer you'd like to receive. The best way to avoid including this type

of question in your survey is to have several people review your questions before the survey is sent out.

- Don't make the questionnaire look too complicated or time-consuming. Your customers are busy. If they receive a ten-page questionnaire in the mail, they'll be unlikely to respond. But if you send a simple, one-page questionnaire that is easy to read and makes it easy for the customer to respond, you'll be much more likely to receive a high rate of return.
- Make your questionnaire *look* important. If respondents feel that they will be performing a worthwhile service by taking the time to answer your questions, they will be more likely to do so.

ESSENTIAL

To the extent possible, try to quantify the cost/benefit analysis of your marketing research expenditures. If the market research firm you're working with can sell you a study of your market for $50,000 and you are confident it will help you boost your customer conversion rate from 5 percent to 25 percent in a market of $10 million, that could be a very good investment.

- Use premiums. Offering something extra as an incentive for a purchase can be a good way to generate sales. For instance: "Subscribe to this publication and receive a free copy of our latest best seller." Premiums have been found to greatly increase response rates. When choosing a premium, make sure it is something the respondent will find desirable—but does not introduce bias into your survey—and is not only small and lightweight enough to be mailed easily but also not so expensive as to make the cost of conducting the survey prohibitive.
- Offer respondents a summary of the results of your survey. This also has been shown to significantly increase response. People are inherently curious and, when they've invested their time in responding to a survey, they naturally want to know how their responses compare to the responses as a whole.

Again, primary research is any information you collect yourself. Other primary inputs might be observation—what you observe your customers doing—or experimentation, perhaps by introducing different products in different markets, or using different types of promotional activities in different markets to see which produces the greatest results. The ability to analyze the results for each of these efforts through online analytics can help you make informed decisions for future marketing activities.

While primary research often yields the results most pertinent to your own unique situation and research questions, it can be very expensive. That's where secondary research comes into play.

Secondary Research

Secondary research is information that someone else has gathered. While not directly related to your specific question, secondary sources of research can still prove valuable. Secondary information is widely available. Published information that could be useful to you includes information on competitors' products and pricing strategies, census data that provides information on the characteristics and size of a target market, government-published data, and data available through market research firms. Some examples of the latter include:

- **A.C. Nielsen** (*www.acnielsen.com*). Best known for its monitoring of TV program viewership, A.C. Nielsen also offers a variety of other research reports and services related to market and consumer trends.
- **Arbitron**, acquired by Nielsen in 2013, is an international media and marketing research firm serving radio broadcasters, radio networks, cable companies, advertisers, advertising agencies, outdoor advertising companies, and the online radio industry in the United States, Mexico, and Europe. It helps media companies, advertisers, and marketers understand media audiences and reach consumers more effectively.
- **Gallup** (*www.gallup.com*). The Gallup Organization has studied human nature and behavior for more than seventy years. Gallup employs many of the world's leading scientists in management, economics, psychology, and sociology. Its performance management systems help organizations increase customer engagement and maxi-

mize employee productivity through measurement tools, coursework, and strategic advisory services.

- **Simmons Market Research**, acquired by Experian Marketing Services in 2004 (*www.experian.com*), collects information on more than 8,000 brands in 460 product categories, creating detailed consumer profiles with over 600 lifestyle characteristics linked to every media genre accessible in the United States. That information is turned into consumer studies, segmentation systems, and advanced integrated marketing solutions.
- **U.S. Yankelovich Monitor** (*www.thefuturescompany.com*). Yankelovich offers database and segmentation solutions for clients, providing insights into consumer motivations and lifestyles to identify specific, tangible opportunities for competitive advantage.

There are countless more. A Google search for "market research firms" results in more than 57,000 hits. Secondary research is available from many of these firms. In addition, the professional associations that serve your industry typically offer their own research reports and information to members.

Before embarking on your own research (which can be time-consuming and costly) it pays to do a thorough job of determining what may already be available to provide you with some of the basic information or direction you need. That secondary research can then serve as the starting point for any primary research you need to do.

Net Promoter Score

While businesses spend a lot of time and resources on research of various kinds and tend to ask any number of questions related to their own situations, markets, and goals, there is one question that engaged audiences respond to. Framed simply, it is this: "Would you recommend us?"

It's a question that companies have been asking for years, but in 2003, a Harvard Business School article, "One Number You Need to Grow," introduced the concept of a "net promoter score." A Net Promoter score (now a registered trademark of Satmetrix) is a reflection of the positivity of your customer base, and it's based on the response to that very basic question of "would you recommend us?"

The idea is that customers fall into three categories—promoters, passives, and detractors. Promoters are those who not only keep buying themselves, but also recommend your business to others. Ideally, you want as many of your customers as possible to be promoters and as few as possible to be detractors. That's the goal. That's engagement.

It's important to note that this same concept can apply to employees. Asking them whether they would recommend your business to their friends as a great place to work can give an indication of employee engagement in the same way that it can indicate customer engagement.

What Research Can and Can't Tell You

Owners of small businesses need to stay on top of what's important to their customers, get to know them, ask a lot of questions, and listen well. The key is gaining a sense of their "pain points": what are your customers most concerned about? What do they most hope for? What keeps them up at night? Finding the answers to these questions can be as straightforward as asking them, or it can involve simply being very observant and reading between the lines.

From a marketing standpoint, it is important for small businesses to recognize the value of doing ongoing research—or environmental scanning—to detect changes in needs and preferences among, and within, target audiences. This is very easy and inexpensive to do these days by conducting online searches, monitoring social media chatter, setting up RSS feeds to track or monitor certain topics, and so on. Another great way to do this is by establishing a group—on LinkedIn, for instance—to engage in conversations with your audience.

While research can be invaluable, there is one very important thing that it cannot tell you. It cannot tell you what people *will* do. It can tell you about people. It can tell you what they believe, at this moment in time, they *might* do. But only their actual behaviors will give you an indication of what they will *actually* do. This is why even very large, very successful companies with very big research budgets have sometimes made missteps in terms of introducing or modifying their product and service offerings. Coca-Cola's attempt in 1985 to introduce a new version of its popular product was a dismal failure as many still remember. Still, research is a critical input in your quest to engage with the customers you currently serve—and those you will serve in the future. There are a wide range of options available to you in gathering this information.

Additional Research Options

Businesses of all sizes and types are concerned with staying abreast of constantly changing customer and consumer expectations. The information age represents both challenges and opportunities for doing this. The challenges are related to the sheer volume of information you have available to use. The opportunities are related to the same thing!

When most people think about research they think about quantitative research, often done with surveys. However, that's not the only form of research that can provide value. There are a multitude of other options. For instance:

- Observation can be a valuable form of information for small businesses and simply involves observing or watching people. So, for instance, a retailer might observe how people shop. What do they look at? How long do they spend in certain areas of the store or with certain products? Do certain displays attract more attention than others? This type of information is important because it reflects *actual* behavior. Surveys, regardless of how scientifically relevant and expertly done, are always subject to respondents' often biased perceptions of what they *might* do.
- From an online standpoint, you can conduct observation research through analytics—a really powerful source of low-cost information about consumer behaviors. For example, you can create tests by using various ads or by sending different types of e-mail marketing messages to see which generate the most response, or you can modify and monitor website copy and content to determine what resonates most with visitors.
- Polling can be a good way to "check the pulse" of your audience. You can easily conduct polls online through websites or through social media outlets like LinkedIn. The results will not be statistically significant, but can provide some insights and information that might direct

future research and, when done on an ongoing basis, may allow you to identify and monitor trends.

- Opinion surveys. Businesses have a ready-made opportunity to gather information from their customers during and after interactions with them. You can do this through comment cards or online surveys. Following up with customers via e-mail and including a link to a brief survey can be a great way to gather information.

With the wide range of information available today through secondary sources and the many opportunities to conduct primary research at a very low cost, there is no excuse for not relying on solid data to make important decisions about your business and its customers.

CHAPTER 5

Understanding Your Competition

Every business has competition. Even businesses or entrepreneurs who introduce products or services that are "first to market" deal with competitive forces. From a customer engagement standpoint, it is very important that businesses have a clear understanding of the competitive landscape in which they operate. Competitive analysis is an important part of positioning.

Direct vs. Indirect Competition

There are different forms of competition that must be considered and different ways to look at competition to help draw conclusions about the effectiveness of your planning. First you need to consider whether your competition is direct or indirect. Businesses tend to be most focused on direct competitors.

If you operate a pizza restaurant, another pizza restaurant down the street is a direct competitor. However, you can expand that competitive net to include other types of restaurants that would also be considered direct competitors (although less so than another pizza restaurant). Then you should expand the competitive net even further to consider a competitor to be any available alternative to what you have to offer. The businesses in that category represent your indirect competition—a very important factor that is often overlooked.

ESSENTIAL

As any business owner should know, your business is both predator and prey. Don't forget the flip side of indirect competition. Your indirect competition should also be seen as a potential market to expand into. For example, maybe your pizza company can implement a drive-through with ready-made pizza to more directly compete with the burger joint down the street.

For instance, for that pizza restaurant owner, other pizza restaurants represent a direct threat and a clear alternative choice for customers, but going further, there are other restaurants that offer a similar choice that must be considered and narrowed. A hamburger restaurant might pose a greater threat than an upscale restaurant because it would be more likely to be included in the customer's "consideration set" when deciding to go out to eat.

A consideration set represents the choices that consumers have to select from once they have identified a need. If the consumer's need is "I'm hungry for pizza," that may be a narrow consideration set. If the need is simply "I'm hungry," the consideration set becomes much broader. Pizza restaurant owners need to consider both scenarios. It is the broader consideration set that brings up the concept of "indirect competition." In this case, that indirect competition might be the corner grocery store or simply staying home and making something to eat.

Why is this important? Because when it comes to attempting to influence consumers to choose you, it's important to understand what their other alternatives might be. That allows you to make sure that when you communicate with them, you are addressing all of their potential objections to what you have to offer compared to other options they may have. In this case, if you're only focused on other pizza restaurants, for instance, you may be missing the opportunity to position yourself against other available options.

The bottom line: don't overlook the impact of secondary competitors.

Porter's Five Forces Analysis

When considering competitors and their impact on your business, *Porter's five forces analysis* can provide a useful tool for helping you think of all of the potential impacts the competitive environment might have on your success—both positive and negative.

In 1979, Michael E. Porter, a Harvard Business School professor, developed a framework for examining and analyzing the competitive nature of a market in terms of five forces:

1. The threat of new entrants
2. The power of suppliers
3. The power of buyers
4. The availability of substitutes
5. Competitive rivalry

Let's examine each one of Porter's five forces and how they provide input for the strategic planning process.

Threat of New Entrants

What is the likelihood that another business offering what you offer will enter your market? You need to consider how difficult it would be for another small business owner to enter your market and offer what you are offering.

Obviously, the easier it is for others to enter your market, the more competition there will be.

A pizza restaurant, for instance, would have relatively low barriers to entry, therefore making it a very competitive market. A software development firm focusing on a specialized niche market, on the other hand, might face higher barriers to entry and be less at risk for competition—but not necessarily!

FACT

A classic example of access to inputs as a barrier to entry is the diamond industry. De Beers Diamonds of South Africa controls roughly 80 percent of the world's supply of diamonds. This makes it extremely difficult for competitors to enter the market.

One common misstep made by small business owners and entrepreneurs is to believe that "nobody is offering what we have to offer." Rarely is that true. It's important to be realistic and objective when considering the field of competition and to be prepared to respond to it.

Power of Suppliers

Most businesses rely on supplies of some sort to provide their products or services. These supplies might include the raw materials required to produce the product or service (in the case of a pizza restaurant, the supplies would be cheese and other ingredients), or the support services required to deliver the product or services (such as an online ordering system). The impact of the power of these suppliers comes into play when the supply is suddenly cut off and business owners must evaluate these risks. If your cheese supply is cut off, there may be alternatives available that you could readily substitute. If your online ordering system goes down, however, the impact on your business could be significant, and competitors—at least for a time—might have an edge.

The Power of Buyers

Suppose you are a business consultant and you have three clients. One of these clients represents 75 percent of your annual revenue. What do you think the impact of losing that client to a competitor might be? Significant. This example illustrates the power of buyers and why it is important to consider the impact that your customer base, or buyers, might have on you in terms of your level of risk should they choose to seek what you have to offer elsewhere.

The Availability of Substitutes

This refers to the direct/indirect issue that was previously discussed. If your pizza restaurant operates within a five-mile radius of several other pizza restaurants, there are many substitutes available. If there are no pizza restaurants within 100 miles, you face an entirely different situation.

Competitive Rivalry

The existing field of competition is another factor that is considered in Porter's analysis. The more competitive the environment, the lower the available profits for each participant. Why? Because competition drives down price. The less you can charge for your product or service because of competitive forces, the lower your margin.

Some issues you may need to consider as you evaluate your competitive environment and consider your level of risk in terms of losing, or failing to gain, customers include:

- Consumer loyalty to other existing brands or companies
- Incentives that may be available from other companies
- Your need for supplies or resources that may be scarce, or at risk
- The high costs consumers might have for switching from one provider to another
- Government restrictions or laws that impact the ability to do business

Each of these factors may work either for or against you. Suppose your pizza restaurant has been serving the local community for twenty years and has a loyal following. As you analyze the potential impact of competitors you might first consider the potential threat of new entrants to the market and recognize that this threat is high. You might also recognize that, due to the loyalty of your existing customers, you may have an edge over a competitor that might emerge. But, what if that competitor represents one of the "big brands"—Pizza Hut, for instance?

What are some common barriers to entry?
One common barrier is scale. Big companies can spread fixed costs such as advertising over a larger operation, and the cost of scaling up can keep potential competitors away. Another one is government regulation. Many utilities are given a sanctioned monopoly to provide power to certain areas. Others include network effect (the ability of their network of contacts to serve as intermediaries to promote/support their brand) and customer loyalty.

If you were the owner of a software firm, you could use this same analysis. Cost might be a factor in terms of attracting and retaining the highly skilled software engineers needed to create your particular product. Switching costs could be a factor here, as well—it can be very expensive both in terms of time and money for businesses to change software providers. Still, due to these factors, the risk of a new competitor in your market might be low.

Sources of Information

There is a wide range of information available about your competitors these days, ranging from firsthand experience to online research and even monitoring what the public is saying about your competition through engagement in social media.

If you operate a grocery store, it's a good idea to check out other grocery stores in the area on a regular basis. One interesting way to do this is through mystery shopping. Mystery shoppers are people who assume an "undercover" role and go into businesses (even including your own!) to evaluate products and services, as well as service provided, and make comparisons. There is much to be learned from mystery shoppers that can help you determine where you excel in business and where you may lag behind. This kind of in-person evaluation can also provide you with information about how consumers are interacting with other businesses, what's important to them, and ways in which you might better engage them through your own business.

ESSENTIAL

Make sure to clear your browser cache when you do online research of your competitors' websites or the results you find will be impacted by the other searches you've done recently. In some cases, depending on the geography you're interested in, you may also want to change your location through your browser's search settings.

Online, of course, there is now a wealth of information available about your competitors, starting with their websites. A review of competitors' websites will give you insight not only into their brand positioning, but also into their products and services, and even in some cases their pricing. It is also very simple to compare yourself to your competitors in terms of how you show up in search results for the types of words and phrases your customers and potential customers may be using when they seek the kinds of products and services you offer.

Here are some additional tips for finding out about your competitors:

- Do an online search for your competitors' business names, and product or service names, to see if they have been covered by the media or if there are comments posted by consumers about them.
- Find out which LinkedIn groups your competitors' key staff members are participating in and join them yourself to monitor their activity.
- Follow competitors on Twitter, Facebook, and other social media channels to track their activity in terms of comments they and their followers are making and the level of engagement they've achieved among their followers.

- Depending on your industry, regularly check consumer ratings sites such as Yelp!, Angie's List, and others to get a sense of satisfaction—or dissatisfaction—levels.
- Use online tools like Google Alerts to stay on top of current news or information about your competitors. You can enter in specific search words or phrases and receive updates ranging from news, to blogs, to videos and more.
- Additional tools such as Hootsuite allow you to easily monitor social media activity related to your competitors based on the key words you enter.

All of these tools and resources provide businesses with information that was literally never available just a few short years ago. Keep in mind, of course, that just as you are spending time monitoring your competition, chances are that they are spending time monitoring you as well! Everything you post in a public forum should be done with this in mind.

What They Have That You Don't

It's important to be continually aware of the competitive environment. You need to know who you are currently competing with, where you are at risk of emerging competition, what the changing needs and desires of your target market are, and how your product or service is better than or different from what your competitors have to offer.

ALERT

The power of suppliers and buyers can threaten the very existence of a business, particularly one in the middle of a supply chain. If you supply brake pads to an automobile company, that buyer might someday decide to develop its own internal supply. What if the company that supplies processors for your PC manufacturing company decides it wants to start making PCs of its own and compete with you?

As you're researching and evaluating your competition, you're likely picking up some good ideas and insights into the products and services they're offering and the things they're doing that may represent opportunity for you.

It's important to position yourself *against* your competition, not attempt to be just like them. But it can be helpful to evaluate what they have that you don't have and use this as input to your ongoing planning processes.

It can also be helpful to identify what your competitors do not have that you either already have or could easily provide. Do you note any gaps in terms of the products or services they provide, or have you heard or read comments from their customers or others online who may be asking about product or service additions or enhancements? By continually monitoring the competition you may find that you get some great ideas for ways to add to or augment what you have to offer, delighting your own customers—and theirs!—in the process.

The Importance of Positioning

Positioning involves making sure that your potential customers see an important difference between you and their other choices—a difference that makes it clear to them that you are the better option.

ESSENTIAL

Just as there are barriers to entry in many industries, there can also be significant barriers to exit that can "trap" a company in a particular industry. For example, a railroad company can't easily liquidate the assets it has tied up in railroad tracks crisscrossing the country. Similarly, a company that has long-term contracts with external partners may find it difficult to get out of those agreements when it wants to leave that industry.

This is another area where small businesses often fail to take the right steps to effectively differentiate themselves from competitors. Instead of trying to be different, they copy what their competitors are doing. Does the competition offer a price break? Then you offer a price break. Did the competition add a new product feature? You add a new product feature.

That "me-too" approach to positioning is rarely effective. The more you make what you have to offer the same as what others have to offer, the more direct the competition is. Effective positioning involves:

- Understanding market needs
- Understanding the competitive landscape
- Identifying or developing ways you can stand out from the competition
- Communicating these differences to your customers or potential customers

Effective positioning can boost the value of what you have to offer in the minds of your target audiences. The more clearly you can differentiate what you have to offer, the more effective you will be at attracting and retaining customers.

Competitors as Collaborators

While you may tend to think of competitors as, well, *competitors*, there are times that it might be a good idea for you to actually work *with* your competition—to collaborate. Collaboration among competitors is not as uncommon as you might think. For example, in 2011 BMW and Toyota announced their intention to collaborate on research into electric motors. Additionally, BMW was to provide diesel engines for Toyota. All of this would occur despite the fact that Toyota's luxury brand, Lexus, is a direct competitor of BMW. As another example, HBR.org has reported that Canon, a business that manufactures imaging and optical products, has supplied photocopiers to competitor Kodak, and American Airlines partnered with Boeing to retrofit Boeing 737s.

The big takeaway: don't view competitors as the enemy—some may represent the potential for collaboration. Those most likely to do so are those that may have skills, competencies, products, or services that might augment your own.

For instance, a florist shop that grows and sells exotic plants might wish to partner with another florist that has a skilled floral arrangement artist on staff. Or a beauty salon may wish to bring in a stylist from another salon to provide specialty services that it does not have the internal talent, or budget, to provide.

Think outside the box. Importantly, spend time to get to know your competitors, personally if possible. As Sun Tzu suggested, as translated in *The Art of War*: "Keep your friends close but your enemies closer." It pays to know what they're up to, and you never know when you might spot an opportunity for collaboration that may benefit both of you.

QUESTION

Why collaborate with competitors? Aren't they "the enemy"?
Your competition is not always the perfect partner; however, don't confuse market share with profitability. To the extent that your market is big enough for both of you, there can be efficiencies and learning opportunities to be gained through collaboration that can increase the bottom line for everyone.

Disruptive Innovation

Competition can give rise to disruption. VHS tapes. Landlines. Encyclopedias. Camera film (the kind used to take photographs). These are all examples of products that have already disappeared from use, or most likely will soon do so. Why is this happening? Because they've been made obsolete due to new advancements, replacements, or changing consumer demand.

This kind of evolution is happening all of the time; sometimes slowly, sometimes rapidly. Just as DVDs signaled the end of VHS tapes, so do new innovations like the iPad and streaming video suggest that DVDs may also go the way of the 8-track tape (remember those?).

How often do you give any consideration to the tenure of your own product or service? Are you aware of emerging or existing innovations that may make your company obsolete? All businesses are at risk of becoming the victims of disruptive innovations. Disruptive innovations produce incremental, radical, or revolutionary changes in products, processes, and sometimes entire industries in ways that are often unexpected and unplanned for.

Vinyl records. Audiotapes. Video rental stores. Typewriters. Carbon paper. That white stuff that Mike Nesmith's mom invented that was once used to correct typing errors. Rotary phones. The U.S. Postal Service (well, not yet . . .). Look back over the past ten, twenty, or fifty years and you'll find countless examples of products and services that simply no longer exist or that have "morphed" into something else.

While there is a tendency to think of disruptive innovation as being driven by technology (and it often is), obsolescence can occur due to other impacts as well. Examples are found in changing fashion trends or changing taste in music, movies, or literature.

ESSENTIAL

Disruptive innovation doesn't have to spell death to your business. Consider, for example, the emergence of online news sources. Many observers saw this as the beginning of the end for traditional newspapers. However, while these organizations have certainly struggled, companies like the *New York Times* have become big players in the online media movement that many saw as fatal to their business.

Whether or not your company is based on, or dependent on, technology, it is at risk of becoming obsolete. The concept of evolution—adapt, migrate, mutate, or die—applies to marketing as it does to biology. Could *your* product or service become the victim of a disruptive technology? Yes, of course it could. The big question then becomes, "What can or should you be doing now to ensure that you are evolving effectively?"

There are two key ways that you can prevent your product or service from becoming an anachronism. First, pay attention. You should continually monitor the external environment and *listen* to your customers, your competitors, and your community. And, as the saying goes, "don't believe your own press"—don't become complacent or satisfied with the status quo. How many organizations die, or products lose their allure, simply because the leaders behind them *refused to believe* that their product or service could possibly ever be replaced? Too many. Iconic brands such as Compaq, Sony, and Saab, for instance, are no more.

You obviously can't accurately predict the future. What you can and *should* do is stay aware and current and continually evaluate the variety of impacts that affect you. Why is it that companies like DuPont (1802), Wiley (1807), and Colgate (1806) still exist after *two centuries* in business while others like Woolworth's (1879) and Compaq (1982) are long gone?

FACT

One nontechnological "innovation" that has had and will likely continue to have significant consequences for businesses is changing attitudes toward environmentalism. A recent Cone Communications study found that 45 percent of American consumers actively seek out environmental information on products they are shopping for. Similarly, 71 percent of survey respondents in the 2013 study said they consider the environment when they shop, up from 66 percent in 2008.

There still are other retail stores, and there still are other computer companies. But there is obviously something different about companies like Saks Fifth Avenue (1867) and IBM (1911) that still exist despite weathering environmental changes and fluctuating economic conditions.

What is it that's different about those companies, and can be different about yours? Paying attention! Refusing to become complacent. Refusing to believe that nobody could *ever* possibly replace or improve what you have to offer. Refusing to hold fast to "the way it's always been done" and, instead, embracing new challenges and resultant new opportunities that could potentially launch *your* company into another century. Easy? No. But certainly worth the effort.

CHAPTER 6

Defining, Refining, and Managing Your Brand

Brands aren't just big names like Google or Target. While you may not realize it, you have a brand! Brands are simply a reflection of what your target audience thinks of you. A brand, according to the American Marketing Association, is a "name, term, design, symbol, or any other feature that identifies one seller's good or service as distinct from those of other sellers." That's the technical definition. The practical definition is a bit more elusive.

What Is a Brand?

You might think of a brand as a personality. Just as individuals have personalities, so too do businesses, products, and services. Brands are a reflection of how the market views you.

You're familiar with brands. They permeate society and are an important part of the culture. Consider such well-known brands as Coca-Cola or Starbucks. In 2013, the top ten global brands, according to Interbrand.com, were:

- Apple
- Google
- Coca-Cola
- IBM
- Microsoft
- GE
- McDonald's
- Samsung
- Intel
- Toyota

Interbrand was founded in 1974 and has been monitoring brands since that time, compiling a list each year of the top brands. It is very interesting to note that there is never any significant change in who makes the list from year to year.

Your Brand

Importantly, while Interbrand's list makes use of the familiar logos of these top companies, and while these logos have become iconic and are widely recognized—even by young children—it is not the logo that defines the brand. The logo is simply a symbol that helps consumers quickly identify and connect with the brands that they have formed impressions about.

You want your customers to identify your brand for years to come. Your logo, and the other elements of your visual image such as the colors you use or your product packaging, are there to convey consistency to your customers.

While your logo is an important element of your overall brand management efforts, it is not the only element. In fact, branding is an issue that involves every aspect of the marketing mix—your product, the delivery of that product (place), your pricing, and, of course, your promotion.

ESSENTIAL

As important as brand is, it generally should follow your core competencies and not the other way around. McDonald's, for instance, would find it challenging to rebrand itself as a healthy dining option. If your core competencies revolve around a lean cost structure and low cost, you are probably not well positioned to pursue a luxury brand identity, no matter how much you want to be the high-end company.

Who Owns the Brand?

While a company might create a logo or symbol to define its brand (think of Apple's apple) companies don't create brands; consumers do. It is the consumer perception of brands that create the brand reality. What companies do, though, is work to understand the brand position that their products and services hold in the minds of consumers and, based on that information, work to enhance the attributes that contribute to a positive brand image or to overcome those that contribute to a negative image.

This is not an easy task. It is often subject to the whims of the marketplace. Consider, for example, how quickly some brands move in and out of favor. Every communication that comes from your organization—whether it is committed to a permanent form as in an advertisement, posted on your website, conveyed via a media interview, or shared one-on-one, as through a customer service center—has an impact on your brand.

Branding is all about differentiation. Strong brands are strong brands because there is something distinct about them that creates differentiation in the minds of consumers. Disney. Starbucks. Nordstrom. They all have their unique brand. The key to developing and supporting a successful brand image lies in understanding what is unique about your organization and its products and services and then capitalizing on that uniqueness through *all* of your communication efforts.

While it can take years to build a strong brand, that brand can be deflated far more quickly through inconsistency or incongruity in your messages and in the experiences that consumers have with your products and services. This happens when a customer's experiences do not support the "brand promise"—the communications the company uses to describe itself or its products and services. Experience creates reality in the consumer's mind.

Brand Management

All strong brands are clear, consistent, and visible. Think of the brand with which you are most familiar and consider the brand attributes that the company uses in its communications. Do these attributes hold true? Maintaining a clear, consistent, and visible brand message is, of course, an ongoing challenge because customers change, customer expectations change, employees change, and the environment in which any business operates is continually undergoing changes that must be monitored and responded to.

The brand management process involves three important elements:

- Understanding what is unique about your products and services (features) *and* how those unique attributes create meaning for your target audience (benefits).
- Developing a plan to make your brand visible to your target audience.
- Managing your brand so that every consumer interaction with your company (your staff and your products) will send the same consistent "on brand" message.

ALERT

Don't assume you are in complete control of your brand and overlook the external factors that play a role in how your brand is perceived. What about the media attention surrounding Target's recent data breach, or all those public service announcements exposing the health effects of cigarettes?

If your brand focus is on simplicity and your billing statements, for example, do not convey that same consistent brand message, that's a problem. If your employee communication materials like your newsletters and intranet sites do not support your organization's brand messages, that's a problem.

Branding isn't just a one-time effort—it's an ongoing process that involves a lot of work. To help support a strong brand, you need to:

- Deliver your products and services in a unique way; don't be a "me too"
- Get to know your competitors so that you can understand what makes you unique
- Focus on a specific audience; don't try to be all things to all people
- Use feedback from customers to understand what your strengths are and what separates you from your competitors
- Make sure everything about your organization is sending the same message (your website, your media advertising, your building signage, your letterhead, your product packaging, etc.)

ESSENTIAL

Your brand and its constituent components can be valuable assets for your business, and they should be protected accordingly. Make sure you have taken the necessary legal steps to protect your brand against copyright or trademark infringement. Do you think McDonald's has taken steps to prevent other companies from using its signature Golden Arches? What about Nike's "Just Do It" slogan?

Effective brand management is about consistency. Every interaction that a customer, or your target audience, has with your organization forms an impression. It is the consistency of those impressions over time, aligned with your desired brand identity, that creates a brand. To support a strong brand you must continue to send the same message in multiple channels over and over again—even when you have become tired of it. And, importantly, you must deliver on that brand promise. It is not just the messages consumers receive that define your brand; it is also their interactions with you and your products and services.

While the concept of branding is relatively simple, the process of effective brand management is not. Effective branding requires a focus on every detail of consumer and customer interaction with your company and its products and services.

Identifying Brand Attributes

Branding is a fundamental task for any business, whether large or small, regardless of industry, and regardless of how long the business has been around. Effective brands drive successful businesses. Get it right and you will reap the rewards. Unfortunately, although the process can seem straightforward from an "academic" perspective, the real work of branding is an ongoing process that involves all areas of the organization and all individuals in the organization. That's what makes it such a challenge.

You've probably heard the expression "like herding cats"—that's exactly what brand management can feel like, especially for service organizations. There are basically four steps involved in the brand management process:

1. Clarify how you would *like* to be perceived.
2. Assess how your target markets currently perceive you. This assessment should include employees (because they play a critical role in serving as brand ambassadors for your organization), customers, prospects, and community leaders, as well as all audiences whose goodwill is important to you. The specific audiences will vary by organization.
3. Identify the gaps between desired and perceived brand image.
4. Develop a plan to close the gaps. This includes both marketing communication and operational strategies and tactics.

Most of this process is fairly straightforward. In fact, it's relatively easy to get to the fourth step, but that's where the challenges emerge. Why? Because most organizations view branding as a communication process. While communication is certainly part of the branding process, it is just a part. Operational issues also play a major role.

For service businesses (healthcare organizations, professional services firms like attorneys or consultants, etc.) brand management is especially challenging because *every interaction* they have with their target audiences serves to form impressions. This includes everything: how clean the parking lot is and how easy it is to find parking; how their staff answers the phone; how staff are dressed; and on and on to encompass every single interaction—every single impression.

Brand management is a worthy challenge though. It starts with determining how you ideally would like to be perceived. The larger the organization, or the greater the number of individuals who might be involved in this process, the more challenging it may be to achieve consensus on a list of desired brand attributes. Put simply: how would you like your target audience to think of you?

For example, suppose you operate a dry cleaning business. Your list of attributes might look like this:

- High quality
- Accessible
- Friendly
- Environmentally responsible
- Cost-effective
- Responsive
- Quick turnaround

Another dry cleaner might have an entirely different list:

- High quality
- Upscale
- Personalized service
- Great value
- Attention to detail
- Satisfaction guaranteed
- Multiple locations

Is there any "magic" to developing your list, or any "right" answers? No. The list is entirely up to you. However, there are two considerations that can help you focus your list appropriately: customers and competition. Your list of attributes should be designed to meet the needs of your target market and should serve to position you against the competition. Your list represents your vision of how you would like to be perceived. It may or may not reflect how you currently *are* perceived. The next step in this process, then, is gathering information about consumer perceptions.

Consumer Perception

An important step in the brand management process is determining how consumers perceive you. This is often done through the use of focus groups and what are called "projective exercises." Projective exercises are a means of understanding inner feelings—even a subconscious perspective—that consumers may have about your brand.

It's one thing to ask people to tell you what they think of your business, your products, or services; it's another thing to use projective techniques to dive deeper into their perspectives and opinions. There is a wide range of projective techniques that might be used to do this. These may include:

- **Drawing pictures.** "Suppose our product was a house. What kind of house would it be? Draw a picture to illustrate how you would view our product as a house." The picture doesn't have to be of a house. It could be of anything that might help to offer insights on perceptions that might be difficult to describe objectively. Through these images, participants will share perspectives that are not impeded by their ability to convey their thoughts through precise words. This allows marketers to understand more subjectively how they—and their competitors—may be viewed.
- **Creating analogies.** Given a list of words or phrases, consumers are asked to describe how the product or service is similar, or dissimilar, to these words and phrases.
- **Personifying the brand.** "If our brand were a person, what kind of person would it be? What would its personality be like?"

Focus Group

A typical focus group setting might include eight to ten participants. After some initial introductions and discussion, the group might be asked to think of some attributes that define the brand being evaluated. They might then share and discuss those attributes. Then they might be asked to either draw a picture or tear pictures out of magazines to convey the attributes they had in mind.

ALERT

One of your biggest branding tools could be right in front of you and largely overlooked: your name! The name of your business could be the first thing a potential customer ever knows about your company. Don't overlook its importance. A name like Dusty's Janitorial, for instance, may send a mixed message.

The ensuing discussion would delve deeper into their thoughts and opinions, providing a much richer range of inputs and perceptions than what would typically be generated through their initial list of attributes.

Quantitative Techniques

Quantitative techniques can also be used to evaluate consumer perceptions. Suppose you have generated a list of five attributes that you would like your product to be known for:

- High quality
- Good value
- Reliability
- Consistency
- Exclusiveness

You might then create an assessment tool or survey that would ask respondents to rate your product along a continuum for each of these criteria; for instance, from low quality to high quality, or from inconsistent to highly consistent.

The aggregated results would provide an indication of where you might need to focus your efforts to change perceptions over time. For instance, if you discovered that your target audience generally perceives your product as being low value, you might want to consider changing elements of what you have to offer. Changing things like product, price, place (availability), or promotion can alter these perceptions over time. This might mean doing a better job of communicating the value of your product, changing packaging or distribution, remodeling or upgrading your storefront (or website), and so on.

Assessing consumer sentiment can be accomplished in informal ways. Simply engaging consumers in conversation or monitoring their comments about your organization through comment cards, online comments, reviews, or similar means can yield valuable information.

It is important that this type of assessment occur on an ongoing basis, because the environment is constantly changing. Consumer preferences and opinions change. Expectations change. New products or competitors emerge—or go away. Continually monitoring these perceptions and taking steps to manage and shift them is a critical component of effective brand management.

Developing a Brand Management Plan

Sometimes, through your assessment, you may find that your audience doesn't perceive you as strongly for a particular attribute as you would like to be perceived. In other cases, the opposite is true. Sometimes, you may find that your audience has a positive perception of you that you weren't even aware of and now wish to emphasize.

The gap between how you would like to be perceived and how you are perceived will drive the development of your brand management plan. This plan will focus on far more than your logo and communication materials (although they will be a component). Your brand management plan must consider issues related to your product itself, how you communicate about that product, and every potential interaction that your target audience has with you.

The first step in this process is often conducting a "brand audit"—a review and critical evaluation of every touchpoint that your audience has with you that may impact their perceptions of your business. During this process it's important to consider to what extent each interaction does or doesn't support your desired brand attributes.

ESSENTIAL

Taking advantage of changing consumer sentiments or attempting to appeal to broader markets does not have to mean changing your entire brand. Consider creating separate brands under your overall corporate brand umbrella. A perfect example is the way Toyota tapped into the luxury market with its Lexus brand without tarnishing the affordable quality image of Toyota itself.

For instance, if you operate a beauty salon that you wish to be perceived as "exclusive," "cutting edge," and "high value," even something as seemingly counterintuitive as being able to get an appointment at a moment's notice could be counterproductive. After all, if you're so exclusive, why is it so easy to get into your salon? The concept of scarcity in marketing tells us that sometimes *not* having our product or service readily available can support our desired brand image.

In this same salon, the exterior of your building and its signage will have an impact on brand perception. So will the way your staff, including your reception staff, dress and appear. Jeans, baseball caps, and having your hair tied up casually in a ponytail probably won't send the cutting-edge message you're hoping to deliver. From facilities, to attire, to every single piece of your communication materials, your brand has an impact along a wide array of consumer touchpoints that must be continually evaluated, measured, and managed!

Consider how effectively some of the top brands align their desired brand attributes with how well they deliver on the brand promise. Consider also the variation in desired brand identity and how this affects the actions of the company—the difference between McDonald's and Starbucks, between Kmart and Nordstrom, between Chevy and Lexus.

There is no right or wrong when it comes to defining your brand. It is up to you. What matters, though, is that however you define your brand, you are ensuring that you are delivering on that brand promise through every interaction with your target audience. For instance, if you want to be perceived as a high-quality provider, your staff should be well dressed and professional, and reflect the image you wish to convey; your facilities should be clean; all of your communication materials should be high quality. If you want to be perceived as offering great value, you would attempt to reflect a more casual image. In that case you would certainly still want your staff to convey a professional image, but it would probably not be consistent with your desired brand identity to have staff dressed in formal business attire.

It is very important to take a broad view of your brand based on the four elements of the marketing mix: product, price, place, and promotion. Each of these elements impacts how you are perceived and all must be managed, concurrently, to convey and maintain a strong brand image. The big brands know this and do it well.

When to Alter Your Brand

Businesses sometimes talk about changing their brand when what they are really doing is changing their brand identity. The two are distinct. Keep in mind that your brand identity refers to the elements you use to communicate with your audience—your logo, your corporate colors, and so on. Changing your brand identity may impact how your brand is perceived, but actually changing your brand is a much more extensive process that involves the same steps already discussed:

1. Identifying your desired brand attributes
2. Determining how you are currently perceived
3. Identifying the gaps
4. Taking action to close the gaps

For example, in the salon example used in the previous section, your assessment may require that you update your signage, clean up the outside of your building (including the parking lot), establish dress codes for staff, redesign your website, etc. All of these, however minor, really do matter.

Since names and logos certainly are important reflections of the brand, it is worth discussing whether a name and/or logo change may be appropriate.

Name Change

Sales are stagnant. New customers are few and far between. Competitors are nipping at your heels. What to do? Must be time to change your name, right? Not so fast.

Often, the desire to change a name—whether of your company or of individual products or services—is driven by the misperception that changing the name will suddenly boost sales, create new customers, and make competitors shrivel up and go away. This is rarely the case.

When *should* a company or business change its name? When the company or business has *literally* changed and the name change will help in communicating that change to audiences that may otherwise be confused. A good example of this would be the merger of two well-known companies; unless one is being "assimilated" by the other, this can be a good time for a complete name change. Another situation that would appropriately prompt the consideration of a name change is the existence of evidence that suggests your potential customers are confused—or worse, put off—by the current name.

QUESTION

What is the value of a brand?
You may be surprised. Apple, which topped Interbrand's list in 2013, has a brand value of $98.3 billion according to Interbrand's survey. It's followed closely by Google Inc., which has an estimated brand value of $93.3 billion. Is it any wonder that these very large companies protect their brand equity carefully? Shouldn't you be doing the same?

When should a company or business *not* change its name? When the name change is somehow intended to magically, on its own, boost business. It won't happen. Companies generally point to well-recognized brand names—Apple, Nike, etc.—as examples of great company names, and they want a great name just like these. However, those names meant nothing when they were originally selected. It is only what those organizations have done over time that has created these strong brands. Name does not drive brand. Actions do.

Finally, never change your name before assessing how much value or "brand equity" it currently has. A name that is widely recognized by your target audience and that reflects your desired brand attributes has significant value. Don't throw that value away simply because you have grown tired of the name or you believe your market has. Find out first.

Logo Change

Recent logo changes by Google and Yahoo! have gotten the marketing and branding communities buzzing. Neither made a major change to the look of its logo, which, from a branding standpoint, is an important point. In fact, if you review most iconic brand logos over time (think Coca-Cola, Starbucks, McDonald's, etc.), you'll see only slight changes—often changes *so* slight that, if these companies hadn't told consumers about the change, it's likely that they would have gone unnoticed.

FACT

While even small organizations should carefully consider their image and brand when just starting out, and invest in a quality image (including logo and other materials), that is often not done. For these organizations, a logo redesign often becomes necessary over time as the organization grows and has access to more resources.

Why is the preference for only slight changes so prevalent among the top brands? Simply because they *are* the top brands. Logos, and other elements of a company's or brand's visual identity (colors, packaging, etc.), serve to help consumers make an instant connection between the brand and all of their past perceptions and experiences with the brand. Change the logo too much and you risk impacting—even breaking—that connection. That can be an expensive proposition for those companies that don't wish to change their brand image.

For those that do, however, changing visual identity can be a very visible way of conveying a shift in image. This happens fairly frequently for small organizations, in which logo changes may be undertaken to provide a more "polished" look.

Logos also are often changed to remain fresh and up-to-date with design shifts, especially for companies that have been around for decades. The danger for companies both large and small when making logo changes is that they may confuse or alienate their markets, or that they somehow diminish the ability of the logo to serve its role of being a visual reminder or representation of the brand. That's exactly why it's most common for organizations like Google and Yahoo! to make only minor adjustments to their logos. Many do this without ever informing their audiences that it has been done. It is only through looking back at the use of their logos over time that we can see these adjustments.

Unfortunately, organizations that are not counseled by large public relations and marketing departments or agencies have a tendency to make these changes too frequently and without good reason. The best advice: exercise caution when you start going down the path of changing your name, your logo, or anything else that serves to connect your audience to your brand. These impressions are formed over time, often over a *long* time. They can be broken in an instant.

Building Community

Brands are the foundation of engagement between businesses or products and their markets. Strong brands are based on strong engagement. There are some iconic examples. Harley-Davidson is one of them. Some Harley-Davidson owners are so strongly engaged with the company that they actually have the company logo tattooed on their bodies. Now that's loyalty!

Individuals or groups may also have strong brands that create a strong community. Consider the "Deadheads," followers of the Grateful Dead in the 1970s, or the "Beliebers," followers of Justin Bieber early in this century. Once you have developed a strong brand that is based on consistency and what's called "living the brand promise," you are positioned to create a community of loyal followers. These followers become advocates, even disciples, for what you have to offer (remember the Net Promoter score from Chapter 4?).

Although these communities sometimes grow organically, without prompting from the business, group, or individual, in most cases they require action on the part of the business to reach out, connect with, and engage with its audiences. That focus on engagement starts inside and grows outward.

CHAPTER 7

Your Employees and Customer Engagement

Companies often spend a great deal of time and effort managing customer perceptions through their marketing communications and other external efforts like media relations and events. This sort of behavior is designed to reflect positively on the company and its products or services. While these efforts are certainly important, there is another important audience that can have a very positive impact on the customer experience: employees.

The Critical Role of Employees

Employees are a critical component of your brand and your ability to successfully engage with your target audiences. Unfortunately, the importance of employees is far too often overlooked for a number of reasons:

- Businesses often fail to recognize that a brand is bigger than a logo and, therefore, overlook the role their employees play in creating and maintaining a strong brand presence.
- Business owners, especially small business owners, may be so focused on driving new business to their doors or websites that they don't take the time to ensure that employees are armed with information to help support their efforts.
- Business owners may take it for granted that employees know what is expected of them and how their actions impact the brand.

Despite the fact that studies by Towers Watson, Gallup, and others continue to support the critical role that employees play as ambassadors (or detractors) for the organizations they work for, not all organizations are as focused as they should be on their staff. If you're interested in boosting your marketing, you need to first start inside, with your employees. Seem a bit counterintuitive? Maybe. But consider that, particularly for service-based organizations (like healthcare providers, consultants, attorneys, etc.), the interaction between employees and customers is a key part of the service experience. If your employees aren't energized and engaged—and serving as passionate brand ambassadors—what kind of service experience do you think your customers will have?

QUESTION

What if my employees don't understand my brand strategy?
Employees, especially "frontline" employees who interact directly with customers, play an important role in communicating your desired brand. If they don't know whether you are positioning yourself as the low-cost leader or the high-quality option, think of the inconsistent messages they could be sending to customers they deal with every day.

A study by *The Forum*, part of the Business Marketing Association, called "Delivering the Brand Promise Influences Consumer Spending" showed a direct link between employee satisfaction and patient (or customer) satisfaction. In addition, this research also supported the fact that those with higher levels of satisfaction are more likely to recommend a product or service to others. That's engagement!

Employees as Brand Ambassadors

There is a lot of talk these days about B2C (business to consumer) and B2B (business to business) marketing, but there's another important market that businesses must engage in to ensure their success: employees. B2E (business to employee) marketing can be thought of as the process of engaging employees and ensuring that they understand and are ready to carry out their critical role as brand ambassadors.

Employees have the potential to "wow" your customers. Without their support and strong performance pushing your desired brand attributes, you'll likely have a hard time engaging your customers successfully. This is especially true in service environments where employees are, essentially, the product.

In addition to the role that employees play in engaging customers through their interactions with them (and for those in back office or support roles, through their impact on product or service quality), employees also have the ability to influence the perception of your brand through their conversations with others. These others include family members, friends, and, increasingly, the online community. When employees enjoy the work they do, respect the leaders of the organization, and have strong relationships with their managers, they are often effective brand ambassadors. When the opposite is true, employees can have a negative impact on the brand.

It's not enough to provide employees with key messages that you'd like them to share with various audiences. They have to believe those messages, get behind them, and care enough about you and the business, and what the business does, to *want* to share positive information about you.

Do you want employees complaining about your processes, your products, or your management acumen? Probably not. But that's exactly what many may do if you have not taken steps to fully and effectively engage them.

Employee Engagement as a Leading Indicator

Conventional wisdom suggests that there is a direct correlation between employee and customer satisfaction. But that wisdom doesn't take the issue far enough. A few years ago an article in the *Harvard Business Review* by Rosa Chun, a professor of business ethics and corporate social responsibility at Manchester Business School in the United Kingdom, and Gary Davies, a professor of corporate reputation at the same school, disputed this conventional wisdom. Their position drew an immediate and strong response from those in the customer service industry, and for good reason.

FACT

Engaged employees provide a better customer experience than do disengaged or neutral employees, and that positive customer experience provides real dividends. A McKinsey study, for instance, found that 70 percent of buying experiences were influenced by how the customers felt they were being treated. The issue is far more complex than the simple, assumed link between "happy employees" and "happy customers." Why? Because "happy employees" represents just one of the variables that ultimately impact customer satisfaction. Certainly employee satisfaction, which is also commonly referred to as engagement, is important for organizations. However, engagement without alignment around the organization's mission, vision, values, and goals will not yield desired results. It's not *just* about satisfaction—it's about *process* and *people*. Satisfied employees alone are not enough.

As Russ Eisenstat, a co-author of *The Critical Path to Corporate Renewal* (Harvard Business School Press, 1990) said, "A lot more needs to be aligned than just satisfying the people who work on the front lines. They also need the tools in order to be able to meet customer needs, the quality of the product and service offering needs to be effective, and the internal processes need to be aligned in a way that allows them to deliver their best."

In short, it's complicated.

Yes, businesses are wise to engage their employees. But they're also wise to recognize that engaged employees are just one piece of an increasingly complex process that ultimately delivers value to customers.

As Chun and Davies note in their article, "Satisfying customers is crucial to a business," there's a great deal of evidence for a causal link between happy customers and higher profits. Of course, satisfying employees is a worthwhile aim in itself for many reasons. To link the two, companies need to engage employees by giving them both reasons and ways to please customers; then acknowledge and reward appropriate behavior.

FACT

Employee engagement is not a given. A recent study reported by Fast Company says that 30 percent of employees claim to be fully engaged in their work, while 52 percent claim to be disengaged, and 18 percent actively disengaged.

Clearly employee engagement, or lack thereof, can be an important leading indicator—and a good starting point—for businesses to begin considering how they can effectively engage with external audiences. And it all starts with recruitment.

Recruitment and Onboarding

Hire a dour employee and you're likely to nurture dour customers. Hire a friendly, outgoing employee and you're likely to nurture engaged customers. In the process of building an organization poised to nurture strong customer engagement, the most critical juncture is the hiring process. Building a staff of employees committed to strong customer service is the best offense against disengagement.

Similar to the branding process, the process of identifying the attributes of engaged employees who are likely to be strong brand ambassadors and likely to interact effectively with customers begins with a list. Your list of attributes will serve as the hallmark of employees who exhibit strong commitment to customer service.

This list then will become the basis of your hiring criteria, and will help you devise questions to ask during the hiring process to screen out the dour prospective employees and pinpoint the friendly, outgoing ones. A good place to start developing this list is by considering current, or former, staff members who exemplified a strong commitment to customer service—those employees who were often recognized by customers and other employees for their great attitude and exceptional service. Those just starting out may want to consider the traits of employees they've interacted with at companies where they have felt well served.

ESSENTIAL

Seeking out employees who are personally interested in your business's line of work can be a great way to recruit enthusiastic employees without necessarily having to break the bank. That amateur musician will probably be very engaging when talking to your guitar customers. The avid outdoorswoman you just hired could be a great resource for your green energy company.

What traits made them so exceptional? Chances are the list might look something like this:

- Strong communication skills
- The ability to deal effectively with conflict
- Patience (and sometimes lots of it!)
- A commitment to win-win solutions

You know these employees when you see, and interact, with them. So do your customers. For any business, the ability to recruit and retain service-oriented employees goes a long way toward building a strong brand and "wowing" customers.

The Manager's Role

Much research has been done to indicate the impact that managers have on their employees. Managers are the people with whom employees have the most contact throughout the day and, of course, managers are the individuals who determine employees' salary, opportunity for promotions or advancement, and even tenure in the organization.

Is customer engagement an explicit priority for your management team?
Businesses have a lot of goals: efficiency, quality, staff development. It's easy for customer engagement to take a backseat to these other laudable goals if your managers aren't consistently reminded of how important it is.

Through this influence, managers also have an important impact on customer engagement. When they hire, train, and coach employees effectively to serve customers well, they boost the odds of engagement.

Managers exhibit a wide array of management styles—some more effective than others. The following sections describe some common management styles along with some of the pros and cons for each. There's nothing necessarily right or wrong about any of these styles, but some are more appropriate in certain situations than others, and all will have an impact on your employees.

Authoritarian

Authoritarian managers simply direct employees according to their judgment and expect that those orders will be followed blindly. This management style can be efficient from a time perspective, but tends to generate low morale, which may ultimately outweigh any benefits. Additionally, the authoritarian style leaves managers with little or no outside input to their decision-making. This style is generally seen as an extreme example meant more to provide context for the other styles than as a practical management approach. There are situations, though, where this style is appropriate and effective—generally associated with the military or high-risk situations like firefighting or healthcare.

Consultative

The consultative manager seeks out the opinions of subordinates and takes them into consideration before making a decision. This management style benefits from outside opinions and is still relatively efficient in terms of time; however, employees can sometimes feel slighted or insignificant if their suggestions are largely disregarded by the manager. Consultative managers need to make sure they're clear about how input will be used (e.g., as "input only" or to influence the decision/outcome).

Collaborative

The collaborative manager directly involves employees in the decision-making process. This could involve a voting system, for example. Depending on the situation, the manager's vote might be equal to an employee's or weighted somehow by saying the manager's vote counts for two. The collaborative approach benefits from employee input and a sense of ownership of decisions, but can potentially force a decision that the manager is opposed to, based on the votes of the employees. It is important for managers to always reserve the right to make the final decision based on multiple inputs.

Laissez Faire

On the management spectrum, laissez faire style is the opposite of authoritarian. Laissez faire management means the manager is completely hands-off, and employees are left to their own to make decisions that will affect them. Laissez faire management can create a strong sense of ownership and self-motivation; however, there are obvious risks of chaos and lack of uniform direction.

The appropriate management style will depend both on the culture of your company and the situation. It is important to note, though, that managers have a significant impact on their employees. Effective management involves ensuring that employees know, specifically, what is expected of them, that they are provided with immediate feedback—both positive and constructive criticism—and that they have opportunity to learn, grow, and clearly see the impact they have on the business.

As managers work with employees to ensure that they meet the expectations they have been given—in this case, expectations related to customer engagement—it is important that managers:

- Are explicit about what effective customer engagement looks like

- Immediately recognize and reward instances of good customer engagement
- Immediately recognize and correct instances of poor customer engagement

It is the manager's actions and examples that pave the way for effective behaviors on the part of employees. Consider a few examples:

- The manager of a small restaurant stresses the importance of great customer service and treats customers well, yet when the restaurant is closed for the evening, speaks dismissively about the evening's customers.
- A manager in a sporting goods store spends so much of the day playing with equipment or online, surfing websites, that he generally has nothing to do with the store or its operations.
- The manager in an auto parts center encourages employees to sell inferior products to move inventory.

These are just a few of the many bad examples set by ineffective managers on a regular basis. Is it any wonder, then, that some businesses seem to continually underwhelm their customers? In most settings, if an employee is consistently delivering bad customer service, a look at that employee's manager might provide some insights into why that occurs.

Arming Employees with Key Messages

Helping employees serve as effective brand ambassadors who are committed to engaging effectively with customers can be a complex process. It's a process that involves everything from your hiring criteria, to training and communication, to employee satisfaction and, ultimately, to constructive feedback (positive and negative). However, it's time well spent because employees have a significant impact on the perceptions of customers and other important audiences.

Just think of how your own perspective of a business is impacted by your interactions with its employees, or the comments employees make to you in both professional and personal settings.

While the entire process of developing employees as effective brand ambassadors is a significant undertaking, there are two foundational steps that can help organizations get started on the right path toward this ultimate goal. First, develop and reach consensus on your organization's "elevator speech." Your elevator speech is a short statement of what your organization is all about, framed from the point of view (POV) of your external audience, that can be delivered quickly and succinctly whenever anyone asks, "What does your organization do?" The next chapter will explain how to put together this statement in more detail. What's important to know right now is that the statement should be based on a reflection of value from the target audience's perspective—what's meaningful to *them*. It's also important that all of the leaders, managers, and supervisors in your company must reach consensus on this elevator pitch. That, alone, can take some time.

ALERT

Your company culture has a huge influence on how your employees represent your brand. Anything from dress code to whether people show up early or late to meetings can find its way into employee behavior that is outward facing. The leadership can mold company culture by incentivizing desired behavior and leading by example.

Once you have consensus, test the internal validity of your elevator pitch. In order for your pitch to resonate with the outside world, it needs to be an accurate reflection not just of whom you *wish* to be, but who you really *are*. A good way to test the validity of your statement is by gathering input from your employees. Don't just ask them, though. Consider, instead, using the type of projective techniques that are often applied in focus groups to get a good, qualitative indication of how employees would define your organization.

Here's how you might do that: Gather a group, or several groups, of employees together in a conference-room type of setting. Provide them with a wide range of magazines to browse through. Instruct them to tear out photos of people, cars, houses, or some other image (pick one image to have them focus on) that they feel best reflects the "personality" or "image" of your organization. Once they've had a chance to do this, have them discuss why they selected the images they did. Consider how closely their selections and descriptions reflect the consensus of your senior leaders around your desired image.

This exercise will give you some indications of where you may need to do additional training, education, and communication to ensure that employees are armed with the right information to serve effectively as ambassadors for your organization, whether talking with customers, friends, relatives, or neighbors via social media.

Another technique for identifying potential key messages is to spend some time considering those things that customers, or your various audiences, don't "get" or don't know about you. For instance, "Why don't our customers know about our 100 percent money-back guarantee?" or "Why don't our customers know that our products are all locally grown?" These kinds of thoughts, which are frustrating and occur all too frequently, can provide you with good insights about the key messages your employees need to know in order to help you convey important points to your customers.

Make a list of these things, along with other key points that you want to emphasize on an ongoing basis through all of your communication materials. Then prioritize them and make sure your employees are aware of their role in getting this information out.

Employees and Social Media

Although there are plenty of businesses that attempted to "hide from" social media for a long time and, possibly, some that are still trying to do so, the fact of the matter is that social media is here to stay, and it has the potential for dramatic impact on how effectively you are able to engage your customers and consumers at large. That impact can be both positive and negative.

You already know that employees have a very important role to play as brand ambassadors, and they can certainly carry those important messages forward through the social media channels. Disgruntled employees, unfortunately, may share messages that are not quite so positive.

Because there is always the chance that some employees will share information inappropriately, spread misinformation, or damage the brand, *and* there are concerns about employees who may be "bashing" the company or its products and services, many companies establish policies designed to guide employees in their social media behaviors both during work time and personally.

ESSENTIAL

Employees can be great sources of social media input as well as output. Not only can they help spread the word about your organization through social media; they can be a valuable source of eyes and ears to help keep your company informed about what others have to say regarding your business.

Social media policies are, in many respects, no different from policies that companies have always had in addressing the role that employees play in representing the company in various settings. For instance, rules about the use of company letterhead for personal business have long been the norm. Similarly, rules about communicating on social media on the company's behalf should clearly indicate who may and who may not represent the company in this way. And, for those who are charged with being an online representative, it is important to convey guidelines about what is and what is not appropriate behavior. Many organizations take the time to consider and develop online "personas" or personalities to provide an indication of the style and tone of conversations that take place online.

ALERT

While employees engaging in social media on your behalf can be a great way to strengthen your brand, you need to be careful. To the extent your employees are using their personal social media accounts to bolster your business, your brand will be linked to those individuals. What else do those employees have on their profiles? Could their personal "brands" tarnish your professional brand?

Legality

Communicating with employees about how to represent the company when they're not at work can get a bit tricky. The National Labor Relations

Board has stepped up to address instances of employees being disciplined, or even terminated, for such actions. And, while employers are sometimes justified in their response to inappropriate comments made by employees in online environments, it's important to understand the laws and regulations that apply.

Generally, employers are not allowed to prohibit discussions of wages or working conditions among employees. Clearly this can be a gray area, and one to tread on lightly. Business owners need to be cognizant of both protecting the image of their brand and not violating employment law regulations. When in doubt, call upon your legal counsel to provide you with sound advice.

"Bad Apples"

Unfortunately, not all employees will be a good fit for your business. Those who do not convey and maintain focus on customer service can be a detriment. Any actions or behaviors that do not serve to positively engage with your customers are actions or behaviors that you must eliminate. Sometimes that may mean eliminating the employees.

There are four important steps to follow here, both to ensure that you are providing employees with the information and guidance they need and to ensure that your customers are being treated well and in alignment with your customer service values and philosophy:

1. **Hire for service skills.** Make sure that all candidates are screened and evaluated based on the skills that you have determined are needed in their roles.
2. **Clearly communicate your expectations.** Employees need to know what, exactly, is expected of them.
3. **Quickly follow up on any service-related infractions.** Employees need to be provided with prompt feedback when their actions or behaviors are not aligned with your expectations.
4. **Terminate when employees do not exhibit the ability to consistently live up to your expectations.**

Your organization should have a progressive disciplinary process leading up to, and including, termination that is clearly outlined in an employee handbook. You need to be sure that employees understand this process, and should also be sure that an attorney has reviewed both the process and your policies.

While terminating employees is never pleasant, it is sometimes essential. Your good reputation may depend on it.

CHAPTER 8

Using Business Development for Customer Engagement

Business development is an important tool for customer engagement. Small businesses have many opportunities to connect with key audiences and establish relationships that can serve them in a variety of ways. Business development efforts can "put a face" to your organization and cement relationships that drive business and positive word of mouth.

What Is Business Development?

Business development is a term that is sometimes used as a synonym for "marketing," although the two are not technically synonymous. Marketing is a broad process that involves product, price, place, and promotion considerations (the "marketing mix" or "4 Ps"); business development is generally directly related to the "promotion" piece of the marketing mix. Basically, though, it's all about reaching out and making connections!

Shel Horowitz, author of *Principled Profit: Marketing That Puts People First*, says that when it comes to breaking into a new community and building new contacts, attitude is key. "Come in with an attitude of service, and not just a 'what's in it for me' attitude," he says. "It won't take long to become visible."

ESSENTIAL

Never overlook any opportunity to make a key business connection. You just never know where you might encounter someone who knows someone who knows someone else who just might be a big prospect. The receptionist at your doctor's office, the car wash attendant, the bartender at the local watering spot—all may represent key connections that could help you leverage your business. Treating them in a friendly, courteous, and respectful manner can reap benefits down the road.

Your first step in establishing a presence with any target audience should involve "getting the lay of the land." What do you know about this audience in terms of what's important to its members, other individuals, or businesses like you that they currently interact with and, most important, how you might stand out and provide value in meaningful ways?

Starting with the network you already have can be a good starting point. These existing contacts can help you both by introducing you to others and by helping you develop an understanding of the community and its key players. For instance, if you're a business consultant offering human resource management advice to small businesses, you might ask your friends and relatives if they have connections who manage small businesses. Once you've gotten "the lay of the land," the next step is to get out and make connections. That means exploring the various organizations and events where your target audience may participate. Become active in community events. Working on nonprofit boards and committees, for instance, can help you contribute to the community while you build a network and—ultimately— customers and clients.

Building relationships through personal contact is key. Even if you're prospecting through phone calls, you should be arranging for face-to-face meetings whenever you can. Of course, while face-to-face connections are important in building your presence, today's networking opportunities allow you to take advantage of electronic options as well, which can be a big benefit when geography is a factor.

The bottom line, though, is this: whether on the phone, face-to-face, or on the Internet, if you're trying to get established and gain awareness for yourself or your business, business development can be the best and fastest method.

Your Customers Are Everywhere

Opportunities for business development are everywhere—even in your own backyard! One of the important elements of business development is recognizing that anyone could be a valuable connection. You never know who knows someone else that might represent an exceptional contact for you.

Associations and Organizations

There are a wide range of associations and organizations that you can join to help you connect with your customers, face-to-face and virtually. The organizations that are most appropriate for you will depend on your industry, your customers, and their interests.

These may range from local service organizations like the Rotary Club, Kiwanis, or Lions Club or they may be large national organizations. For instance, if you sell products to beauty salons, you many want to join the Professional Beauty Association (PBA). If you sell services to the funeral industry, you may be interested in the National Funeral Directors Association.

There are thousands upon thousands of organizations that may serve your markets. To find them, simply do an online search based on your target audience. The search results can lead you to their websites, where you can find out about membership requirements and costs, whether they hold regular conventions, meetings, or seminars (most do), and how you can get involved.

Associations also often have proprietary networking groups on their websites where you can connect with and learn from members. You can do the same thing on LinkedIn, which has almost 2 million groups representing various professional interests.

QUESTION

Where and how did Rotary originate?
Paul Harris, an attorney in Chicago, formed the Rotary Club of Chicago in 1905. He intended the group to provide a gathering place and network for professionals with a wide range of backgrounds. The name "Rotary" came from the group's practice of rotating meeting locations among members' offices. Today there are 1.2 million members around the world.

Professional Networking Groups

Professional networking groups like local chambers of commerce or BNI International also represent opportunities to get in front of various audiences. Chambers of commerce generally offer a variety of training, educational, and social events for members, as well as opportunities to participate on various committees.

BNI International is the largest networking organization in the world and is focused on generating referrals for its members, which form local groups comprised of members who meet with each other over breakfast or lunch and share referrals. Group members are limited to one from each profession. So, for instance, a group can have only one health insurance provider, or one marketing consultant, or one car dealer.

Trade organizations and associations also allow the opportunity for networking through various meetings and events that are held on a regular basis. These can be leveraged through attending the educational sessions, exhibiting at conferences, or even making presentations.

Community Involvement

Community involvement also can be a great way to make connections with customers and potential customers and to demonstrate your interest in and commitment to various causes. Corporate social responsibility (CSR) has become a strong area of focus for many companies, large and small.

Consumers are increasingly aware of, and interested in, the causes that their favorite businesses support. Your support, or lack thereof, of various types of organizations can either positively or negatively impact customer perceptions. Consider companies like TOMS Shoes, which provides one pair of shoes to a child in need for every pair it sells.

Involvement may range from making donations or contributions to volunteering. Many businesses also encourage their employees to support local organizations and may provide paid time to allow them to volunteer. In addition, they may sponsor various events or arrange for the business and its employees to participate in community-sponsored activities as a group. All of these opportunities provide ways to both connect with various audiences and demonstrate support in alignment with your business's mission, values, and brand.

Developing Your "Elevator Speech"

Remember that networking can occur at any time, so it pays to be prepared. As mentioned in the previous chapter, one important tool for effective networking is an "elevator speech"—a brief statement of what it is you do or sell. This is an opportunity to support your desired brand perception. The steps to take in developing this statement are similar to the steps you would take in any branding initiative.

First, identify the specific target audience (or audiences) you wish to influence. You may have more than one and, depending on those target audiences, you may need an elevator speech for each of them. Based on one of these specific target audiences, identify your desired brand (or personality). How do you wish to be perceived by others? Start with a list of about ten words or phrases that describe your "desired brand." In considering the development of this list, think about how your competitors are currently "positioned." What attributes do they use, or do others use, to describe them? Your goal should not be to constantly say "me too" in terms of how you position yourself, but to come up with different attributes that you can own.

Next, identify how your target audience currently perceives you. This is somewhat more challenging from a personal standpoint than it is when doing branding for a product or organization (for which you could use focus groups, interview, or conduct surveys), but it can be done. Some suggestions: ask trusted customers, clients, advisors, or colleagues for their perceptions; if possible, arrange for a group meeting with other colleagues where all could give and get input—even in an anonymous way—by passing around a sheet of paper with your name at the top and asking others to write down their impressions of you. Finally, based on how you would like to be perceived and how you currently are perceived, identify the gaps and prioritize areas of improvement.

ALERT

You may recall your parents telling you that the people you associate with reflect you. The same is true in a business sense. As you make connections and establish relationships with others, make sure that these individuals are aligned with your own business values and that they can help, not hinder, your efforts. Not all business associates may be supportive of your core values.

In terms of actually creating the "copy" for your elevator speech, it's important to start with the end in mind. In what way do you wish to influence or impact your audience? What do you want them to think or believe about you? This influence should be framed from the standpoint of benefits to them. It's not (and never is) about you. It's always about what's important to them (your audience)! So, just as when advertising any product or service, you want to turn your features (from the list you developed earlier) into benefits and ask, "What's in it for them?"

Here's another key point that may be somewhat intimidating: individuals attempting to develop or refine their "brand presence" are faced with the same challenges that service organizations face when attempting to manage their brands. Individuals are multifaceted; it's more challenging to create a successful brand image for you, as a person, than it is for tangible products.

Your "brand" is, ultimately, influenced not only by what you say, but by how you look—the clothes you wear, the car you drive, your office decor, your website, your online communications, and everything else that others see. Your elevator speech should be designed to convey the benefits you provide to a specific target audience and supported by all of the myriad other elements that make you *you*.

Effective Networking

Effective networking is a critical skill for any business person to learn. People like to buy from people they know and like, so developing a wide and active network is critical for effective customer engagement. Networking, whether through traditional, face-to-face methods or online, benefits from a solid understanding of your "personal brand" and your objectives, as well as the ability to effectively engage others in positive and rewarding relationships.

Three Key Factors

It's likely that you are aware of people who have broad, expansive networks—they're continually getting new business, picking up new clients, and making connections that simply aren't coming your way. Why is it that some can be so successful at these efforts while others flounder? There are three key factors involved: confidence, the desire to be of service, and interacting with others.

The confidence factor is readily understandable. To connect effectively with others, it's important to have a positive and outgoing demeanor. That is, of course, easier for some than for others. The second factor, the desire to be of service, may not be so readily understandable, but can help build the first.

Effective networking is not about selling. That's good news for those who simply are not naturally gregarious people. Effective networking, like marketing in general, is about providing something of value to others. That stems from a sincere desire to be of service.

The third factor, interacting with others, is also readily understandable. In order to be effective at networking, you need those interactions. You can't sit in your office staring at your phone and e-mail inbox hoping for something to happen. You need to get out and among people to help them develop awareness of you and, ultimately, preference for your services.

FACT

The Small Business Administration (*www.SBA.gov*) offers a broad range of services for small businesses. Chances are there's an office near you. If you visit one of the offices, you can get assistance in developing business plans, financial packaging, lending assistance, and much more. In addition, this is a good resource for connecting with other local businesspeople who may own small businesses, or who might have additional useful resources.

Networking is all about people. The more people you meet, the more options and opportunities will present themselves. Of course that makes sense. The more people you meet, mathematically speaking, the more opportunity there should be to make connections. While your marketing efforts should generally be very targeted, your networking efforts should be broad!

Sometimes people make one fatal error when networking: they are too exclusive. For whatever reasons, they discount the value of some individuals compared to the value of others. In the process they may be missing out on opportunities to exponentially expand the number and value of their contacts.

That's understandable, of course. It's human nature. There is a tendency for people to gravitate to others who are like them; they are more comfortable with people who share their background and perspectives. So, when they encounter others who are not like them, or who don't seem to fit the mold that they've determined defines their "best networking prospects," they dismiss them. That's a mistake. If you've ever found yourself thinking about how "lucky" someone else has been in making a key connection, think again. That connection likely didn't occur because of luck, but because of a broad and diverse network.

The big takeaway should be that you never know when you might be sitting next to someone on a plane, train, or bus, or at a restaurant, sporting event, or other activity, who could have a positive impact on your business. Being alert to opportunities often means stepping outside comfort zones and interacting with people who are not typically part of your social circles.

Adopting a personal philosophy focused on effectively reaching out to connect with others will serve as the foundation of success here. Two key principles apply.

Principle #1: Be Prepared to Give

Effective networking is about giving—as you meet with people, you should take the approach of wondering how you might help them. Others will give you tips on how you might help them through their conversation. Your goal in these interactions, therefore, should be focused more on listening than on talking. By listening to others you can pick up clues about what's important to them, what's of interest to them, and how you might be able to help.

ALERT

Business development is all about giving. One key best practice in business networking is recognizing that others will reward you if you are able to provide something of value to them. That means understanding their needs, connecting them with people and resources that can benefit them, and taking a "soft sell" approach to any interactions you have. Make it all about them!

The concept behind this principle is known as the law of reciprocity. When you give, you get. Listen to what others have to say, identify needs they may have, and do something to help them address those needs. That might be suggesting someone else they should make a connection with. It might be sending them some information that would be relevant, or it might be offering to do something for them yourself.

Principle #2: Be Patient

The results of effective networking won't be evident overnight. It takes time to build and nurture a network and to see the fruit of your labors. You may find yourself benefiting years from now from a connection you make today. You just never know.

The goal of networking is to meet as many people as you can and to develop a community of contacts that satisfies your needs; a community that brings together people who may be prospects, or future customers and clients—or who may know potential prospects, or future customers and clients.

Once you have engaged with people, staying in contact over time will help keep you "front of mind." Just seeing you at an event or hearing from you via e-mail means that your name is part of a contact's consideration list. For instance, if your business is a law office, it's more likely that contacts who find themselves or others in need of legal assistance will think of you first if you have stayed in touch with them.

Networking is a lifelong process. Results will come from persistence and a commitment to connecting with people in multiple settings—even when those people may not represent "the likely suspects."

Generating Positive Word of Mouth

Initially, your network will consist of new contacts that you will nurture over time. Ultimately, your network will contain current and former clients to whom, hopefully, you have provided exceptional service. Their positive word of mouth means everything to your continued success. When it comes to making an impact on consumer buying decisions, word of mouth matters.

ESSENTIAL

Thought leadership can be a great way to generate new business. Thought leaders are those who have established themselves as experts in a certain area or topic through the creation and generation of information, which might include blog posts, articles, white papers, webinars, and more. The good news is that even small, solo practitioners can effectively establish themselves as thought leaders.

If you think of your own personal experiences when purchasing goods or services, you can easily recognize how important word of mouth is. How often do you turn to colleagues, friends, or relatives to ask, "Who did you use?" or "What did you think about this product/service?" The significant impact of word of mouth can be good news to some marketers. If you have a great product that is readily available and meets consumer needs, generating positive word of mouth is virtually free marketing.

On the other hand, word of mouth can be bad news for some businesses. Given the influence that others have on consumer buying behaviors, it certainly behooves marketers to make sure they're spending time and effort both on creating and delivering exceptional service to every customer, every time, and continuing to "woo" the customers they already have.

Learning from Your Customers

Not creating exceptional experiences for every customer every time or continuing to "woo" the customers you already have is critical. But what's even worse than not doing these two things is doing what many, many businesses do: either spending a lot of time and money promoting and delivering products and services that are not meeting customer needs and that customers do not value, or not providing customers with the level of service, or outcomes, they had hoped for. That will create word of mouth, but not the positive kind. A good way to assess the value of your services on an ongoing basis is to follow up with customers to ask them about their experience, and to be open to their feedback. What you learn can provide direction for leveraging the things that are working well in your business practices, and improving the things that may not be working so well. Here are some questions to ask:

- Did your overall experience provide the value you expected?
- To what degree were you satisfied with the outcome?
- What could we have done better to serve your needs?
- Would you recommend our products or services to others?

Sometimes you may not like the answers you receive, but you should still seek this input. You can only fix what you know. Don't shut yourself off from the input of others.

Networking Best Practices

Effective networking is an ongoing process that takes time, effort, and attention. As you're connecting with others, be sure to make a good impression during the interaction as well as after. Follow up with a quick e-mail or personal note, as appropriate. Keep good records. As you're making new connections and building a network, don't commit these names and faces to memory; put them in a database.

FACT

There are literally millions of small businesses in the United States, with new businesses emerging every day. According to the U.S. Small Business Administration, small businesses provide 55 percent of all jobs, occupy 30–50 percent of all commercial space, and have increased almost 50 percent since 1982. Since 1990, as big businesses eliminated 4 million jobs, small businesses added 8 million.

Customer relationship management, or CRM, is a bit of a buzzword in the marketing industry these days, but the concept is sound. It involves building a database of contacts to help you track your progress and provide you with a valuable repository of information about potential customers or clients, their needs, their interests, and, of course, their contact information. Use the database to help you stay in touch on a regular basis. Set up a contact schedule and reach out just to say, "How are things going?" Send clippings or share information you know your contacts would be interested in.

Recognize that every interaction you have is an opportunity for business development—regardless of how unrelated it may seem. Connections are made in some of the most unusual places! Here are some additional tips to help you boost your business development practices:

- Connect with current contacts or colleagues to see how you might be able to meet their needs once you start your business development effort. Cast a wide net—friends, family, and even casual acquaintances can provide you with useful leads.
- Broaden your search by including connections from your past: school, early jobs, associations, and so on.

- Don't overlook building up your presence on social media (just don't expect immediate results).
- Commit to providing exceptional products and services to ensure repeat business and referrals (word of mouth is the biggest driver of business in most industries).
- Pay it forward: Reach out to help others whenever possible and have an abundance philosophy, recognizing that there is more than enough business to go around. Despite a weak economy, there is still plenty of work to go around!

CHAPTER 9

Using Traditional Media for Customer Engagement

In the "old days," before the Internet and social media, the best way to engage with a large number of potential customers was through traditional media outlets: newspaper, radio, and television. While these outlets have been augmented with a wide range of other alternatives that provide easier and less expensive opportunities than ever before, there is still value in the use of traditional media, and it should be part of your marketing mix.

The Role of Traditional Media

The media mix, according to the American Marketing Association, is "The specific combination of various advertising media (including network television, local television, magazines, newspapers, specialty advertising, etc.) used by a particular advertiser and the advertising budget to be allocated to each medium." Simply, it's the combination of all media communications used to get a message out to consumers.

The media mix is most commonly associated with advertising. A "medium" is a specific media element that carries a message to consumers or, more precisely, to target market segments. Some examples of media are television commercials, newspaper advertisements, and flyers in the mail. Poor media selection can undermine the best marketing plan. For example, using newspaper ads to connect with a millennial audience is unlikely to achieve desired results. Similarly, advertising on Instagram may not connect well with an elderly market. There is a proliferation of media available to marketers today as media offerings become more specialized to specific consumer audiences. This can be both a benefit and a drawback. It's a benefit in that marketers are now able to tailor messages to very specific segments of the population, targeting those most likely to respond to their product and service offerings. It's a drawback, though, because with so many options the decision-making process can be extremely complex.

The key to making appropriate media selection decisions lies in having a clear understanding of your objectives and your target market. However, before you can successfully match your media needs to your market, you need to understand the unique characteristics of each media type.

Print

Print media includes newspapers, magazines, and other printed publications like brochures, fact sheets, etc. Print is the oldest form of media, and although its use has been challenged by the growth of the Internet and electronic technology, it still plays a role for certain types of messages. It is not likely that the electronic media will completely replace the need for print communication any time soon.

Newspapers

Newspapers remain the most prevalent form of print media. A key benefit of newspaper advertising is the ability to be geographically selective with your messages. Newspapers are appropriate for "destination" advertising—that is, for advertisers who rely on direct traffic to their place of business. (e.g., retail and grocery stores, restaurants, healthcare organizations, and car dealers are among the businesses most likely to benefit from the use of newspaper advertising.) For organizations that operate within small and well-defined market areas, newspapers offer the ability to communicate directly with an audience that is likely to be interested in the product or service. A quick look at your own local paper on the weekend will give you a good idea of the types of businesses that find this form of media effective.

ESSENTIAL

Elements like QR codes can be a great addition to printed advertising, whether in ads, direct mailers, or even on billboards. QR codes are a type of barcode that can be scanned through a smartphone app to direct users to additional information that comes in the form of ads, videos, or landing pages. Consumers can scan the codes with their smartphones and find additional information about the product or brand. Be creative here, though. Don't just take people to your webpage—take them to unique and useful content.

Newspaper offers the advantage of a short lead time, allowing advertisers to produce messages for which timing is important. Most newspapers are published daily—although in rural areas of the country weekly papers are prevalent—meaning that advertisers can share timely messages such as notices of sales and promotions and have the flexibility of quickly changing offers/messages to increase effectiveness.

There are disadvantages to newspaper advertising, however, even for those businesses that find this medium most effective.

Newspaper offers limited segmentation. Beyond segmenting by geography, newspaper offers a limited ability to further segment the market by sex, age, income, etc. This can be done, of course, to a limited degree by careful placement of your advertising messages in specific sections of the newspaper. For example, you might run an ad for a health-food store in the health section of the paper, or an ad for a financial services firm in the business section.

Newspaper also has constraints in terms of the creative options available. Print quality is often uncertain, meaning that photos, particularly color photos, may not reproduce well. This is one reason why inserts are so prevalent in many newspapers—advertisers who depend on the ability to accurately show their products (e.g., furniture stores, clothing retailers) need to carefully control the quality of the printed materials they use.

Another disadvantage of newspaper is the cluttered environment it offers for your message. When your ad is in the newspaper you are not alone. Ads and inserts are prolific and yours can easily get lost within the clutter. Because of this clutter, newspaper advertisers need to use frequency—exposing audiences to their messages multiple times—to increase the chance that their messages will be seen. This, of course, increases the cost of getting your message to your audience, yet another disadvantage of newspaper.

Magazines

Magazines and trade journals offer another print media option—one that provides the advantage of additional segmentation options. A trip to the local grocery or bookstore will illustrate the wide array of magazines available targeting a multitude of audiences and interests. Consumer magazines are generally used by business-to-consumer advertisers, and trade magazines generally by business-to-business advertisers.

Additional advantages for magazine and trade journal advertising are increased production values (the print quality is generally high) and a longer "shelf-life." While newspapers are generally thrown away after a day or so, magazines will be kept for longer periods of time, offering your ad greater opportunity to be seen. And, to a greater degree than you'll find with newspapers, magazines and trade journals provide the value of pass-along readership. Readers will frequently share their copy of the magazine with others.

There are disadvantages, of course. You'll still be competing with many other advertisers within a relatively cluttered environment. And lead times are longer, meaning that you're not able to quickly get out information or messages about new products and services or to introduce changes in marketing strategy.

Radio

Radio advertising offers the advantages of low cost; high reach and frequency; the ability to target audiences selectively; flexibility; and timeliness, due to short lead times and the ability to be more creative in delivering messages with the addition of sound.

Radio offers segmentation options based on the format of the radio station (e.g., country, easy listening, hard rock) and time of day (morning drive time to target business commuters, weekend afternoons in the summer to target youth, etc.).

QUESTION

Are there any companies that don't use advertising?
There are actually quite a few. Some companies have products so popular and brands so strong that they don't need to advertise (although they still communicate with their audiences in other ways). Examples include Krispy Kreme, Rolls-Royce, and even Spanx. And, of course, the product with the brand name that says it all: No-Ad Sunscreen.

Poor audience attentiveness is a factor with radio, of course. People listening to the radio have a tendency to "tune out" commercial messages and, with many stations promoting longer music blocks to appeal to listeners, advertisements are strung together, adding to the likelihood that listeners will tune out (or switch stations).

Sponsorships and promotions through radio stations can offer an opportunity for increased exposure. These might include contests and giveaways of certain products/services, live remote broadcasting at local events, etc.— all of which are opportunities to increase reach and frequency when using this medium.

Television

The big advantage of television is impact. Television combines sight and sound and offers many creative opportunities and options. Because of the proliferation of cable networks and specialized programming, television also offers the ability to target specific audience segments. And, because of the large viewing audiences for many programs, reach can be quite large and, based on cost per contact, a good buy.

In general, though, television advertising is expensive. While local stations often provide production at no charge when ads are run on their stations, businesses should be careful to weigh quality against cost. Your ads need to convey the right image for your business, and local stations aren't always able to produce the quality that your product or service requires.

Another big disadvantage of television, similar to radio, is audience attentiveness. Perhaps with the exception of the Super Bowl advertising, consumers generally avoid commercials. And there's a lot of clutter out there. Your ad really needs to stand out in order to have an impact, and standing out can cost a lot! The cost per contact with television advertising can be low, but don't let this mislead you. Because of the large viewing audience, the total dollars you spend divided by that viewing audience might be low. But, unless those contacts are appropriate, they provide no value to you and represent wasted dollars. An ad for a new car presented during the evening news, for example, will impact only a small percentage of the total viewing audience.

FACT

Traditional media is not dead! Despite the proliferation and popularity of social media, traditional media outlets still play a role for small businesses hoping to connect with their audiences. In fact, Pew Research reported in 2014 that local news viewing on television was on an upswing. This represents a great way for small businesses in local markets to connect with their customers.

Advertisers are able to segment, of course, by selecting placement within certain programs most likely to appeal to their target market segments. *Desperate Housewives* will have a viewing audience decidedly different from that of *Fear Factor*. Advertisers capitalize on those different audiences through thoughtful placement of their ads.

While advertising on national programs can be prohibitively expensive, particularly for smaller businesses, cable television can offer advantages in terms of both greater segmentation and lower costs. A cable commercial can be purchased in some markets for as little as $4 for 30 seconds. Spots are purchased in bundles called "zones" that allow advertisers to target their messages to very specific geographic areas. A zone could include just a few small towns. Combining zones lets advertisers extend their reach. The selectivity that cable television advertising provides offers great benefits to marketers. When advertising on television, the cost of airtime isn't your only consideration, of course. You must also factor in production costs, and television production is the most expensive of the three forms of media advertising.

In any medium, but particularly in television, production is not the place to attempt to cut corners. Because of the high visibility and impact of television advertising and the proliferation of high-end players in this medium, image rules. A cheaply produced spot can reflect negatively on your business and its products and services. While the same is true with newspaper and radio advertising, television—by virtue of the fact that it is so noticeable—presents greater challenges in this regard (and, consequently, higher costs).

Outdoor

Outdoor advertising includes traditional billboards as well as messaging on bus shelters and kiosks and in transit settings (buses, airports, wrapped vehicles).

According to the Outdoor Advertising Association of America, Inc. (OAAA; *www.oaaa.org*), digital technology has transformed the industry. "Hand-painted boards are replaced by computer-painted outdoor advertising formats. Outdoor companies offer an increasingly diverse selection of advertising formats including: bus shelters, transit and kiosks; airport advertising, mall displays and taxis."

Billboards are the cornerstones of outdoor advertising (62 percent of outdoor advertising is in the form of billboards according to OAAA). They offer the advantages of repeated exposure and the ability to target specific areas and types of commuters. Consumers driving to work use the same route regularly; your message, whether promoting a product or service, can be right in front of them for long periods of time, at a relatively low cost.

Obviously any lettering on outdoor signage must be large enough to read and prominent enough to stand out against any graphic elements used.

And locations need to be carefully selected to target the consumers you consider your best prospects.

ALERT

With so much information and so many images readily available online, opportunities for copyright infringement abound. It's important to understand that whenever you want to incorporate words, images, sound, or video that you did not originally produce, you must have permission to do so. Infringement can lead to lawsuits if permission is not explicit (as through the use of stock images) or attained by asking the owner of the material for permission for use. On the downside, billboards cannot be used to convey a great deal of information. Your message needs to be simple and visual. When using outdoor in your media mix, brevity is a must. Although you'll certainly see exceptions, common wisdom suggests using no more than seven words and no more than three elements for an effective billboard design. The intent with billboards is to provide brief, essential information. Advertisers should focus on the most important product benefit and communicate that benefit with words, visually, or in some combination of the two. With billboards, that old saying "a picture is worth a thousand words" is especially apt!

Yellow Pages and Directories

Many businesses consider telephone directory advertising a necessary evil. In reality, though, your telephone directory advertising can be an important part of your marketing arsenal. Some products and services are more appropriate for telephone directory advertising than others. For example, businesses that people turn to in emergency situations (plumbers, locksmiths, etc.) still attract customers through their yellow pages listings, whether in traditional hard-copy format or online. However, the Internet has had a significant impact on the ways in which people search for information, and the decision of whether or not directory advertising makes sense must be an individual one for each business and its audiences. As with any other communication decisions, this one will be based on a thorough understanding of your target audience and how they seek information.

ALERT

The Federal Trade Commission (FTC) governs truth in advertising and is on the watch for advertising messages that are misleading or just plain inaccurate. While a certain amount of "puffery" is allowed (e.g., "We're the best!") advertisers must be careful to ensure that the claims they make in their ads are accurate and can be substantiated.

Plan your directory advertising in relation to your competitors. What benefits are they emphasizing? What can you emphasize to set yourself apart? What headings are they listed under? Do those same headings make sense for you or are they missing a segment of the market by not listing under a certain category? What buzzwords is the competition using that you could include, or respond to, in your advertising?

Your directory ad needs to break through the clutter and help you stand out from your competition. Here are some tips that can help you do that:

- Choose a headline that offers a clear, meaningful benefit to your audience. Don't use your business name as your headline.
- Include all pertinent information such as where you're located, hours of service, etc.
- Be cautious about using space for photos or clip art. Directory space is pricey—use it wisely. A graphic illustration can help to attract attention to your ad, but it can also take up valuable space that could be used to differentiate you from your competition.

A good way to decide what to include in your ad is to pay attention to the questions that potential clients ask when they visit or call you. Your answers to those questions can serve as a good starting point for your directory copy.

Start small and measure religiously. If you're trying too many directories or too many variations, it will be difficult to determine what's really working for you.

Direct Mail

Direct mail was the shining star of advertising in the 1980s and although its use has been impacted by the Internet and by consumer backlash against "junk mail," it continues to be a very cost-effective and very selective form of media. In fact, with exceedingly cluttered online mailboxes, some marketers are strategically turning back to traditional mail as a means of connecting with their potential markets in a much less cluttered environment.

Direct mail allows advertisers to specifically target their promotion to people who are most likely to be interested in their product or service. It's a one-to-one communication alternative (as opposed to other forms of advertising, which are one-to-many). Direct mail offers the marketer the chance to fully explain the product offering and direct the offer to a specifically targeted market at a fraction of the cost of television or telemarketing campaigns.

ESSENTIAL

Traditional direct mail can be a great way to connect with audiences. Advertisers can stand out through the use of three-dimensional formats, bright colors, and interesting packaging. Before finalizing your design, though, make sure to check postal regulations to be sure that your piece can be sent through the mail and to understand cost impacts for special sizes and formats.

Direct mail relies on the use of carefully selected mailing lists to reach prospects. You might use your own client lists for direct mail or you might rent lists through outside sources. Lists are generally defined as either "compiled" or "respondent." Compiled lists are simply a list of names and addresses. Many of these lists are created from telephone directories or association membership lists (a state bar association list, for example). Respondent lists are lists of people who have responded to other offers. The value here, of course, is the ability to select people who have purchased products or services similar to those you are attempting to sell. People who have purchased items through Nolo.com, for instance, might represent a good target market for certain attorneys.

A good source of information about the wide array of mailing lists available is the Standard Rate and Data Service (SRDS). Although SRDS does not directly rent or sell lists, it provides listings that allow marketers to locate those lists that represent their target markets.

Despite the fact that the United States Postal Service (USPS) is struggling and may cut back on delivery, there are those who believe that traditional direct mail still holds benefits for both marketers and consumers. In an increasingly cluttered e-mail environment, after all, marketers will be challenged to come up with new ways to "capture eyeballs." Traditional direct mail may hold some opportunities for a number of reasons:

- **Direct mail is intrusive.** It can't be ignored! It's in your mailbox and you have to do something with it, so it must be handled. And that creates an impact. Messages in online advertising media are fleeting. In fact, research conducted by Millward Brown, a global research agency, has found that reading something that can be tangibly and physically held has been proven to be more long-lasting in a consumer's mind than is looking at something on a digital device.

- **Direct mail is personal.** You can touch it and feel it; it can have dimension and texture. You bring it into your home or office, where it requires attention and some sort of interaction. Think about this: with an e-mail marketing message you never know if the recipient ever even sees it; it may be screened at a company's firewall or end up in a junk mail file, never to be seen. That's not the case with traditional direct mail. It has to be seen. It has to be handled.

- **Direct mail can be much more descriptive, persuasive, and emotional than online messaging.** You can motivate people to action using compelling messages and emotional hooks with more detailed copy and images.

- **Direct mail can be extremely targeted.** Through a thorough understanding of your target audience, and careful list selection techniques, you can precisely pinpoint those individuals most likely to respond to your offer.

- **Your direct mail messages can be personalized and relevant to your prospects or customers.** You can take a personal, direct tone, focused specifically on key benefits that are important to the recipients.

- **Direct mail can be readily tracked and measured.** Based on testing and your response data, you can focus or expand your list to set the performance level you want to hit.

- **Direct mail is trusted.** Online communications are becoming more and more annoying to many consumers who are dealing with cluttered inboxes, frustration over spam, and concerns about privacy.

The bottom line? Well-executed direct mail programs can bring big benefits! Don't give up on traditional direct mail. There may be opportunity for you in reaching both B2B and B2C audiences through the relatively uncluttered environment of the traditional mailbox!

Best Practices for Traditional Media Engagement

The challenge with all media, both traditional and new, is how to stand out. Media is cluttered, and consumers (both B2C and B2B) are quick to ignore or overlook advertising, especially when it's perceived as being "all the same." Advertisers need to consider ways of being different to attract attention. Being different, of course, is not enough in and of itself. You must be different with meaning. So, for example, getting attention with a television advertisement that begins with ten seconds of "dead air" might attract notice, but if the message and offer doesn't appeal to the people watching, the next time your ad airs it will be ignored.

QUESTION

How much does a Super Bowl ad cost?
A 30-second ad can cost as much as $4 million—and that doesn't include the cost of producing the ad!

The same is true of the very clever or entertaining television ads that have come to be associated with the NFL Super Bowl game. Clever may attract attention, but if that attention doesn't positively impact marketing objectives (e.g., increased awareness or increased sales), the advertising dollars are misspent.

Rarely will one media option serve all of the communication needs of an advertiser. The power of advertising occurs when media are used in combination to ensure that the message reaches the target market regularly and consistently. Repetition and reinforcement are key in generating awareness and encouraging sales.

Clearly the decisions you will face will be complex. Which media should you use? Which media should you use together? Which should you avoid? The following are some key questions, which, in addition to the advantages and disadvantages outlined in the previous section, can help you to make sound advertising choices:

- Who are you trying to reach? What are the specific traits and characteristics of your target audience? Are they male or female? How old are they? What is their household income? Do they work outside the home? If a B2B audience, what industry are they in? What size is their organization (in terms of both employees and revenue)? What are the titles of individuals within the organization most likely to make decisions related to what you have to offer?
- How do they spend their time? Are they sports-minded and therefore likely to watch football games on the weekend? Are they interested in the arts? Do they commute regularly? Do they listen to the radio? What programs? Do they read the newspaper? What sections?
- When do you want to reach them? At home? At work? In the car? When would your prospects be most amenable to hearing your message? When would your message be most likely to resonate or connect with this particular target group?
- How are their purchase decisions influenced? For example, prospects for attorneys who work with clients to set up their businesses are not likely to feel as "time pressured" as prospects for attorneys who represent drunk driving cases, or plaintiffs involved in automobile accidents.
- How often do you need to reach your target market? Is your service "top of mind"—something for which the market has an ongoing need (e.g., employment law issues for businesses), or is it more situation-specific (e.g., family law representation during divorce)?
- What information do you need to share? If you need to provide detailed information about your product, it's likely that radio, television, and billboards won't be the best options for you. Newspapers or

brochures would be more likely choices. If your product needs to be "seen" to be appreciated, then television or full-color print (magazine) might be obvious choices.

- How much money can you spend? Your advertising budget will automatically rule out certain media. Keep in mind that you must always consider both the cost to run the ad and the cost to produce the ad.

Selecting the right medium or combination of media for your message involves careful analysis of your target audience, identification of the geographic scope of your market, and a determination of the level of exposure that market will require to influence the desired action. Selection of media is, arguably, both the most complex and the most critical element of an effective advertising effort.

It is important at this step to think beyond the obvious. It's far too simple, and often ill-advised, to decide to run a newspaper ad or develop a billboard or create a television commercial. For certain objectives these tools can all be quite effective. But they're not necessarily or always the right choice. The right choice depends on your target market, and it relies heavily on your understanding of who your current customers are.

FACT

According to Nielsen research in 2013, the most influential force on consumer spending was recommendations from those the consumers know, followed by online consumer opinions and then ads on television, which showed up third. Perhaps surprisingly, ads in newspapers was in fifth place (behind branded websites), indicating that traditional media still has its place in the twenty-first century.

The key point is to look beyond the obvious based on a thorough understanding of your target audience. Your goal is to maximize the effectiveness of your marketing communication efforts by identifying those promotional opportunities that allow you to reach the most highly qualified prospects at the least cost.

CHAPTER 10

Using Social Media for Customer Engagement

The question of whether using social media makes sense for you is not an easy one to answer. Like many marketing-related questions, the first response that comes to mind is "it depends." That response is not meant to be facetious; it is true. Whether or not to engage in any form of communication always depends on your goals and your target audiences.

Should Your Company Use Social Media?

Obviously social media has taken the world by storm, with Facebook, Twitter, and LinkedIn leading the pack, but other options abound and are continually emerging: YouTube, Google+, and Pinterest, to name a few.

Research by American Express OPEN Small Business Monitor indicates that while only half (50 percent) of entrepreneurs surveyed were using social media in 2013, those who do are taking an increasingly targeted approach. Here's how some entrepreneurs are using it:

- 71 percent use it to attract new customers
- 59 percent use it to drive sales
- 55 percent use it to create a dialogue with customers
- 36 percent use it to create communities where customers can talk to each other

Whether you should take part in any of these venues can be somewhat of a chicken-and-egg issue. Should you establish a presence in social media and attempt to entice your audience to "follow" or "like" your business? Or should you look to see if your audience is already "out there" and find ways you might connect with them?

QUESTION

Are there any people who are not engaged in social media?
Yes, actually, a fair number. According to Pew Research, 65 percent of those who are Internet users use social networking sites. This means that 35 percent are not and, given the sheer number of those who are online, that's a big number. The big question for you is: Are your customers online? If not, there may be better ways to engage with them.

While there is no necessarily right or wrong way to go about making this decision, and best practices are continually emerging, there are some basic principles that can help guide you to the right decisions for your business.

Who's on Social Media?

Not surprisingly, age is a factor when it comes to online participation in social media channels. If you're hoping to engage a market of people ages eighteen to thirty-four, chances are they're out there and active on social media. If, however, you're targeting an older demographic—say fifty-five and older—the news isn't quite so good, although it's getting better.

Research released by the Pew Research Center in 2013 should send a wake-up call to all marketers who have been, or may find themselves becoming, overly enamored of the power of social media. Their research shows that 67 percent are on Facebook, 20 percent on LinkedIn, and 18 percent on Twitter, leaving a significant audience not engaged through these channels. While social media may have its place for many, there are some marketers who are far too eager to jump on the social media bandwagon without appropriate consideration to whether or not a significant percentage of their audience is out there. If a tweet enters the Twittersphere and nobody's there, does it make a sound? Sadly, no.

Watch the Research

According to the research, even among those under the age of thirty, only 61 percent indicate that they use social networking sites in a typical day. Compare that to the popular wisdom that suggests that all young people are using social media. They're not.

What does this mean for you? Well, it really doesn't matter whether "everyone" is doing something or not. What matters is whether *your* target audience is doing something—like actively participating in Twitter, or reading the local paper, or watching the local news, or listening to particular radio programs, etc.

It is a best practice to be familiar with the various communication options available to you, including social media, and to understand how those options work and what benefits they might have to offer for reaching your market. But don't just blindly follow the herd when it comes to adopting social media as part of your promotion mix. If you do, you may find that wiser competitors are connecting with your audience in other, more relevant ways.

The point is this: it pays to not make assumptions. Chances are that certain social media sites, depending on your needs, are able to put you in front of your desired target audiences, while others are not. When considering joining social media, you should ask yourself several questions:

- Who are you trying to reach (specifically)?
- What do you want them to do, think, or feel (your goals)?
- What communication channels are available to you to connect with them and compel them to some type of action?

Assessing the Value of Social Media

You should not wonder about specific things, like whether you should be on Google+, but rather answer questions like "Who are you trying to connect with, and what tools will be most effective in making that connection?" Having a varied list of options to select among is good. Simply using an option because it's the "latest thing," or because your number one competitor is using a tool, isn't a good reason at all.

If you're not yet an active participant in social media, don't feel bad. You're not alone. However, you should definitely take the time to learn about social media, in its various forms. In particular, you should pay attention to the audiences each social media outlet reaches and how those audiences are engaging with these sites (what they're doing online, what they're talking about, etc.).

FACT

What started as the BBS led to what we now know as social media. No, not the British Broadcasting System, but Bulletin Board Systems, online forums that allowed people to connect with each other online. Long before Facebook came into being, these early, iconic sites included America Online (AOL) and CompuServe. Both brands are still out there, but they've morphed over the years.

Remember, when it comes to marketing communications of any kind, the right question to ask yourself is always, "What communication tactics will be most cost-effective in reaching my target audience?" While communication tactics will change, and do change rapidly in our technology-driven environment, that question won't.

Social Media Myths and Misconceptions

Is social media better than traditional media? Well, it depends. Is television advertising better than radio? Are billboards better than newspaper? Is direct mail better than e-mail marketing? These are all "it depends" questions and, frankly, if you ever see what seem to be definite answers to questions like these you should exercise a healthy dose of skepticism. These questions simply can't be answered with any degree of certainty without some additional information. Before you can determine what form of media to use, you need to know, at a minimum, the answers to two fundamental questions: What are you attempting to accomplish? (What are your goals and objectives?) And who are you attempting to reach and influence? (Who is your target audience?)

If you're attempting to connect with college students, text messaging might be a good option. If you're attempting to reach businesspeople in the fifty-and-over crowd, advertising during the local news might be a good option. And social media might work for either of these audiences. But it depends!

Managing Misconceptions

The hype and attention that social media has generated over the past few years has led to some common misconceptions. One big one is the feeling that you need to be on social media or you'll be missing out. But think about that in the context of a different medium. For instance: "Gee, you're not advertising on television—are you missing out?" Social media is the same. It is simply another medium that may or may not be right for you.

Starting with the tool (social media) and wondering whether you should be using it is backward communication thinking. Instead, marketers should always first consider their objectives and their audience and then determine which of the many communication options available to them, often in combination, make the most sense in terms of:

- Likelihood to effectively reach the desired target audience
- Likelihood to effectively engage the target audience in the content
- Likelihood to generate the desired response

In many ways social and traditional media are very much the same: they are channels to get messages out to desired target audiences. One very important way they are fundamentally different is that, with social media, others can observe the interactions taking place between the marketer and its social media audience. In addition, the audience can be privy to the conversation whether it's positive or not so positive. But, that said, social media is neither better nor worse than other forms of communication. It all depends, as noted earlier, on the objective and the audience.

Social Media Best Practices

The first step in considering whether social media holds opportunity for you or your business is to clarify your goals and objectives. What are you trying to achieve through your social media presence? The answer may seem obvious (customers), but, while that is the ultimate goal, there may be other drivers. For instance, some business professionals may want to establish themselves as experts, or thought leaders, in a particular area. Others may be hoping to raise awareness for a new business, products, or services. Are you hoping to position yourself relative to a particular competitor? Interested in establishing a reputation for strong community support? Resist the temptation to focus, at least initially, on the end game. Customers will come, but marketing is a building process.

The first step is always building awareness, then preference and, ultimately, some type of action that impacts your bottom line.

Once you've clarified your initial goals and objectives, the next step is to think about whom you hope to influence. Who are the key decision-makers, or influencers, related to your business that you want to move toward some ultimate action? The more clearly you can define who these people are, the better you will be able to consider their attributes and, most specifically, their communication preferences. How are they interacting with online media? Which sites are they active on? What type of information are they most interested in?

This analysis may lead you to believe that social media is not the place for you. Or it may point to various opportunities across a number of channels. More specifically, it may suggest that one particular channel is likely to hold the most promise.

ESSENTIAL

Take the time to analyze your audiences online. It makes no sense to spend time building communities and creating conversations if those you've engaged with don't represent your target audience. If you're interacting primarily with spammers, advertisers, and your own company representatives, you may not be getting value from your efforts.

B2B Engagement

In certain industries, business professionals, particularly high-level business professionals, are simply not spending a lot of time online. They don't have time and, frankly, many do not see the value in it. In 2013, the *Huffington Post* ran a piece titled "Why Don't CEOs Use Social Media?" If this is, in fact, true and CEOs are your primary audience, you may determine that social media is not the best communication channel for you.

If, on the other hand, your target audience is young professionals starting small businesses, the situation could be quite different. Perhaps your target audience is college students who are generally very active on social media. If this is the case, you should get on Facebook or other social media sites as quickly as possible. Regardless of your target audience, the key is to take the time to find out if, and how, they are engaged! It makes no sense to spend time and effort on building a social media presence if your audience isn't there.

Why Connect Online?

Another important, threshold issue for consideration is *why* consumers (B2C or B2B) would want to connect and engage in conversations with you and your business online. While most businesses can come up with creative ways of generating conversation, some have more obvious, and less challenging, paths than others. What about your audience? What is the likelihood that you can offer them a compelling reason not only to initially like or follow you, but continue coming back to your site to listen, learn, and engage in discussion? Think creatively and don't automatically think you have nothing of value to offer.

ALERT

What you say on social media stays on social media. Never post something that you will regret later. Particularly when responding to what may be negative or critical online comments about you or your business, make sure to take a deep breath and consider whether what you are about to say will reflect favorably on your brand. If not, let it go.

Communication through any medium, including social media, has always been and will always be about deciding which information a business has that the target audience is likely to value. That seems simple, but businesses often struggle to get to this point, erring instead in thinking more about what *they* want to tell their audiences than what their audiences need or want to know. A good starting point is a brainstorming session with your partners, staff, or, better yet, with current clients to determine areas of interest that you may be uniquely positioned to deliver.

Questions to Ask Yourself

The following is a summary of the key questions you should consider as you evaluate your current social media activities or as you consider becoming engaged in social media:

- **What are you hoping to achieve through these efforts?** What's the goal? If you don't have a goal at the outset, there's no conceivable way you'll be able to measure or evaluate results. Your goal should also give you an indication of the audience you hope to impact or influence: "We want to increase our customers' levels of satisfaction with our products and services by 25 percent," or "We want to increase awareness among noncustomers in our market area by 30 percent."
- **Is there value for your target audiences in connecting with you?** That question should be considered long and hard—and realistically.

There may be some customers who have ongoing needs that make them eager to stay engaged with you. Others may not have these ongoing needs or interests. For instance, consider the difference between customers of a grocery store and patients of a heart surgeon. Based on your target audience, what value would you able to provide that is significant enough to get them to connect with you and stay connected?

- **With whom do your audiences wish to interact?** Often (but not always), the answer is going to represent individuals or groups, not your organization as an entity. We don't develop relationships with organizations; we develop them with people. That may mean managing multiple profiles and balancing the need to protect your brand with the value of allowing individual staff members to reflect their own unique personalities to their audiences.

- **How will you evaluate results?** This ties back to the first question, of course. Before launching a social media initiative you should think about how you will determine whether your goals are being met.

- **How do you avoid risk?** Yes, there are risks involved in online communications. The risks themselves are really no different from what they've been in the past with other forms of communication. Businesses and individuals have always been concerned about their reputations and about how to best respond to disgruntled consumers, but with social media the potential impact has increased exponentially. It makes sense to develop a plan *up front* for how you will address creation and posting of information, responses to feedback and input, and various types of potentially reputation- and brand-impacting issues that may arise.

Your Social Media Strategy

Miley Cyrus (@MileyCyrus) has more than 17 million Twitter followers. *Harvard Business Review* (@HarvardBiz) has 1.4 million. Midwest Dental, a dental clinic in the Midwest, has 150. What does this all mean? Absolutely nothing!

Evaluating social media effectiveness based on "the numbers" is like evaluating whether the television ads that run during the Super Bowl are "good" or "bad." Unless you're privy to the strategy behind them, your opinions are pretty much irrelevant. Without an understanding of the advertiser's objectives and the results attained, the opinions of whether the ads are "good" or "bad" are simply based on personal preference. To the marketers, that may be interesting, but is not what really matters. And while many are still enamored with the numbers (likes, pins, retweets, and +1's), the truth is that in social media, as in any form of marketing communication, it's the real results that matter—increases in awareness, preference, leads, and, ultimately, sales.

Effective Tactics and Strategies

It's difficult for many people, even those in the marketing world, to get their arms around strategy. Some effective social media marketing tactics often include elements such as these:

- Track your leads from social media by tagging your URLs.
- Sponsor user-generated content contests.
- Have a pin of each of your blog posts on your Pinterest account.

While these may be effective tactics, they are not strategies. And that's the problem with much of the social media content on the web today. It's an amalgam of presumably "good ideas" promoted and perpetuated by those with good intentions, but presumably without a solid strategy. Developing a solid social media strategy involves the same steps as developing any other communication strategy. These steps include the following:

- **Know your audience.** Know whether they're on social media, which channels they use, and how they engage with those channels.
- **Know your competitors.** What are they doing? What's working and what's not? Who is engaging with them, and in what ways?
- **Define what success means to you.** Certainly success is not about number of followers. But then, what *is* it about? Number of leads? Number of flow-through purchases tracked through your website?

In short, a solid social media strategy involves establishing measurable objectives, clearly understanding the target audience and their social media consumption habits, and monitoring and measuring results. Importantly, these results need to be based on return on investment (ROI). Having millions of followers or friends is not an ROI measure. What is a good measurement of ROI? New customers, clients, subscribers, or sales.

QUESTION

Did Al Gore invent the Internet?
Well, opinions differ and he has both supporters and detractors. However, what he did say in March 1999 during an interview with CNN's Wolf Blitzer was, "During my service in the United States Congress, I took the initiative in creating the Internet." What he meant by that statement is the subject of some debate.

However, new followers, click-throughs, and requests for information can provide an indication of future downstream impacts—things like requests for more information or actual sales. In fact, you might consider assigning some value to these types of actions based on the outcomes you are seeing. For instance, what is a new client worth to you? How many prospects or leads do you need to interact with, on average, before a new client is landed? How many online impressions or visits are required to generate a lead? Monitoring the various touchpoints along the pathway to a sale can help you establish metrics that provide leading indicators of downstream revenue. Is this a perfect science? No. But it can be a helpful barometer to provide you with some indication of the value of your social media efforts.

Keep in mind, though, that you can't know what to measure if you don't first have a strategy. That's the starting point. It's the price of admission for those who wish to drive real results through their online activities.

Your Website

Your website plays an important role in your customer engagement efforts. In fact, many small businesses consider their websites to be the hub of all activity. This is where they ultimately want to channel their customers and potential customers.

The twenty-first century marketplace allows consumers to find and form impressions of you online without ever encountering you either face to face or voice to voice. That can be a good thing if, through those online encounters, their impressions are positive. It can be a very bad thing if they're not. And, sadly, you may never know the difference.

Online Presence

Your online presence speaks volumes about you. If you don't have a good idea of how your website stacks up against your competition and how prospects or customers might perceive you in contrast to your competitors, it's important to take the time to find out.

The biggest problem for many small businesses is that their sites do not adequately convey their desired brand identities. New and small businesses are often cash-strapped and may take a low-cost (or even a no-cost, do-it-yourself) approach to the development of their websites. This can be a big mistake, even for brick-and-mortar businesses, because many consumers check out businesses online before actually going to them.

FACT

Social media often isn't really that social. In fact, if you monitor much of the activity going on through various social media channels, you'll see that it is usually businesses and individuals sending messages out with few or no responses. Your challenge is to find ways to effectively create those conversations that give social media its name.

Businesses have to ask themselves, "When our customers go online to look for what we have to offer, what are they seeing? How does our website stack up?" The purpose and role of your website will vary depending on your type of business and your business objectives. For instance, if you sell products online exclusively, your website is the hub for customer activities. It is where interactions occur. Your goal will be to drive those interactions to your website through a variety of other means, like traditional advertising, social media activities, blogs, etc.

Blogs

Web logs, now commonly known as just "blogs," represent a great opportunity to not only stay in front of your target audience, but also to establish yourself, or your organization, as a "thought leader." A blog provides you with a forum that you can completely control. You get to pick the topics, you get to create the content, and you get to regulate the interaction with those who choose to weigh in on what you have said.

For customers, blogs provide a forum to share relevant information about their products and services, which can help other customers use those services more efficiently. A beauty salon might blog about trends in hair and makeup. A dog groomer might blog about ways to keep pets healthy. A massage therapist might blog about healthful living.

Blogs can also be a way to reach out to noncustomers, or prospects, who might become customers at some point in the future.

SEO

In addition to the ability to engage with audiences, blogs provide a big boost for your website's search engine optimization (SEO), or the ability to drive increasing amounts of traffic to your website. Because blog content is frequently changing—or should be—search engines view it as fresh content, which means it's more likely to get noticed. In addition, by ensuring that your blog posts contain the types of words and phrases that your audience is likely to be using when looking for the kinds of products and services you provide, you boost your searchability online. Much of the traffic to your website will be driven by the results that users receive from a search engine when they search for various words and phrases. Searchability is basically their ability to find you and your ability to be found online. It is the holy grail of online marketing.

Brennan Enterprises (*www.brennancorp.com*), an exterior remodeling company based in Texas, created a blog to educate homeowners about the remodeling industry. It included content about how to shop for the company's products, what the best products are, and fun articles about decorating or DIY projects. Blogging has definitely had an impact on web traffic, according to Erin Reid, an account manager for Marketslice.net; one of her clients, Brennan Enterprises, a remodeling company, saw an increase of 125 percent in website visits and a 54 percent increase in leads over one month. "Visitors enter our website through our blog more frequently than any other page on our site," she says.

ALERT

You do not own social media sites; corporate giants like Google own them. That means there is always the potential that rules will change in ways you may not like, and those changes may have an impact on the way you communicate with your customers. With any of the social media channels you are on, it's a good idea to stay up to date on what those rules are and how they impact your customer interactions.

SEO isn't "rocket science" (although some firms/consultants try to make it seem like it is)! You basically need to think about who your target audience is and what types of words/phrases they might be using when they're seeking what you have to offer, and then just make sure that you're using those words and phrases in your copy (web content, blogs, etc.). And, guess what? This is *exactly* the same thing that you would be doing if you were writing copy for any channel—print, direct mail, etc.

It's important, though, not to be solely focused on SEO when you create content for your blog. Focus on relevant content for your audience and SEO will follow!

A blog provides a number of benefits from a marketing standpoint. Blogging can help you hone your perspectives on issues that are related to your industry, products, and services, and that are relevant to your target audience. It can also help you strengthen and support your brand by putting a little edge and personality into your communications on a more personal level than traditional marketing materials would do. As your blog gains traction, it can provide the opportunity for others to link to you or to ask you to be a guest blogger on their sites, which expands your thought leadership exponentially.

Content

What should you blog about? As with any form of communication, consider the topics and information that your audience is likely to find valuable, and that is also related to what you have to offer. The most important consideration, though, is to be sure that once you commit to blogging, you continue your commitment. You will need to provide content on a regular and reliable basis to ensure that your audience will grow and keep coming back for more.

An added benefit to blogging is the fact that generated content can be used for other purposes. Blog posts can serve as a foundation for content that can be multipurposed in various ways. You can pull snippets of your blog posts to use in social media posts (and, in some cases, you may want to link back to the blog). You can pull sections of your blog posts to use in e-letters or newsletters. Once you've built up enough copy, you can pull that copy together to create white papers, or even full-length books that you either self-publish or pitch to an editor. With all of the benefits inherent in blogging, the only reason not to blog is if you can't commit to producing and publishing content on a regular basis.

The Role of Video

As consumers increasingly turn to tablets and smartphones to consume content, the importance of video is emerging and growing exponentially as a key way of staying in touch with existing customers and attracting potential customers.

In fact, a 2013 study by Accenture (*www.accenture.com*) revealed that 90 percent of consumers surveyed watched video content on the Internet regularly. Increasingly that content is being viewed on small devices, on the go, and in what is being referred to as "second screen" situations, which refers to viewing video content on small devices while watching television content. Consumers are increasingly multitasking as they consume content, and content providers are taking maximum advantage of this trend. So are small businesses!

These days it is not only easy to create video content; it is also inexpensive. With the growth in consumer-generated video, it is no longer necessary to spend thousands of dollars to hire professional videographers and editors to create video material that consumers will watch. Businesses are increasingly doing it themselves. Social media tools like YouTube, and, more recently, Instagram, are fueling this trend. YouTube, for example, offers ease of access and use for your audience; a more intimate, human experience; and an enormous reach.

ESSENTIAL

Looks matter! Whether you have a physical business location or do all of your business online, it pays to ensure that the image you're presenting is consistent with your desired brand. Do-it-yourself websites may be tempting, but if you don't have web or graphic design skills, you're better served in the long run by working with someone who has the ability and experience necessary to properly establish your online presence.

Using video services like YouTube will be covered in more depth in chapters to come, but in the meantime, here are a few tips for deciding whether you should employ video as a way to communicate with customers:

- Is your product or service visually appealing or oriented? Products that can be shown through demonstrations, for instance, could benefit from video display.
- Can you convey your message succinctly in a visual manner? Viewer attention span is limited so if you can't convey your message in a few minutes, video may not be the route to take.
- Is your audience likely to consume content via video? Busy nurses working in a hospital unit or construction workers are not likely audiences—homemakers, students, or office workers on the other hand may be.

CHAPTER 11

Using YouTube for Customer Engagement

Created by three former PayPal employees, YouTube emerged on the social media scene in 2005. The site became very popular very quickly, so much so that Google recognized its potential and purchased it in 2006. Less than ten years later, YouTube is the go-to source for viewing video ranging from user-generated content to popular social memes, movie and television clips, news, and much more. According to YouTube's own data, more than 1 billion unique users visit the site each month, and more than 6 billion hours of video are watched each month on YouTube. Is YouTube a good platform for you to reach your customers? Maybe!

The YouTube Platform

YouTube literally provides small businesses with the opportunity to create their own "television stations" accessible to anyone, anywhere, twenty-four hours a day, seven days a week. Better yet, the cost of establishing this presence is nothing! The only cost is creating and posting the video, and monitoring and responding to comments that may be received.

Taking your ideas online in video format is a great, inexpensive way to promote your business and gain exposure. Many businesses have found that drafting white papers or putting useful information on a website can help boost exposure and build awareness. Moving to a video format is simply a natural progression of this marketing technique.

FACT

YouTube may never have existed if it weren't for PayPal. It seems like an odd combination but, in fact, YouTube's founders, Chad Hurley, Steve Chen, and Jawed Karim, had previously worked together at PayPal. It was that connection that brought them together to launch the now very popular video-sharing site.

This visual social media option offers significant benefits for business such as ease of access and use for your audience, a more intimate, human experience than simply reading text, and an enormous reach.

Watching Videos

Every minute, 100 hours of video are uploaded to YouTube. There's certainly something in this mix that is bound to be useful to the small business owner. From do-it-yourself content on just about anything to training and educational videos on marketing, social media, and other pertinent topics, YouTube is a treasure trove of free information.

Viewers can take advantage of:

- Subscriptions. If you like the videos someone produces, you can subscribe to that channel to get updates when new video is uploaded and new content is posted. (Hint: this can be a good way to track the activities of competitors!)

- Playlists. Playlists allow you to separate your video content into categories that you can organize and easily access later.
- Watch Later. No time to watch the entire video now, but don't want it to get lost among the millions of videos out there? Add it to your Watch Later playlist to remind yourself about it when you have the time to view it.

Once you've begun using YouTube and have created an account, the site will start to track and recognize your behavior, recommending videos and channels based on your tastes and the content you subscribe to. It will also track your history, which can be helpful if you want to go back to a video you've previously watched.

A wide range of videos have proven to be useful for marketers. These range from how-to-use videos to travelogues or tours to educational or training videos. Movie trailers are a natural for a video format, as are other entertainment-related videos, but businesses can use video to produce company profiles or to introduce key personalities. Health care organizations, for instance, have found videos to be a good way to help consumers get a sense of a doctor's personality before making a choice of whom to seek care from.

Uploading Video

Uploading video to the site is easy. For small businesses wishing to establish a presence on YouTube to help them engage with various audiences, the first step may be to establish a channel there. If you're already on Google+ and go to YouTube to set up a channel, YouTube will immediately offer you the opportunity to establish a presence for your Google+ account. If you're not on Google+, you simply have to enter the desired name for your channel. The videos you upload are automatically added to your channel.

YouTube has continued to make enhancements to the site to make it easier for users to create and upload video to engage viewers. You can upload video from your computer, phone, or even directly to the site via webcam. You can create photo slides directly on YouTube by uploading photos.

Changeable settings on photo slideshows include music, transitions, and slide duration/effects. You also have the option to use tools to add text and effects to your video through the site's video editor, which also allows you to cut and trim parts of your video.

If you've never dabbled with video, this may all seem intimidating at first. The best way to learn is to just dive in! There's really nothing to lose. Until you actively begin promoting your video, it's unlikely that many will see what you're up to. So feel free to play and experiment—and don't overlook the opportunity to learn from what others are doing.

ALERT

Whenever you upload a video to YouTube, it is automatically made public. If that's not what you want, you need to adjust your privacy settings so you can limit who is able to view the video. It's easy enough to do. Go to Video Manager, find the video you want to make private, click Edit, and change your privacy settings.

Whether your business is B2B or B2C there's an audience waiting to see what you have to offer.

Creating Video

When it comes to creating and publishing content in the twenty-first century, it's not just producers of print content that now face competition from "citizen journalists." Broadcast media has been equally impacted. With the cost of a video camera at under $200 and online video editing software available at low or no cost, pretty much *anybody* can produce video content.

But, just as a keyboard doesn't make someone a journalist, a camera and some editing software doesn't make someone a videographer. There is a wide range of quality represented through the nearly eight *years* of content that has been uploaded to the YouTube site by *millions* of users. Those are staggering numbers. And they represent opportunities for you.

Creating your own video may seem initially challenging, but don't be hesitant to give it a try. Careful planning and a well-developed and clearly articulated strategy will help you achieve success with your videos. While do-it-yourself video may bring up concerns about quality, the good news is that expectations of quality are on the decline.

Overly produced, super-high-quality videos don't always work in the new YouTube environment, and even the big corporate producers are taking a less "slick," more genuine approach to the video content they develop. "Business casual video" is a term that has been popularized by David Meerman Scott, an online marketing strategist who attributes the term to Cliff Pollan, CEO of VisibleGains. Business casual video comes across as very honest.

ESSENTIAL

Boost the SEO value of your YouTube videos by leveraging the use of the Google Adwords Keyword tool to determine the popular keywords currently in use by your audience. Then include those keywords in your titles, tags, and descriptions. Once you draw consumers to YouTube, make sure you then move them to your website, where they will take some specific action. A simple link can do the trick!

Despite a preference for less showy, more real video content, there are some things that demand your attention. You want to make sure that the audio is loud enough and clear enough. You also want to make sure that your lighting is bright enough and free from unwanted shadows.

Maintain a Customer Focus

While quality standards are lower than they used to be, it's still important to ensure a positive experience for your customers, and potential customers, and to provide content that is consistent with your desired brand image. Many people prefer viewing content via video rather than reading static information, but not everyone. For most small businesses video will augment, not replace, other forms of content.

In addition, certain types of businesses lend themselves more to video than do others. Businesses that sell products or services requiring demonstration are a natural fit. JustBlinds.com, for instance, offers a number of videos on its website, and also through its YouTube channel, that provide instruction on proper installation.

But even organizations that may not seem to provide such a natural fit can provide value via video. It has become increasingly common for health-care organizations, for instance, to provide video interviews with doctors to give potential patients a feel for the doctor's personality.

QUESTION

What's the most-viewed video on YouTube?
It's "Gangnam Style" by PSY, a video that was initially uploaded in July 2012 and had almost 2 billion views in 2014. The music, but particularly the unique dance moves of PSY, sent this video viral. It's followed in popularity by "Baby," a Justin Bieber performance with Ludacris; "On the Floor" with Jennifer Lopez; and a noncelebrity video "Charlie Bit My Finger—Again!"

As with any other element of your communication mix, your use of video should be carefully considered in terms of its ability to effectively engage with your audience and deliver a relevant message designed to achieve some desired outcome. Video should be used when the ability to include sound and motion will enhance your message—not just because you can use it. When considering the use of video:

- Take a look at what others are doing. Take note of what seems to be effective to you and pay attention to research information YouTube provides: How many people have viewed the video? What kinds of comments are they leaving? How many people "like" or "dislike" the video?
- Brainstorm the types of questions you think most of your customers would have, or the topics that would be of most interest to them. You can get some clues from the types of questions you may already receive from customers. For instance, if you receive a number of calls about how to use your product, that might suggest a how-to video.
- Think of the keywords that are most likely to be used when consumers are looking for information on this type of content (just as you would with other online communications). Once your video is developed you will use these words and phrases to tag your video to help with search results.

- Consider how you will make the video available. Certainly it will be on your website and most likely on YouTube, but are there other channels that you might use and other ways that you might promote the availability of this content?

Production Tips

When you get to the point of actually preparing to produce your video content, some important considerations to keep in mind include these:

- Be prepared and organized. What information do you want to convey and how will you convey it in an organized and meaningful way that will be most useful for your audience? Thinking from the point of view of your audience, as with any communication effort, is key.
- Think visually. What elements will be necessary to "tell the story" effectively? "Talking heads," or people sitting in front of a camera just talking about a topic, are often overdone and may not provide much interest for viewers. Screen shots with voiceover can provide some visual interest, as can the use of graphics, animations, etc.
- Think broadly. Effective video communication encompasses words, sounds, and images. You want to use those three elements, in combination, not only to convey your message but also to maintain your audience's interest.
- Create a script. Literally write out the scenes and words that will be used to convey your message. Don't "wing it," regardless of how comfortable you are with the subject matter.
- When shooting the video, keep the camera at about head level of anyone speaking on camera, and watch what they are wearing—no patterned clothing, which can create a sense of vibration on screen.

In addition, don't be afraid to separate the video and audio. In other words, when editing it's not necessary to simply let the sound continue as actually recorded over the image as it was actually recorded. For instance, a voiceover might be used while a demonstration of some sort is occurring, even though the two did not actually take place at the same time.

Don't overdo the transitions and special effects. Just because you can, doesn't mean you should. Do use a variety of types of shots and scenes.

Change camera angles, change rooms, shoot different scenes—keep it interesting.

And finally, don't try to put too much into the video. Less is more.

Consumer-Generated Video

In addition to video that you might produce yourself, consumer-generated video is becoming a trend that is taking hold among even very large companies. PepsiCo's Doritos brand, for instance, has solicited consumer-generated video for the past several years as part of an annual "Crash the Super Bowl" competition. The spots were first introduced in 2007 and remain highly popular. In 2014, the company's "Time Machine" ad scored big in terms of fan favorites. The entire campaign and its ongoing coverage has done much to maintain brand awareness for the company. Each year Doritos invites consumers from around the world (the competition was extended to 46 countries in 2013) to create an ad—two are chosen to air in the Superbowl, one by the Doritos marketing team and one by fan votes.

Engaging consumers in helping to share messages about your company and its products and services is a possibility for companies of any size.

YouTube for B2B

YouTube isn't just for consumer viewing. Many B2B businesses have well-established and well-trafficked YouTube channels. In fact, the B2B Marketing Community on YouTube has more than 370 subscribers and a wide range of videos offering advice, insights, and examples of how businesses are using the site to effectively connect with the business market.

Large B2B businesses like Cisco and IBM have a strong presence, and while the B2B participants tend to represent technology firms there are opportunities for others to connect as well. As with any other form of communication, it's all about understanding your audiences' interests and providing video content to meet their needs through information, tutorials, or pure entertainment.

Importantly, that content needs to be more directed toward the useful than self-promotional. From a customer service standpoint this approach provides ample benefits, including the ability to provide visual demonstrations as well as responses to common questions and concerns expressed by your customers and clients.

FACT

The first video that was uploaded to YouTube was taken at the San Diego Zoo. In it, one of YouTube's creators, Jawed Karim, is seen in front of the elephant enclosure where he talks about elephant trunks. That video clip, titled "Me at The Zoo," is still online and has generated more than 13 million hits since it was posted in 2005.

Are some of your customers having a hard time figuring out how to install one of your products? Create and post a demonstration online. Are some of your business prospects having a difficult time understanding the intricacies of how your product works and how it might save them time and money? Create and post a demonstration online. Not only does this type of information get your name out in front of people; it also provides strong customer service, which is a critical part of ongoing engagement.

For some small businesses, the ability to share visual content can be an important part of the prospecting process. Baird Group (*www.baird-group .com*), for instance, a healthcare consulting firm based in Wisconsin, sells consulting and training services to hospitals and healthcare organizations around the country and uses its YouTube channel to show clips of training programs to give organizations an idea of the depth and breadth of its presentations and the consultants' delivery style. Businesspeople, of course, are also consumers, and YouTube has been widely embraced by consumers around the globe.

YouTube for B2C

Over the recent years, consumers have flocked to online video sharing sites like YouTube. The same benefits that drove the adoption of television in the 1950s contributes to the popularity of these sites. Consumers simply like being able to see and hear information through moving visual and audio content. Add to that the ability to see unfiltered content from other consumers, often offering late-breaking and otherwise unavailable glimpses into trending topics, personal experiences, and news, and you have an unbeatable combination.

Small businesses have begun recognizing the power of online video both for conveying messages and for driving website traffic. YouTube can be a big player here, particularly for the B2C marketer. YouTube viewership grew from 8 million views per day in 2005 to more than 3 billion views per day in 2011 according to Pew Research. That's a lot of "eyeballs"!

Marketers can take advantage of the ability to put their messages in front of these eyeballs by sharing information they generate as well as by offering their audiences an opportunity to contribute user-generated content.

YouTube is Traverse Bay Farm's preferred method to engage with customers. Traverse Bay Farms is a cherry farm and the owner of the number one viewed super fruit channel on YouTube says owner Andy LaPointe. The farm's gourmet fruit products are made from antioxidant rich fruit. Over the past year the company has produced more than 150 videos, ranging from teaching consumers about its products to providing recorded webinars, in-store demonstrations, and education about how its products are made. Most important, says LaPointe, the videos are about "having fun."

ALERT

Don't be a Domino's! In 2009 some bored Domino's employees filmed themselves doing vile things to the food and then uploaded the video to YouTube. You can imagine what happened next. Domino's response was quick and effective, but some damage had already been done. Domino's has effectively recovered from this mishap, but they, and others, learned an important lesson about making sure employees are well aware of the rules and guidelines governing their social media use.

"We believe video allows us to make that personal connection to our customers," he says. "They not only get to learn about our product, but more important, they get to see the people behind the product." Since 2008, the company has won twenty-three national food awards at large national competitions. Video, says LaPointe, "allows us to showcase our awards without looking like we're bragging." The videos include testimonials provided by celebrities and well-known figures like Kevin Sorbo, an actor, and Vincent DePaul, an actor and producer.

YouTube for Building Community

YouTube offers an opportunity to build community with various audiences in a very visual and often real-time way. The key is generating interesting and relevant content on a regular basis—content that users interact with and, importantly, subscribe to.

How do you keep your consumers and viewers coming back? By being explicit through a call to action! Wayne Ford, who writes Udemy Blog, says that video content is a way to capture attention, entertain, inform, and build a relationship. The blog offers tutorials on a wide range of technical topics like using C#, a programming language, to experimental probability. To create a community on YouTube with your customers, create a clear call to action. Make sure your viewers know what they need to do next. This is, after all, the main benefit of sharing online content—driving your viewers to your product or service.

Another best practice: subscribe to the channels created by your regular customers, reply to their comments, and keep up with their activity!

Sharing Videos

YouTube makes it easy to share on other social platforms. Each of your videos will have a unique URL that allows you to copy and paste it wherever you please, including other social sites, your website, or documents that you can share.

Even if you maintain a YouTube channel, it's also a good idea to post your videos on your website. Visual content is highly valued and can add interest to your site. Having this kind of cross-platform can also generate traffic between these two online sources of information about your company and its products and services. When it comes to social media, more is better!

To drive viewers from YouTube to your website, let viewers know at the beginning, end, and throughout your video that they can find more information on your website or by contacting your company. Tell them the name of your site in the video and include a link in the description.

ESSENTIAL

While you may think of YouTube as your own private television network (and, in fact, it really can take on this role), your videos should be focused more on information than on infomercials. Advertising-focused videos don't do well on YouTube (unless they're for the iconic brands). Focus on sharing useful information with your audiences.

And, remember, this is a two-way street. Include links to your YouTube videos on your company website to not only add content, but also to increase the number of views your video receives.

Best Practices for YouTube Engagement

There are a number of ways you might use YouTube to effectively engage with your audiences. Here are some examples:

- **Interviews and feature stories.** Interviewing your staff can create a more personable experience for your viewers. In the case of B2B marketing, promote your staff through interviews to introduce the faces behind the company. It may give businesses an interest in working with you!
- **Demonstrations.** Is your product or service a little confusing or too complex to put into words? Use YouTube to post videos demonstrating it! This can help your audience, including other businesses, better understand what you sell and how it could benefit them.
- **Collaboration.** As explained earlier, teaming up with other businesses, sometimes even your competitors, can add value to your products or services. Because you would be reaching more than one audience, you can multiply your viewership and increase awareness of your business among a new audience.
- **Reaching out in crisis.** Your customers should usually be among the very first to know when something bad has happened. YouTube gives

you the capability to share video instantly with the help of its direct webcam record. Seeing and hearing from the people behind the scenes instantly can ease consumers' minds in times of crisis. These kinds of videos also are great for formal statements and apologies.

- **Event recap.** If some of your customers missed an event you sponsored or hosted, use video to recap it. Showing them all the fun they missed will help bring them in next time! Those customers who did attend will enjoy seeing themselves on your video, and in the process you'll be nurturing strong relationships.

While using YouTube is a modern marketing technique, it is far from new. That presents significant advantage for small businesses interested in learning what others are doing and getting a sense of the effectiveness. They can do this just by looking at the number of views, likes, and comments the various videos have generated.

QUESTION

When did Google buy YouTube?
YouTube has been owned by Google since 2006. The search giant bought the popular video-sharing site for a whopping $1.65 billion. That connection is another good reason to add YouTube to your marketing arsenal. It's all about search, and with Google holding the purse strings you just know your content has an edge when it has a YouTube connection.

Finally, make sure you are leveraging the significant SEO value of YouTube. Always fill out your YouTube description and make sure it contains the relevant keywords and phrases your audience is likely to be using. Brainstorm the types of questions you think most of your customers would have. Think of the keywords that are most likely to be used when discussing that topic, and fill your description with those keywords to increase the likelihood that your video will appear in a search. The more you appear, the more awareness of you grows, and your community will expand exponentially!

CHAPTER 12

Using Facebook for Customer Engagement

Started in 2004 by Mark Zuckerberg from his dorm room at Harvard University, Facebook was originally designed for Harvard students to interact with one another and then morphed into a tool for students at campuses around the country to do the same at their own schools. The rest, as we all know, is history. The platform went public in 2012, raising $16 billion in its initial public offering (IPO). In 2014, as Facebook celebrated its tenth anniversary, participants included everyone from tweens to Traditionalists (those born before the Baby Boomers), as well as companies large and small.

The Facebook Platform

Facebook is a very "social" social media tool. Much of the activity taking place on it is more related to social interactions than to business connections. Nevertheless, Facebook *can* offer good opportunities to certain types of marketers, particularly those who have a combination of something "visual" to present to an audience (because Facebook is so visually oriented) and a business/product that lends itself to engagement/interest.

FACT

In 2010, the movie *The Social Network* was made about the creation of Facebook and the conflict between Zuckerberg and his collaborators. The film won three Oscars: Best Adapted Screenplay, Best Original Score, and Best Film Editing.

While Facebook is a very multifaceted tool, at its core it is a social networking site that allows users to create their own pages and join common interest groups. With well over 800 million regular users worldwide, Facebook represents a huge marketing opportunity for any business. The site provides a number of free resources for businesses. Facebook allows businesses to create their own page, which acts as a sort of second website for the business to provide information and learn more about the customers and potential customers who visit the page or join as "fans." Facebook also lets users target customers with paid advertisements tailored to specific demographics and locations, utilizing the site's enormous data mining abilities. And Facebook allows businesses to augment their sites with custom apps and plug-ins and utilizes member activity to help generate buzz around their pages.

ESSENTIAL

Encourage key employees to engage in Facebook on your behalf. In addition to a business page, individual employee representative pages can help put a personal touch on your online interactions. For instance, you might have profiles for your customer relations manager, your human resources manager, and other key connections.

The Basics

On Facebook, you can create and customize a profile including a profile photo and cover photo (more like a background photo). Your profile tells and shows people who you are and what you do, including a biography, work and education, family and relationships, contact information, and more. You can also share your interests by picking your favorite books, movies, hobbies, teams, and more.

Your profile also showcases your Timeline. Your Timeline is a collection of your activity over the years as well as your interactions with your friends. A main component of Facebook is posting statuses. Facebook asks you "What's on your mind?" so that you can easily share your updates with your friends.

ALERT

Facebook, like any online form of communication, can be subject to both risks and rewards. One risk is how your employees use the site when they're "off the clock." While there are limits to the direction you can give them, having clear policies and communicating them regularly can help you avoid embarrassing situations online.

Facebook business pages offer the same type of functionality, but focus on portraying a business "personality," rather than that of an individual. Business pages don't offer the ability to add "friends," but those engaged or interested in your organization are able to "like" your page, signifying their support of your organization and what it has to offer.

In addition to establishing a presence on Facebook through a profile or business page, business owners may also find value through advertising on Facebook, depending on their target market. Facebook advertisers have the ability to very narrowly target their messages to specific niche audience segments (because of the information that Facebook gathers about its users), and the cost for advertising can be very low. In addition, you will be able to track how many people read your ad, follow the links to your website, and take some action.

A relatively recent addition to Facebook is hashtags, popularized by Twitter. As on Twitter, Facebook hashtags allow you to tag words or phrases to make it easy for those interested in your topic to follow it.

Facebook also offers a built-in analytics tool, Insights, to help you monitor and measure the effectiveness of your activities by showing you which posts generated the most interest, activity, and sharing; which links were clicked on; and even when your fans tend to be online.

Facebook for B2B

Because of the characteristics of Facebook already mentioned, it does not serve as a good platform for B2B interactions. B2C is where it's at in the Facebook community. Still, there are some businesses that have been successful at connecting with a B2B audience on Facebook by thinking creatively about how best to engage with a business audience through this very personal social media tool.

QUESTION

Are contests a good way of engaging customers through Facebook? They can be. It's important that your contest is aligned with your business and its brand, and that you're not just attempting to engage the masses; you want to engage them with meaning. In addition, it's important to make sure that you are following Facebook's contest guidelines.

Cisco's "Cisco Networking Academy," for instance, is a good example of how businesses in the B2B space can effectively connect and engage with target audiences online. Cisco, a company that manufactures and sells networking equipment, and other successful B2B users of social media platforms, like Facebook, know that even in B2B marketing, it's all about connecting with *people*, not businesses. The distinction is that the people represent a business audience. In this case, Cisco delivers technology education to its followers, often around very specific and technical topics.

HubSpot (*www.hubspot.com*) is another example of a company in the B2B space that has learned that connecting through Facebook, or any social tool, is really about P2P (people to people). With more than 570,000 fans,

HubSpot delivers information to help companies better market their products and services. HubSpot creates a lot of content and generates a great deal of interest among the interested businesspeople, entrepreneurs, and marketers that follow them.

Many of the B2B companies on Facebook are in the technology space, but not all of them are. Corning (*www.corning.com*), for instance, made a big splash back in 2011 with its "A Day Made of Glass" video, which was posted to its Facebook page. Since then the video has garnered more than 23 million views. Still, despite some successes among the big players online, small businesses might want to look beyond Facebook to more B2B-friendly social media outlets like LinkedIn and Google+.

Facebook for B2C

While businesses generally find it a challenge to connect and build relationships with other businesses on Facebook, there are definitely opportunities for many, and varied, types of businesses to connect with and engage the consumer market.

WaterField Designs (*www.sfbags.com*), owned by Gary Waterfield and based in San Francisco, is a small manufacturer of bags, cases, and totes. The company has found Facebook to be a good venue for interacting with customers and engaging them in the promotion of its brand. One of the company's most popular ways to generate this engagement is its "Where in the World" series. The series asks customers to send in photos of their bags in use in interesting places. The photos are then posted to the Facebook page, and followers are asked to try to figure out where the photo was taken.

It's a unique way to position an unusual product.

Who would think that a company that sells cremation urns could generate buzz on social media? But Artisurn (*www.artisurn.com*) has done just that. Owner Irina Jordan says "social media is critical for me as it helps my business stand out from all the other mass produced and traditional urn companies." Jordan connects with her audience on Facebook by showcasing pieces made by Artisurn's artisans and is not afraid to sprinkle some black humor into the conversations.

Even products as seemingly "dry" as mortgages can reach audiences through Facebook. Jennifer Nagle is director of marketing with Centennial

Lending Group (CLG). "When I started, one of our initiatives was to create and launch an innovative team approach to sharing our CLG culture and branding throughout our staff, friends and fans," she says.

FACT

Some states are more active on Facebook than others. According to a 2012 Mashable piece, ten states were driving the most traffic to the site: California, Texas, New York, Florida, Illinois, Pennsylvania, Ohio, Michigan, Georgia, and North Carolina.

Shortly after joining the company she launched a Facebook business platform for CLG and for each of its loan officers to promote CLG's mortgage products and services. The Facebook pages are linked directly back to CLG's website (*www.clg-llc.com*), including to an online mortgage application.

"We treat our CLG Facebook business pages like an electronic billboard to share experiences and resources that enable our fans to interact and become engaged in our everyday events," says Nagle. "Our postings can consist of everything from customer testimonials, to pictures and videos, to interest rates trends, to name a few."

These are just a few examples of how this tool can be used creatively to engage with both existing and potential customers.

Connecting with People

There are a number of features of Facebook that make it a popular way both for individuals and for businesses to connect with people:

- **Messages/Chat.** Facebook chat is an easy way to instantly connect with your community. Similar to an instant messenger, chat connects you with friends faster than ever before.
- **Photos.** Because of its large capacity, Facebook allows you to create albums and fill them with up to 1,000 photos. Because Facebook is especially useful for companies that have some interesting visual appeal (e.g., apparel companies or restaurants), this is a big boon. Photos also can come into play during contests in which you might invite your community to share and tag photos of themselves and oth-

ers interacting with your business through its products, services, and people.

- **Events.** Holding an event? You can easily create detailed events and invite your connections to them. You can also encourage them to share the news with others. They'll get a reminder when the event is approaching!
- **Groups.** If you want to share content with a specific group of people (perhaps a group of long-term customers, or a group of prospects, or a group of customers who love a particular product), Facebook allows you to do just that.

Small businesses have the opportunity to bring their businesses to life on Facebook through their business pages and the use of photos, which are a good way to connect with your audience and make them feel like they know the people with whom they're doing business. These photos could be of your staff, your everyday workplace, your recent activities or events, and more. Just be sure to keep the focus on people. People like to interact with businesses—not with products or buildings!

Building Community

Facebook is all about building community, but it takes some attention and effort to make sure you are nurturing your community effectively. Pay attention to the people who "like" your page. Who is interested in your organization? What demographic or location are they from? What are they looking for from you? This is a simple way to find your target audience and discover what interests them about your company.

One of the best ways to create a community with your customers is to build Facebook groups. Groups can be used to bring people with similar interests, goals, or intentions together to discuss or share content. You can also invite your customers to an online support group. People can talk to other people about your products and services, and you can assist by answering their questions. This can not only boost customers' satisfaction and engagement, but can reduce the number of calls to your call center or service representatives, which will have a positive impact on your expenses.

Jacob Markiewicz is the head of media relations for start-up Exert (*www.exertco.com*), which manufactures a product called Exert Smart Body coolant for the treatment of hot flashes, physical exertion, and underarm stains. Because the product is so versatile, he says, "we can appeal to multiple groups of people." Social media, particularly Facebook, helps create that appeal. "We are networking and connecting with influential women bloggers, writers, and general health advocates through the use of humorous images and informative links in our joint mission to keeping women informed as they go through this change of life," he says.

ESSENTIAL

If you're advertising on Facebook, make sure to target effectively. With so many options available to finely segment the large Facebook population, there's no reason not to take the time to think about those specific segments that are likely to be most interested in what you have to offer.

Importantly, he notes: "We use social media in order to individualize our reach to the specific people that we want to connect with. We don't make a blanket post and hope that everyone connects to it. We use our social networks to connect our content with specific groups."

QUESTION

Who is using Facebook?
According to Pew Research surveys, Facebook is the biggest player in the social media space, with 71 percent of adults online using the site in 2013. The age of these users is trending upward, though, with users fifty-five and over growing at the fastest pace.

That attention to the specific needs of niche market segments helps build community. In social media it is, ultimately, all about relevance.

Sharing on Facebook

Facebook was built on sharing. Originally dominated by the college crowd, the Facebook population has expanded to included participants of all ages, as well as businesses of all sizes. Businesses build community on Facebook through posts, photos, and competitions designed to engage visitors through likes, comments, and shares.

Visitors can leave feedback or reviews of your business and its products and services directly on your Facebook page. Best practice suggests that you review and respond promptly to these posts: the good, the bad, and the ugly.

Because Facebook is so visually oriented, the use of compelling photos and images can help generate interest and encourage shares. It's important to not post pictures of just any kind—they should have some relevance or tie-in with your business. Include captions with your images, along with links embedded within the captions that lead to other material that may provide additional information, again aligned with your overall goals and objectives.

Generally, businesses feel they have achieved success when there is a good balance between their own posts and the posts of others. Invite your Facebook community to share and care. Ask them to forward information to their followers, ask them to "like" your page, and ask them to participate. Most important, provide them with a reason to come back again and again because of the valuable, interesting, and unique information you offer.

Facebook Ads

Facebook, like other social media channels, maintains its free platform by making revenue through other means, specifically advertising. Online advertising has become increasingly prevalent and popular, primarily because it is so easy to very specifically target certain audiences and deliver what hopefully will be relevant messages to them.

Advertisers on Facebook can create ads and ask to show those ads to specific audiences based on such factors as where they live, their age, gender, education, work history, and even interests. Every bit of information that Facebook gathers about its users can then potentially be used by advertisers to create and send messages to their customers.

Sponsored stories are another option that Facebook has introduced. This is an opportunity for marketers to boost the distribution of stories that have been shared. Sponsoring extends the reach of these stories beyond the Facebook user's own network, increasing opportunities to build awareness and generate new followers.

ALERT

Facebook can be a scary place. Consumers are understandably concerned about online privacy and the protection of their personal information and data. Facebook has often been in the hot seat over concerns about how it shares information as well as breaches to the site that have left personal—and business—data at risk. Be careful out there!

Privacy concerns and pushback received from Facebook users has caused Facebook to continually adjust its policies related to advertising. Users also have a great deal of control over what they will, or will not, see. Users can opt out of ads. They may also mark ads that don't interest them. All of these options are available through Facebook settings where users can control what they see and who sees them. Facebook gathers this information and uses it in an attempt to more closely match the ads shown with users' interests.

As a Facebook user, you can learn a lot about how the ads work by monitoring your own ads. These appear on the right-hand side of the page and contain images with a very brief headline and short body copy. They're designed to attract attention and, ultimately, generate a click-through for the advertiser. What you click will also impact the future ads you see.

Facebook ads are built as campaigns, generally including as many as ten different ads with varied copy and images. Monitoring the results you're seeing in real time can help you to modify, add, or delete ads that are either underperforming or generating good results. For your campaigns you will want to track the length of time the ad was run, the total amount you spent, the reach of your campaign, clicks, and, ultimately, click-through rate. Those click-throughs go to your website or landing pages. After this point you will also want to track whether the click-through resulted in an inquiry or sale.

Whether using Facebook ads or simply attempting to engage through your Facebook posts, it is possible to generate sales through this tool—and you don't have to have the most "sexy" product to do so.

Jenny Lind Walsh, president of Legacy Contracting, Inc., in Westminster, Maryland, says: "We are a septic and excavation company. We have been using Facebook, especially through this winter, to try and keep our crews busy with snow removal. We've had a lot of success and are also now getting calls for septic services as a result of the visibility. Honestly, I'm not sure what the picture for this winter would have looked like without the opportunities that our Facebook base provided."

As one of the oldest and still most popular social media sites, Facebook offers plenty of opportunity for both B2B and B2C marketers.

Best Practices for Facebook Engagement

Illustrating the global nature of social media, Aditi Kapur, the founder of the start-up DeliveryChef.in (*www.deliverychef.in*) in India, uses Facebook, Twitter, Instagram, and Google+ to help get the word out both to customers and to potential customers.

DeliveryChef.in is a site where users can order food for delivery from neighborhood restaurants, through collaborations with more than 600 of India's most popular dining spots. Social media, says Kapur, helps the site reach out to new customers and engage with existing customers to keep them on the top of everyone's mind.

Kapur has found that contests and promotions can be a great way to drive customer engagement. Contests help the company reward existing customers and reach out to new customers. Promotions on social media can help drive new customers. In addition, informative posts are used to provide information on current trends and, of course, to share appealing images of food.

Here are some best practices for using Facebook most effectively:

- The use of personal profiles on Facebook makes it easy for you to interact with and get to know your audience. Take advantage of this by inviting people to like your organization's page and seeking out those who could use your services.

- Engage visitors through interactive options like provocative questions, polls, and contests. Just be sure to make the contests relevant to your business and its products and services.
- Remember to reply when others reach out to you on Facebook. That direct, personal connection helps to make them feel like part of your inner circle.
- Use Pages as a way to create or enhance your brand. You can have multiple pages to represent various aspects of your business and its products and services.
- Use photos that are appropriate and professional, yet creative and colorful, for your profile and cover photos. It's a great way to attract people to your page and give them a sense of your "personality."
- Make sure your Facebook activities are designed to drive traffic back to your website or to your brick-and-mortar location, and that all of your activities are aligned with your other brand messages.
- Keep it personal. Even if you're in the B2B space, remember that people like connecting with other people, not companies!

Facebook offers a variety of opportunities for small businesses to engage with target audiences through personal and business profiles. As with other social media sites, the key consideration about Facebook's value will involve careful analysis of the audience, their presence on Facebook, and the type of content most likely to resonate on this very social, social media tool.

CHAPTER 13

Using Twitter for Customer Engagement

Welcome to the world of tweeting, without all the birds. Twitter is a social platform that allows you to send "tweets," or rather, write thoughts to your followers. Unlike Facebook, where both users must accept to be "friends" with one another, Twitter allows people to follow and unfollow whomever they please. Who would have thought that a platform that allowed abbreviated messages of only 140 characters would have captured the hearts of people around the globe and become such a part of the culture that it is turned to by millions during times of both celebration and crisis?

The Twitter Platform

Twitter is a social media tool that many find perplexing. What value can be gained by sending such short messages out to the world? Well, in reality, while Twitter is not for everyone, it can be a good way to build awareness and establish credibility and thought leadership by building a relevant group of followers and sharing pertinent and valued information with them regularly.

FACT

Twitter was created and launched in 2006 by Jack Dorsey (who later founded Square), Evan Williams, Biz Stone, and Noah Glass.

Twitter is called a "microblogging" site because of the brevity of its messages. Twitter is like the blurb factory of social media. It allows users to post brief messages to whoever may be interested at no cost. While 140 characters might seem like an insignificant amount of data, Twitter can be very useful for businesses communicating with customers. For example, customers who "follow" a business's Twitter feed can comment on positives or negatives they experience with the company. Additionally, using Twitter's search function can help you put your finger to the pulse of consumers or competitors in your industry simply by searching for certain terms associated with your business.

Keep in mind that it can be challenging to engage others in interaction on Twitter, since much of the "conversation" is very much one-way.

QUESTION

What are trending topics?
Trending topics on Twitter represent the most popular topics currently being discussed across the "Twitterverse." It can be a good idea to monitor these trends to uncover potential phrases and hashtags to incorporate into your own tweets. Just be sure you're making relevant connections to the trending terms.

Nevertheless, simply pushing your thoughts out into cyberspace can help to build followers, which in turn can drive awareness and, ideally, traffic to your website. The bottom line is that you want to produce a steady flow of relevant items that are of interest to the people following you. Your goals are twofold, really: to keep those people following you and, hopefully, to encourage them to "retweet" your postings, boosting the odds that your audience will broaden even further.

Twitter Basics

The first thing you'll notice when you start using Twitter is a timeline of tweets. These tweets are updated as they are written (this is known as Live Update) by the people you follow.

On the top of the Twitter screen, you'll also see three tabs:

1. Connect: This tab allows you to see who has been talking about or interacting with you.
2. Discover: Twitter tracks what people are talking about online and shares this information by region. This tab allows you to explore topics and find others you'd like to follow.
3. Me: This is a collection of your tweets, aggregated into a timeline.

Twitter allows you to interact with those you follow in a number of ways:

- Replying to tweets: When you see a tweet you'd like to comment on, replying will do just that. The person who posted the comment will get a notification from you to continue conversation.
- Retweeting: When you see something someone else has tweeted, and would like to share it, you can "retweet" it. Essentially, this means you repost someone's tweet to your timeline, where all of your followers can see it.
- "Favoriting" tweets: If you simply like something someone says, but don't feel the need to share it with your followers, you can "favorite" the tweet. This sends a message to the poster that the post made an impact.

Twitter offers a lot of useful how-to information on its site, along with best practice examples of how businesses, large and small, and in various industries, are successfully using the tool. With so many users to engage with there are ample opportunities to get new ideas and test various options to see what will work best for you.

Businesses are now also able to advertise on Twitter through promoted accounts and tweets. Payment is based on those who follow a promoted account or retweet, reply, favorite, or click on a promoted tweet.

Your Twitter Profile

On Twitter, as with other social media, your profile rules. Those few words you say about yourself really help to position you in the social media space and send an important message to followers and potential followers.

It's critical that Twitter profiles are designed to be consistent with your existing desired brand identity and in consideration of your overall communication objectives. It is really the same process that should be used when designing any communication.

Your Twitter profile is just one element of what is hopefully a multifaceted communication approach in support of the brand—whether building a personal brand or a business brand. So, in terms of look and feel it's important that the profile is consistent with other images (your logo, your company colors, etc.). The content of your profile should be designed based on the perspective of the desired audience. You want to use terms that would be important for them and that they know and understand. Links are helpful due to space limitations and the need to quickly connect with the audience.

FACT

Popular culture is one of the most talked about topics on the site. Celebrities rule, with followers numbering in the millions. Lady Gaga is one of the most popular users; it has been said that she gains followers faster than Twitter adds new accounts. She had about 41 million followers in 2014.

Approach the development of your Twitter profile like you would an "elevator speech" (see Chapter 8). Briefly describe what you do that is valuable to your target audience. The link to your website can then further support that brief bit of information. While it's okay, and often advisable, to include a few personal details, be careful here. You don't want those personal details to send a message or create an image that is disconnected from your desired brand.

Another important point: always, always include a profile picture. This can be your logo, but in any case, don't overlook including an image; making that mistake marks you as an amateur. And be cautious in your use of avatars unless they mirror your brand.

Your profile on Twitter or any other site establishes who you are and creates a first impression that leads others to decide whether you're someone worth connecting to and someone with whom they want to do business. Take the time to give some careful consideration to what you want your audience to know, think, or believe about you, and make sure that however you handle this through social media is consistent with what you're doing through all of your communication channels.

Twitter for B2B

Twitter is a useful social media tool for B2B companies, allowing the ability to build a following for both sharing information and learning from others. Thought leaders have a significant presence here with experts and authors such as Guy Kawasaki, Seth Godin, Daniel Pink, and many more having followers that number in the millions. Twitter represents a great opportunity for them and other B2B marketers to raise awareness and establish a platform for sharing relevant news, information, and opinion with the masses.

The key for them and other B2B marketers is to place the emphasis on information. General Electric (GE) is a good example of this. With about 184,000 followers, GE's posts focus heavily on technology and innovation, offering unique examples and perspectives that readily engage its audience.

B2B marketers on Twitter are engaging in conversations in much the same way as their B2C counterparts. The difference is that these conversations generally revolve around business-related issues or concepts and the marketers participating are focused on providing useful, relevant information related to their products and services. The more helpful you can be, the more followers, mentions, and retweets you'll receive.

It's all about generating buzz!

ESSENTIAL

Since it's unlikely that all of your followers are in the same time zone, are online, are on Twitter, and are engaged with your posts at the same time, a good practice is to repost your tweets to broaden their reach. Do so judiciously, though. There is balance to strike between reaching new audiences and spamming those you are regularly connecting with.

Twitter for B2C

One of the big benefits of Twitter is its ability to create buzz, which can be a big boon for small businesses. For example, Mix 'N' Match Creamery, based in Portland, Oregon, uses Twitter, in combination with Instagram, to build relationships with customers online. "We'll often follow and tweet at tweeps who would be interested in our liquid nitrogen ice cream," says owner Genevieve West, who owns the company along with Eric West. When these "tweeps" come to their food cart and introduce themselves, she says, "we Instagram a photo of them or their ice cream for a social media shout-out just for stopping by." That's a great example of how to cross the line between virtual and *real* reality.

Social media is the new word of mouth, says West, who adds that with an advertising budget of zero, the business has been very successful in its first season. "Some of our more publicized successes included being featured in a local reality show, being interviewed on a radio station's Food Cart Friday segment, and being asked to cater a radio station event where we YouTubed one of the popular radio personalities making his own liquid nitrogen ice cream."

Jay Skowron is the founder of Hospitality Defender, a company that helps other companies in the hospitality industry with their online reputation and social media management efforts. Twitter is a commonly used tool with his clients. For instance, he says, "Every time someone checks in with Foursquare, Yelp, Twitter, or Facebook, we send out a tweet responding to them, saying that we hope they have a great visit." Skowron also keeps an eye out on Twitter for people who may mention pizza in the area and then suggests that they try their pizza restaurant. "We have numerous examples of impressed potential guests saying that they will eat at this pizza chain due to the great social media interaction," he says.

FACT

In 2013 Twitter launched its much-anticipated IPO. The stock rose from an initial offering price of $26 to $44.90 per share at the end of the day, and boosted the value of the company to $25 billion—despite the fact that the company was rumored to have never shown a profit.

Building Community

The best way to build a following on Twitter is to follow others and hope they follow you back! Follow your customers. Follow your vendors. Follow your employees. And follow industry experts and analysts who are likely to have big followings themselves that you may be able to leverage. When you find an individual or business with a large number of followers, you may also want to review and follow their followers.

An important point to keep in mind, though, is that it's not all about the numbers despite the fact that many "Twitterers" build up massive lists of followers. What you most want is a community of customers, or potential customers, who are interested in what you have to say. A small, loyal following comprised of your customers is far more valuable than a massive following of people who have no interest in you at all.

Sharing Information

Building a strong community on Twitter, as with any community, of course, requires sharing information that provides value. That requires a balance of information about you (which should be minimal) and information of interest and use to your audience. Much of what you post should point your audience in the direction of interesting facts, information, and knowledge related to your product or service.

So, for instance, if you operate a beauty salon, you might provide tips on hair or nail care, share links to new style information, and, every once in a while, talk about special offers or new services you are providing. If you're a physician you might provide healthcare tips, updates on the Affordable Care Act and other industry issues impacting your audience, and links to new studies or information about healthful habits—and, again, every once in a while something about your services.

ALERT

Avoid the use of automatically generated tweets that might be used, for example, to thank someone for following you or retweeting one of your posts. These auto-generated comments have a tendency to turn off followers and, in fact, Twitter discourages their use. Better to be engaged in real, rather than robotic, time.

A good balance to strike is one post about you to two posts not about you (1:2 ratio). You'll need to keep adding new content to continually engage your community. Two to three posts per day is a minimum number. And, of course, you should also "retweet" posts from others. That's a good way to make connections and build an audience.

Hashtags

The use of hashtags is a good way to start, become part of, or monitor a conversation on Twitter. The hashtag (#) is a symbol that is used in front of words and phrases that allows the Twitter community to easily find, follow, and engage in a conversation. During events, for instance, hashtags are used to tag conversations. For instance: #superbowl2014, #Olympics, etc.

Your own events can also benefit from the use of hashtags to help your followers easily find information before, during, and after the event. The same is true of conferences and speaking engagements. Or, you can use hashtags to draw attention to a particular concept or issue, or your own brand. Use hashtags sparingly, though. Overuse can turn off your audience and lead to disengagement!

Suppose you're speaking at a conference. You might want to include the conference hashtag in any related posts you generate so that those interested in the conference can easily aggregate or find all related posts. Instead of saying, "Excited to be speaking at the National Conference of the Most Brilliant Speakers in the World about (whatever your topic might be)," you could tweet, "Excited to be speaking at the #NCMBSW conference about my views on . . . (whatever)." In this case, the use of the hashtag not only helps you become part of the conversation, but also leaves you with more space to share additional content, perhaps even a link. Most important, your post will appear in the streams of anyone following that particular conference.

ESSENTIAL

Live chats can be a great way to engage an audience around a specific topic. These can be used to engage with authors, participants in a panel discussion, and even television viewers. The cast of the CBS series *Under the Dome*, for instance, live-tweeted their premiere episode to drive viewer engagement around the show's launch. It worked.

Here's another example. Suppose you want to create your own group of followers around a specific topic, like strategic planning. You might create your own hashtag—#MakePlansWork—and hope that, over time, the hashtag becomes adopted and used by others.

Whatever strategies you devise for building communities, keep in mind that it is all about sharing and caring.

Sharing Content

Twitter is one of the best social sites for sharing content. You can easily "retweet" items, or simply put, repost them on your profile. To make Twitter more of a two-way conversation than a one-way download of information, get to know your followers and their interests. That may seem like an overwhelming task, but tools like Hootsuite, SocialBro, and TweetDeck allow you to create streams based on key words, phrases, or segments of your audience that you can readily monitor and evaluate.

Using those same tools, you can determine which of your posts generate the most attention through retweets and mentions. You can also monitor what time of day seems to work best for your posts and then schedule your content to be posted at those times.

ALERT

Beware the rules of engagement on Twitter. While you want to build an audience, and may want to build an audience quickly, there is a limit to the number of people you can follow in one day. Twitter also frowns on the practice of "buying" followers, a strategy that was commonly practiced in the early days of the site's popularity but is now becoming a social media no-no.

Most important, you will want to engage with your audience. When someone adds you to a list or mentions you, follow up with them to thank them for their attention and, whenever possible, to engage them in a conversation. Respond to interesting and relevant posts of others. Stay involved and stay engaged!

Best Practices for Twitter Engagement

The more you use Twitter, the more comfortable you'll get with its format and the more you'll learn about what works best for you. Different types of businesses will attract different types of audiences, and what works for one will not necessarily work for another. Testing, monitoring, and evaluating *your* results is the best way to learn. Still, there are some best practices that are relevant for all. They include the following:

- Don't be afraid to repurpose content. You can find good material to share with your followers on your website, your blog, or from ideas generated through customer comments. The more provocative or unusual (yet relevant), the better.
- Consider short "teasers" designed to pique people's interest and get them to go to your site. With each of these you would include a link to your site, your blog, or a good review. For instance: "Learn 10 Ways to Draw Rave Reviews," or "Guess the Mystery Ingredient in Our New Cocktail and Win a Dinner for Two."

- Use a tool like Bitly.com to shorten the URLs and links that you use so you can monitor how many people click on those links.
- Come up with ideas for postings by reviewing the feeds of people you are following and then "retweeting" items that appear relevant or interesting.
- It's a welcomed courtesy to retweet other people's tweets and a good way to "make friends" on Twitter.
- You might also monitor interesting news items related to your company/interests and include links to those items for your followers. Following news/survey feeds like Pew Research (*www.pewresearch.org*) or Top-Ten (*www.toptnereviews.com*) can provide you with a lot of potential material.
- It can also be helpful to monitor the tweets that other people are posting. Find a few people with a lot of followers and then go through their tweets to see the type of thing they're doing to get an indication of what appears to be working. Then model their style or approach in your own tweets.
- Get visual. A great feature of Twitter is that it displays photos very well. As users scroll through their feeds, they are far more likely to stop and look at something with a colorful or interesting photo rather than just text. Use photos and graphics often to increase your engagement with your customers, but not every time you tweet.
- Participate in Twitter chats. Twitter chats allow you to follow a specific hashtag in real time to ask and answer questions with groups of others interested in the same issue or topic. This is a great way to find people or businesses to collaborate with and learn from.
- Create lists. Twitter provides an opportunity to create lists to help you easily follow people with shared interests or those you'd like to learn from. For instance, if you're a writer, you might create a list of authors who inspire you. These authors will be notified that you've added them to your "Motivational Authors list," and they may also reach out to you. This is a great way to create new connections!
- Do market research. What does your audience want from your business? What do they want to see more or less of? How can you position your company to better fit the needs of your consumers? Twitter is the perfect platform to ask them this! Don't be afraid to use Twitter

to poll your consumer audience about their interests and opinions. This can be a great way to not only engage the audience but to learn more about them.

Generally speaking, people of the "Twittersphere" love interacting with their favorite people and businesses online. That's why when one of your customers interacts with you, either positively or negatively, it's important to respond appropriately. Getting personal with your audience makes them believe that you care about them and their opinions—and it will keep them coming back!

FACT

Twitter users broke a record, and the site, during the 2014 Oscars when host Ellen DeGeneres gathered a number of celebrities together for a selfie and encouraged viewers to retweet the post. They did, racking up 3 million retweets. The activity took down the site during the telecast, resulting in an apology from Twitter to its followers.

There are many, many tools online to help you master Twitter. A simple Google search of "track Twitter unfollowers" will lead you to programs that track those who have unfollowed you to help you stay up to date on what kinds of people follow and unfollow you. The program Hootsuite is a little more complex, but gives you the ability to schedule future tweets, track hashtags, display multiple keyword searches, and more. Take full advantage of these tools to make your social engagement experience better!

CHAPTER 14

Using LinkedIn for Customer Engagement

Originally used primarily by job seekers, LinkedIn remains a tool widely used by recruiters, HR professionals, and hiring managers to find and connect with potential employees, but it has evolved to be so much more. Unlike Facebook and other more B2C-oriented sites, LinkedIn is primarily a B2B tool used by professionals in a wide range of industries to find and connect with those they know and would like to know. Also unlike other social media sites, LinkedIn offers some payment options. While you can use the site at no cost, you can choose to upgrade to get access to additional services and options like the ability to send messages to those you are not connected to and the ability to view more detail about your connections and those who have viewed your site.

The LinkedIn Platform

LinkedIn was launched in 2003 by Reid Hoffman and team members from PayPal and Socialnet. Since then it has grown to more than 260 million users in more than 200 countries around the world. There are four options for engaging with others through LinkedIn:

- Through a personal profile
- Through a company page
- Through LinkedIn groups
- Through advertising

LinkedIn provides small business owners not only the ability to connect with other businesses that may represent customers or prospects, but also the ability to find employees, contractors, or vendors.

ESSENTIAL

You can, and should, join up to fifty groups on LinkedIn. The groups you join allow you to connect with others on the platform and increase both the number of search results your people searches can generate, and make it more likely that your own profile will show up in search. You can choose whether or not to include the group's logo on your homepage.

Personal profiles are for individuals and can be a good way for key people in your company to engage with others. Your personal profile offers you the opportunity to include information about your:

- Experience
- Education
- Organizations
- Skills and Endorsements
- Honors and Awards
- Volunteer and Causes
- Projects and Publications

What you post plays a role not only in telling others about yourself, but also in search. In the same manner that SEO drives people to your website through organic search, those who search for people or businesses on LinkedIn can best find you if your profile contains the right key words and phrases. Organic search is when a user finds your website by entering in search words or phrases in a search engine like Google, rather than coming to your site through your URL or a link from another site.

Company Pages provide the ability to create a profile for your business, where you can share updates about the business and its products and services. LinkedIn users can follow your company page and also can recommend products or comment on your updates.

Groups offer the opportunity to connect with like-minded people around a broad range of business-related topics or issues ranging from AARP to Zynga. The group with the most participants is "Job Openings, Job Leads and Job Connections!," boasting 1.6 million members, but the number of people in a group, the content, and the participation varies widely from group to group. You may also choose to create your own groups, which can be a great way to build communities on this popular social media network.

Advertising on LinkedIn

Businesses may also advertise on LinkedIn through sponsored updates and pay-per-click ads that may contain text, images, or even video. Ads can be targeted to LinkedIn users based on elements of their profile, allowing you to put your messages before your desired target audiences.

LinkedIn ads work in much the same way as ads on Facebook. Because of the data that LinkedIn gathers about its users through their profile and online activity, advertisers are able to target the reach of their messages very specifically to reach a B2B audience based on job title and function, industry, company size, seniority, and geography.

Ads can be text only, or can include visual images or even video. Advertisers set their own budget and can pay based on pay-per-click or impressions. LinkedIn's analytics allows advertisers to monitor activity and adjust or close campaigns based on this activity.

LinkedIn for B2B

LinkedIn is primarily a B2B tool. For B2B (business to business) marketers, as well as job seekers, LinkedIn remains the most viable option when attempting to select the social media tools that will help generate the best results.

B2B LinkedIn users should have both a personal profile and a Company Page. Your personal profile, as explained previously, presents you and your background and interests and is designed to help you engage with those interested in what you have to offer. It is a good idea for as many members of your company as possible to build and maintain personal profiles on LinkedIn.

Your Company Page (which can be and is used by B2C marketers on LinkedIn) lets you help other LinkedIn participants learn about your business, its brand, and its products and services, as well as about job opportunities. The Company Page has five main sections: home, careers, products and services, page insights, and analytics (these last two visible only to you).

ALERT

Don't get cute, clever, or too personal with your LinkedIn profile photo. Unlike less professionally oriented social media sites (Facebook, for instance), LinkedIn has a professional tone. That means business attire, no pets, no avatars, and no photos of you and your significant other. This is about business!

LinkedIn also allows companies to create Showcase Pages, which are subpages to the Company Page. Up to ten Showcase Pages can be created. Both of these can help to contribute to SEO and lead to page discoverability, broadening your online reach.

There are about 3.5 million companies with pages on LinkedIn. The top companies represented are IBM, Microsoft, Hewlett-Packard, Oracle, Accenture, Deloitte, Bank of America, Dell, GE, and Google, representing a mix of B2B and B2C target audiences.

LinkedIn's many groups (there are about 1.9 million) also represent an opportunity to connect with others online. Groups run the gamut from special interests to association and membership groups as well as individually created and managed groups.

Getting involved in various groups can help you connect with and monitor the perspectives and interests of those in your target audience. Establishing your own LinkedIn groups can help you create and engage with those who have an affinity for what you have to offer and can be a great way to stay in touch with target audience segments.

LinkedIn for B2C

Unlike Facebook and Twitter, there is not a lot of B2C marketing taking place on LinkedIn. The LinkedIn audience is a decidedly business-focused audience, so you're not going to see many, if any, posts about retail products and services, restaurants, or other hospitality services.

FACT

While LinkedIn doesn't strongly lend itself to connecting with consumer markets, there are a number of consumer-facing companies that have a well-established presence on the site. Why? They're looking for employees. LinkedIn was, and in many respects still is, an employee recruitment tool designed to connect recruiters and hiring managers with candidates.

While the 2014 B2C Content Marketing Institute study "2014 Benchmarks, Budgets, and Trends—North America" indicated that 71 percent of the B2C companies surveyed said they use LinkedIn (compared to 89 percent for Facebook, 80 percent for Twitter, and 72 percent for YouTube), only 42 percent believe it is effective for them.

Most of these companies are on LinkedIn not to sell their products and services to this audience, but to fill open job positions in their organizations. Still, keep in mind that all of those business professionals on LinkedIn are also consumers. You may find some unique and untapped opportunities to engage with these consumers through this social channel.

Amazon, for instance, has a presence on LinkedIn, and while it is primarily a B2C organization, its products certainly have appeal for consumers engaged in a B2B platform. Its almost 680,000 followers support this. Amazon's posts are focused on sharing information about the company and its services, as well as information about staff members. And, as might be expected, jobs are a primary focus. Another popular B2C company, Best Buy, also has a presence with about 120,000 followers. As with Amazon, the focus is on service and policy, as well as company news and news and information about staff members.

If you're a B2C business, should you have a Company Page presence here? It really will depend on your goals and objectives. If you need to recruit hard-to-find candidates, LinkedIn is definitely the place to be. If you're trying to sell consumer goods, though, this may not be the place for you.

Building Community

One of the big benefits of LinkedIn is the ability to form and join groups to build community and engage with followers. There are 1.9 million groups on LinkedIn, and the number is continually growing. You should join up to fifty groups. When you join groups you expand your network based on the number of participants in those groups, providing you both with better search results and increasing the odds that you will show up in others' searches.

ALERT

Although LinkedIn automatically populates e-mail text boxes with generic messages when you're attempting to connect with someone through the site, don't use that automatic text. Instead, replace it with something personal and relevant that indicates how you know the other person and why you would like to connect.

Belonging to LinkedIn groups can add credibility to your profile and increase the likelihood that your profile will be viewed by those interested in the same types of groups, potentially leading to network or career opportunities. The downside is that the sheer number of groups on LinkedIn can make it difficult to identify those that offer the greatest potential benefit for users.

Groups can help you find and build connections, provide you with exposure through the comments and insights you share, and provide you with useful information about your industry, the business issues you face, and even your competition.

Finding Groups to Join

There are three primary ways to find groups on LinkedIn. The first and most basic is to use the groups directory on the LinkedIn homepage. The box on the top right-hand side of the homepage allows users to search LinkedIn for groups as well as people, companies, jobs, and updates. Users can enter specific keywords to find the relevant subject matter and geographic location of groups they may be interested in.

The second way to find groups is through groups the user has already joined. Members of groups are provided a list of similar groups that may be of interest to them. Once users join a particular group, they may find that there are several similar groups listed that are even more relevant to their interests.

Finally, users can look at groups that their connections belong to. Many connections may be in similar industries or professional fields and may belong to groups focused on those areas. Not only does using connections to find groups make it easier to identify which groups to join; it also provides an opportunity to strengthen relationships with connections by creating yet another thing that two individuals have in common.

QUESTION

What is passive recruiting?
Passive search is a commonly used term in the Human Resources world that refers to the recruitment of job candidates who are not actively looking for jobs. These candidates have been traditionally hard to find, but LinkedIn has changed all of this. Today, through LinkedIn, recruiters, HR professionals, and hiring managers can search and find candidates who already hold positions at other companies and reach out to them to let them know about opportunities at their organizations.

It's important to think of the groups that you belong to as part of your overall brand image. You want to join groups you're interested in, of course, but you also want your participation to reflect positively on you. The exclusivity of a group should be taken into consideration when deciding which ones to join. Some groups are open, meaning anyone can join, while others are restricted, meaning that a LinkedIn user must request permission to join the group. Membership in restricted groups is often more valuable than membership in open groups because restricted groups tend to lend more credibility to the members, as certain qualifications need to be present before one can join.

Another consideration for selecting groups is the size of the group. While larger groups may offer exposure to a larger member base, smaller groups tend to be more specifically tailored to member interests and often provide more useful updates and information to users, whereas larger groups often provide information that is primarily promotional or irrelevant.

Group Etiquette

Before jumping into the conversation in any group, take the time to simply monitor conversations for a while to get a sense of the topics being discussed and the "etiquette" of group discussions. Then, once you have a good feel for the group dynamics, you can start to actively participate and position yourself as a knowledgeable member of the community. What are the key topics being discussed, and what might you be able to add to the conversation? Do group members acknowledge contributions of others? Make sure to read and follow the group rules, which will give an indication of the style of the group and what is and is not allowed; often, for instance, blatant marketing of personal products or services is frowned upon and can result in being "kicked out" of the group.

ESSENTIAL

LinkedIn groups have rules or codes of contact established by group managers to provide participants with insights about what is and is not allowed in the group. Before jumping in to engage in conversations in any group, make sure that you understand these rules. Not doing so can get you kicked out of the group.

You may also choose to launch your own group or groups. For instance, you may want to invite your customers to participate in a closed group, where they can ask questions and share information with each other about how they use your products or services. This is a great way to build a community to engage with your own audiences.

Sharing with Connections

Because LinkedIn is such a business-oriented site, your best opportunity to connect effectively with others is by sharing business-related information that is designed to address their interests, needs, and concerns. It's no different, really, from any other social media site *except* here the focus is "strictly business."

As you build your list of connections, think carefully about the audience you hope to engage with and be selective in terms of how you build this audience. This is important (as it is with any type of communication) to ensure that the posts/updates you generate will be meaningful and of interest to your audience. If you don't have a specific purpose and a clearly defined audience, you will struggle to connect with any of its members. A very clear understanding of your target audience and their interests can help you be more successful in forming strong relationships.

You may find that you have multiple audiences with whom you need to connect. If this is true it may be a good idea to establish separate accounts. Again, it is important for your messages to be focused. If you're attempting to communicate both with HR managers and with IT directors, for instance, it may make sense to do so separately.

FACT

Much of what you can do, and the value you can attain via LinkedIn, is at no cost to you; it's a free service. However, if you want to add functionality such as the ability to see more of the people viewing your profile, or the ability to send direct messages (called In-Mails), you'll need to pay a monthly fee based on the level of service you desire.

Make a commitment on LinkedIn to giving more than you get. While most of the people engaged in social media sites, including LinkedIn, are hoping to "get" something—a job, clients, etc.—social media success is based on building relationships, not on "selling." Consider what's of interest to your audience and how you can provide value, and then do that.

Finally, make a commitment to participate regularly. This can be a challenge because social media involvement does take time and, inherently, contains many potential distractions. It's important, though, that once you've committed to participating in social media you have a plan to ensure that your presence will be regular.

This can be done by scheduling time when you will check updates, activity, etc. Tools like Hootsuite, TweetDeck, and others can help with this by allowing you to schedule posts in advance. But nothing takes the place of personal, real-time engagement. If LinkedIn is the site for you, make sure you are using it to engage effectively and meaningfully with your audience.

Targeted Advertising

Like Facebook, LinkedIn offers members the opportunity to advertise on the site, serving up ads to specifically targeted groups of individuals who can be selected based on criteria ranging from type of company, to position within the company, to location, to groups they belong to, and more.

Ads are displayed to LinkedIn users based on the information they've included in their profile. A look at your own LinkedIn homepage will give you a good indication of the types and range of ads in use and also provide you some insights into best practices. The ads will appear at the bottom of your right-hand sidebar.

As you scroll through your newsfeed and refresh the page, you'll see that the ads you're shown will change. All have been sent to you, though, because the advertisers believe that based on your profile characteristics, you represent a potential customer!

As with Facebook ads, you don't have a lot of space to convey your message. You'll rely on a combination of an attention-getting visual and brief content (a twenty-five character headline and up to seventy-five characters displayed on two lines). The link in your ad will take those who click on it to either your webpage (or a specially designed landing page) or a page on LinkedIn. For each campaign you can create up to fifteen variations.

Choosing Your Ads

You set a daily budget that indicates the maximum amount you wish to spend based on either impressions or click-through rates (CTR). Impressions refer to the number of people who have had the opportunity to see your ad—the same concept as "reach," a term that advertisers are familiar with in the traditional media world. Since most LinkedIn advertisers are looking for response and not necessarily just awareness, CTR may be the most logical and economic route to take.

The analytics that LinkedIn provides will let you review the results for each of the variations of your ad and will show you the number of clicks, impressions, CTR, average cost per click (CPC), and the total amount you've spent for each ad. You can also see the referral path that brought a person to your ad (if that person clicked on it).

ESSENTIAL

Use the information you can glean from analytics to help you determine which ads are working well, which aren't, and how you can incorporate these lessons learned into future efforts. Experiment, as well, with different audiences. Because you have the ability to very finely target audiences, and run ads immediately, you can learn a lot.

A relatively new advertising option on LinkedIn is sponsored updates. Sponsored updates allow you to reach users through their news feeds. Scroll through your own news feed and look for the word "Sponsored" in gray type next to the name of the person or organization whose posts you are seeing. These are sponsored, or paid-for, posts, delivered to you like ads based on your profile attributes. As with LinkedIn ads, you will set a budget for these sponsored posts and pay based on either a CPC or CPM (cost per impression) basis. Again, your analytics will give you an indication of what worked and what didn't, allowing you to adjust your strategy as you learn.

Best Practices for LinkedIn Engagement

Think of your personal profile or your company page as your "webpage." The same general principles apply, including SEO. Stay on top of what your competitors are up to by following their company pages and participating in groups that members of their organizations participate in. When viewing profiles of others, consider changing your security settings so that you show up as "anonymous" when they look at who has viewed their profiles. You can turn this setting on and off to keep yourself private at certain times and visible at others.

Take advantage of groups to build audience and establish a network of people with shared interests. But, make sure that the information you share is valuable and focused more on information than promotion.

Don't overlook the significant opportunity to use LinkedIn as a marketing research tool. There is a great deal of information to be gleaned here about not only your target audience, but also your competition. Keep in mind that LinkedIn had its roots in recruitment. This can be a great place to seek and source candidates for a range of positions.

Remember that you're not the only person in your area of specialty or type of business engaged in LinkedIn. This can present a few challenges, but also many benefits. The biggest challenges relate to the fact that your competitors can monitor what you're doing and saying online, who is interacting with you, and, depending on how you've set your security settings, who you're connected to. That's the downside. The upside, though, is that you can do the same type of monitoring and assessment in terms of what your competitors are doing—and what's working, or not working, for them.

CHAPTER 15

Using Google+ for Customer Engagement

Google+ is the search engine giant's latest attempt to crack into the social networking world to date. Google announced the project in 2011. While similar to Facebook in many ways, Google+ allows users to divide their friends into "circles," such as "family," "friends," "business contacts," and "neighbors," for example. Additionally, Google+ has created a feature called "Hangouts," which utilizes Google's group chat function to allow up to ten users to videoconference with one another. These types of tools seem well suited for informally managing business contacts across departments or divisions and having quick meetings with a handful of key individuals via a Hangout. Google+ also has various tools to help you track who visits your page and how their activities affect your brand.

The Google+ Platform

For some time, Facebook, Twitter, and LinkedIn have been the "big three" of social media, but this new and very powerful player—Google+—has changed the social media landscape. The clout of this site comes from the fact that it is a product of Google. Just three years after its launch it already has more than 540 million users, according to Google.

However, skeptics point out that all those who have Google Mail accounts are, by default, Google+ users whether they actually "use" the tool or not. On top of that, Google recently created an online uproar through its requirement that users of its other property, YouTube, have a Google+ account in order to access YouTube to post content. And, those who use Google+'s most popular feature—Hangouts—are also considered Google+ users, whether they actively use other features or not.

FACT

Google is a massive company and like any successful person or organization, it has its detractors. In fact, the sheer size of the site and its significant power to influence online search—often to the detriment of a business—have generated plenty of detractors, even haters. In fact, there is a "Google Haters Club" on Facebook.

Still, while the site's statistics may involve a lot of smoke and mirrors, most believe that it's an option that can't be ignored, primarily because of its impact on SEO. Given Google's move to "hide" organic search results for those who use Google Analytics, the SEO boost that Google+ is said to bring can be a big reason to become engaged through this social media channel.

SEO

The big benefit of Google+ is SEO. From a search perspective, Google+ has an obvious edge. Google+ communities are indexed within Google searches, meaning that your participation can help boost search results for your business. Perhaps even more important, the more you comment within a Google+ community, the more Google begins to recognize you as an authority in the space. The benefit may not be readily apparent, but what this means is that your participation in Google+ can boost the ability for *any-one* to find you—whether they participate in Google+ or not.

As Penny Sansevieri, a content marketing expert and the author of a number of books, including *Red Hot Internet Publicity* (CreateSpace Independent Publishing Platform, 2013), says, "From an SEO perspective, Google+ is mandatory. If you want to show up in Google, you have to be on Google+. There's no way around that."

QUESTION

How can I know what search words or phrases my customer might be using?
Listen to them! Listen to the types of questions they ask you and your staff. Listen to the conversations you may be able to hear them have with each other. Engage with them in online forums and pay close attention to the language they use. These are your keywords!

In addition, if you're a business that wants to show up as a local result on Google Maps, you must have a Google+ profile! If you also rely on reviews, Google+ is the place to be. Google's recent addition of Zagat ratings means that reviews will appear more prominently in Google search results. And, again, if you're active and engaged on Google+ and are getting likes and shares, you'll rise in Google search results.

You can test this yourself: if you have people in your circles on Google+ and you do a search on Google, the top items that appear are likely to represent content from those in your circles. That's a big benefit for those who are engaged, or a big drawback for those who are not.

Benefits of Google+

Participation through Google+ itself can also provide big benefits. Joel Stein, SEO Campaign Manager with Tecmark in the United Kingdom, shares an example based on a blog he has been involved with—*ManchesterLaLaLa*, a team of writers from around the world. Since the blog was created in December 2013, Stein has been building audience through social media with a goal of driving traffic to the blog through a mix of social and organic search.

"While the highest traffic driver for us so far has been Reddit," he says, "we have seen that visits from Google+ tend to be more engaged, with lower-than-average bounce rate, higher-than-average pages per visit and above-average visit durations." In addition, he says, "Users are also highly engaged on Google+ itself with articles posted into relevant communities averaging five comments or more." When it comes to building community online, it's all about the numbers!

Circles

One important feature of Google+ that other social media tools don't offer, at least not yet, is the ability to segment and target specific audience segments with unique messages through its "circles." This allows users to easily communicate different messages to different segments of their connections. For instance, small businesses may share certain messages with prospects and different messages with customers. They may even share different types of messages with prospects for certain products or services than for others. You may set up circles for media contacts, for professional contacts, for family and friends—the options are entirely up to you, and you can move contacts from one circle to another with ease, or have contacts in more than one circle.

ESSENTIAL

Here's an important tip for Google+ users. Your contacts don't know which circles you may have them in. So, for instance, if you want to create a circle for "difficult people" you could do so and they would be none the wiser (at least not until Google decides to change the settings on the site). You can also place people in more than one circle.

Because Google is incorporating e-mail into the contact information on Google+, you also have the option of e-mailing contacts as well as connecting with them via your circles. That way, even if they are not logged in to Google+ they will still receive your message.

Communities

Another important distinction exists between Google+ Communities and LinkedIn groups. Only individuals can interact in LinkedIn groups, but *brands* can join and engage in Google+ Communities, just as individuals can. Brand participation on LinkedIn is, by default, disjointed. Individuals can spread messages but there is no opportunity to share "brand" messages. Not true on Google+. Here the brand can have a voice, which can be a big benefit for many organizations.

Communities can range from the personal (groups of individuals interested in cooking certain types of foods) to the technical (groups of individuals interested in learning how to use C++ or other software); from the fun (cartooning) to the very serious (fighting cancer).

As on LinkedIn, you can join other communities or create your own.

Authorship

Google Authorship is another element of Google+ that can boost search results. The authorship function allows you to link content that you have created on or for another domain to your Google+ profile. All that is required is that your profile include a recognizable headshot, that the name in your byline and on your Google+ profile are the same, and that you have an e-mail address on the same domain as your content *or* you link your content to your Google+ profile.

ALERT

If you're using links of any kind in your Google+ account, but particularly authorship links, make sure that you occasionally check to make sure that the links are still active.

You can link content from a blog or articles you've published that appear online or virtually any source with a URL. This is a good way to expand awareness of yourself and your business and, as you've seen, to boost your searchability so more people find you when they're looking for what you may have to offer.

Hangouts

Google Hangouts are an important, and popular, part of the platform. Hangouts work like video chats, allowing a number of people to get together to take part in a single event. These events may range from informal conversations among friends to formal conferences across multiple locations. For small businesses, Hangouts can be a great way to connect more intimately with your followers through the use of video.

Google+ for B2B

At this time it is difficult to say whether Google+ provides more of a B2B or B2C platform, since it is still very much in its infancy. Both are prevalent. If you go to your Google+ page and click the "Local" icon in the dropdown menu on the left-hand side, you'll see a list of the businesses in your area that have a presence on Google+. Keep in mind that anyone with a Google mail account will be considered to have a presence.

ALERT

Just because you don't see any other B2B organizations engaging with customers or consumers online doesn't mean there's not an opportunity for someone (maybe you) to come up with a unique and innovative way to break through. If your audience is there, there's a way to reach them. You just need to think creatively.

Still, it can be instructive to look through the business listings that pop up to see how others are positioning themselves, along with their number of followers and their likes and comments.

Check out, also, the big players in the space. Again, as with other large B2B companies involved in social media, these tend to be technology companies. Cisco Networking Academy is there with about 28,000 followers, IBM has about 40,000 followers, and Hewlett Packard (HP) has more than 500,000.

There's not much engagement going on here, though, just posts. Many of these are simply repurposed from other social media sites like Facebook and Twitter.

Google+ for B2C

While it's still tough to tell who is really using Google+, one thing remains certain: Both B2B and B2C marketers can benefit from the site's ability to boost search traffic. Because the site is owned by Google, and unlike other social media platforms, the engagement that occurs doesn't occur only within the confines of the Google+ platform. If you have a Google+ account, what you share on Google+ can, and does, extend into the broader reaches of cyberspace.

Here's an example from Jenna Bechtholt, a Los Angeles–area wedding photographer who uses Google+ to market her business online. Instead of focusing on getting more page views, she says, Google+ helps her website "behind the scenes." For example: "I take a lot of time optimizing my blog and each post using various SEO strategies, so whenever I create a new post I make sure to share it via Google+ so that it will be indexed right away through Google. In doing so, I'm more likely to climb the ladder for the keywords that I am targeting and rank higher on Google."

FACT

In 2011 Mashable did an analysis of the top users of Google's just-launched Google+ tool. They found, quite surprisingly, that user number one was none other than Mark Zuckerberg, the founder of Facebook. This may be a good example of keeping an eye on the competition, although as Mashable pointed out, there was no guarantee the profile was really his.

Google+ Companies

Mayo Clinic, an early adopter of social media in the healthcare industry, has a prominent presence on Google+, where its posts focus primarily on patient stories and health-related tips and information. Nordstrom, a high-end retailer, has a strong presence with more than 12,000 followers. Its posts are focused primarily on products and make use of high-quality images to draw attention and, presumably, drive visitors to its website, where they can purchase those products.

Nike has an exceptionally strong presence here with 2.2 million followers. Other B2C sites have a presence but not yet much of a following. Taco John's, for instance, has just 107 followers.

Building Community

Community on Google+ is built primarily through circles, hangouts, and communities. Your circles are groups of people you know. You can divide your circles into friends, family, work, acquaintances, and more. Dividing people you know into circles allows you to share specific content with specific groups of people. You can also use a Google Hangout to video-call these circles, interacting with just one or several at a time.

Communities are groups of people with similar interests or lifestyles. For example, if you're a photographer, you might join a photography community. Google uses your profile information to recommend communities you might be interested in.

ESSENTIAL

To build your Google+ community, identify those in your circle whose audience is likely to match yours, view the names of people who have them in their circles, and add them to your own circles. You might establish an "I copied these" circle and then move these people into another, more appropriate, circle once they add you to their list.

Again, one of the big benefits of Google+ over other sites is the ability to segment your audience into circles that may overlap—one individual may be a member of a number of circles. This allows you to more specifically target your messages to, for instance, your active customers, your inactive customers, "lost customers," prospects, vendors, employees, etc. Doing this through other sites would be far more challenging and time-consuming. Google+ also has a number of "bells and whistles" that help to boost interactions among communities, including private meetings, social webinars, and live demos.

The general principles of engagement remain the same among the sites, though. It's all about sharing information that is valued by the group of people you're interacting with. Arguably you may be able to do this more effectively through Google+ because of its many features. However, many feel that the critical mass of participation in Google+ is just not there yet.

Sharing and Algorithms

Even if you're not impressed with the current levels of engagement you're seeing on Google+, it's still a good idea to jump in and become part of the mix. Do what you can to build a following and monitor the results you see in terms of search results for your content, products, and services.

Sharing on Google+ involves a combination of building relationships and benefiting from algorithms. Google is using Google+ as its primary method to personalize search results for Google users based on their Google+ contacts (the people you follow and those who follow you). Building your following on Google+ will help you get those favorable personalized search results. In addition, as your information is shared within the network, you also get a boost in ranking. So it pays to build an audience!

QUESTION

What if I'm a Google Mail user and I don't want to be on Google+? Unfortunately, the stars and Google's clout may be aligned against you. The best bet is simply to ignore the site and not participate, although given the role that Google+ plays in generating and boosting organic search results, that may be a shortsighted strategy to take.

Build an audience by reaching out to those you know. Search for and follow them. Look for influential people on Google+ and follow them; tag them when you post something relevant to their companies and their products and services. When you post on Google+, make sure you're primarily posting to the world at large (public vs. posts to your own specific circles). This can help to generate awareness and, hopefully, interest in your profile.

Content

Of course, to build followers you need to provide engaging content. Much of the sharing on Google+ relies on the distribution and redistribution of content. You want your content to be liked and shared by others so you can build viral flow, not just on Google+, but through search results. To succeed here, as with any communication channel, it's all about understanding your audience, what they're interested in, and how you can deliver valuable content that keeps them coming back for more.

Google+'s integration with other Google products, most notably YouTube, means that you can quickly share information across these pages. So, for instance, you could share a document from Google Docs, add your location from Google Maps to your Google+ page, or share a video from YouTube on your page. Each of these shares creates a unique URL that, hopefully, will be spread around cyberspace by your followers.

ALERT

Google+ will allow you to see who is engaging with others' articles. Just type the URL of the article into the search box to see every Google+ post with that link. If the link has been shortened, try searching using both the short and long version of the link. This is a great way to monitor the traction that competitors may be having with their communities.

One unique feature of Google+ is that it also makes it very easy to monitor how others are engaging with your content. You can tell who is sharing and resharing your content, who is giving it a "Plus One," who is commenting, and who the key influencers are among your circles.

Best Practices for Google+ Engagement

Because Google+ is still so new, the *best* best practice is to simply get on board, establish a presence, and begin to learn about the site and how it works. In addition:

- Learn from others. Follow some local brands, as well as organizations or individuals you're interested in, and learn from what they're doing.
- Be sure to add a Google+ +1 button to your website.

- Leverage your YouTube activities through Google+. Because of Google's partnership with YouTube, your profile displays a direct link to your YouTube site.
- Go wild with photos. One of the little-known features of Google+ is the phenomenal photo editor. Not only can you do basics, such as crop, adjust, and fine-tune images, but you can also adjust color, create a focal point, add drama or frames, tilt-shift, make it appear to be vintage, and more.
- Offer a visual, 360-degree tour, with interactive photos. This is a distinct feature that can help you stand out from the crowd and bring you closer to your audience by giving them a sense of your physical presence.
- Use the events page to create and join events, and then promote the events through your circles and communities.
- Use Hangouts to hold videoconferences and meetings, provide one-on-one support to customers, and more. If your business and part of your audience are in different locations, answering your customers' questions on Google Hangouts can be a personal way to interact with and help them.
- Google+ is relatively new in the social media environment and is changing frequently; it's definitely one to keep your eye on!
- Get your name out there through Google Authorship. With authorship, engagement for high-quality, relevant content rises and pushes you, and your avatar, higher in search results. Over time, those with authorship will appear higher in search rankings.

While the jury is still out on whether Google+ will eventually become a major player in social media, for small business marketers it is certainly a tool to consider and one to experiment with.

CHAPTER 16

Using Pinterest and Other Visual Platforms

Pinterest is a relatively new entrant to the social media market, as the site was launched in 2010. Described as basically a "virtual bulletin board," Pinterest describes itself as "a tool for collecting and organizing the things that inspire you." Users have found a wide range of unique ways to use the site: gathering ideas for home remodeling projects, planning weddings, collecting recipes, and more. Other uses are springing up regularly as individuals and businesses find new, and increasingly practical, uses. One particularly interesting and practical use of Pinterest is recruitment. While LinkedIn still has a massive lead in this category, some organizations are finding Pinterest's visual appeal a good way to literally "get in front of" job candidates.

The Pinterest Platform

Imagine sixteen different bulletin boards all over your home, each categorized differently. One has new recipes you want to try. One has travel destinations you want to start looking into. Another has DIY projects you've wanted to try. Now imagine these bulletin boards compiled in one place through an online database. Convenient, right?

Pinterest is a social site that allows users to explore a very wide variety of topics and find ideas, inspirations, and tools to use in their daily lives. Usually, clicking directly on a pin will lead to an outside source or website. When users find ideas or information they'd like to save, they can virtually pin it onto one of their boards. Categorizing these boards makes it easy to organize them.

Users' homepages represent a collection of pins from those they follow. Users can follow and be followed by other Pinterest users, and can easily search for specific pins or categories of items. Pins can be added directly from websites or apps by using a Pin It button app, which becomes part of the user's browser. So, for instance, book lovers on the Amazon.com site might find books they're interested in, click the Pin It button, and add the images of the books to their "Books I Want to Read" boards. Members of Pinterest can follow others' boards, either all of them or selected boards they are most interested in.

All of this clearly represents obvious and immediate value for businesses offering the types of goods and services that attract the attention of pinners. From fashion to food, electronics, travel, and more, your customers and potential customers can find it here. Better yet, they can readily share what they find with others, increasing your reach exponentially.

FACT

There are some unique and, some might say, disturbing boards that have generated a following on Pinterest. For instance, Oddities and Fascinators is a collection of strange and unusual things, like creepy trees, and gas masks for babies tested in an English hospital in 1940. On a brighter note, the Colors account offers some truly breathtaking images in striking, vibrant tones.

Successful use of this social media tool demands captivating images designed to pique the attention and generate user pins. That can be more challenging for B2B marketers than for B2C, but not impossible.

Pinterest for B2B

Think that Pinterest couldn't possibly hold value for B2B marketers? Think again! While initially Pinterest related primarily to fashion and food, the site has grown far beyond these early beginnings to encompass a wide range of topics and creative concepts. And, of course, as with any new thing, there can be an early adopter challenge—those who are first to try something are taking a risk; it may work out, or it may not, and that can mean wasted time, energy, and lost opportunities. It pays for B2B marketers, therefore, to think creatively about how they might leverage this popular tool.

GE and Constant Contact are two examples of B2B companies in this space, both building large, strong, and loyal followings on this platform. Constant Contact is primarily directed toward small, independent businesses, a particularly good niche on Pinterest. These companies are all building a solid following through a combination of great content and practical audience-based tools. That direct connection with audience needs and interests is important and can be leveraged to build strong online communities.

ESSENTIAL

Pinterest is just like any other communication tool, just a lot more colorful! Before going live with a Pinterest site, take the time to think about not only what your audience is interested in, but how you can incorporate visual imagery to convey those interests. Then consider where you will get the images that communicate your messages, establish clearly delineated categories (boards), and you're ready to go!

What to Share

One of the challenges for many B2B companies, of course, is how to find something that's visually appealing enough to be shared through a visually driven platform like Pinterest. Enter the infographic, a colorful, graphic-laden means of representing even the driest information in a visually appealing format. Infographics have taken the world by storm, likely driven to a large degree by Pinterest and the desire of B2B marketers to find appealing ways to connect with their audiences. These graphics are not limited to use just with the B2B market, of course. People in general are attracted to interesting visual images.

Pinterest for B2C

Pinterest is a natural choice for B2C marketers, and many were early adopters. Any business with visually oriented products to sell can quickly and effectively establish a presence and begin pinning attractive, evocative, and even provocative images to generate interest, repins, and followers.

Jenna Bechtholt is one example. As mentioned earlier, Bechtholt is a wedding photographer based in Los Angeles. She uses a variety of social media tools, including Pinterest, to promote her services. "As a wedding photographer, I know that visual forms of social media are very important for my business, whereas others might find only text, videos, or a combination more useful," she says.

Since her primary target market is young women who are planning a wedding, she focuses her energy on Facebook and Pinterest because she knows these sites are most likely to appeal to her audience. Both are visually oriented, but Pinterest has the added value of allowing people to share and reshare their pins.

ALERT

Don't make it all about you! While you may offer a wide variety of photographically pleasing products, resist the urge to make your Pinterest site all about your product. Sure, throw some product images in from time to time, but consider other ways that you can provide useful visually oriented information to your audience that isn't all about you, you, you.

"More people are likely to visit my website when they see an image that they really enjoy or can relate to," she says. Pinterest helps Bechtholt gain a larger following, which results in new business.

A good way to determine whether Pinterest might be a good fit for you is to take a look at what others are doing on the site. Examine the size of each community that draws your interest, who's represented in each, and what types of boards and images seem to be most popular based on how many repins and likes they're generating.

Once you dive in, the next step is building community for yourself.

Building Community

The best way to build community on Pinterest is to share visually appealing and useful images and to be actively engaged yourself. Follow and repin from others' boards. Comment on boards and pins that you like. Find people to follow through search or through the boards and pins that your friends and others have liked. Pinterest is a very viral community!

Another good way to build community is to search the site to find people with like interests, follow their boards, and then repin or like their posts. They'll receive a notice that you've done this, and there's a good chance that they will follow you in return. Post visually interesting content aligned with their interests and you're likely to find your boards being followed and your pins being repinned.

QUESTION

Is Pinterest just for small companies and individuals?
Not at all! In fact, a number of *Fortune* 500 companies have Pinterest accounts. While some of their content might seem dry, some have learned to be both creative and practical when creating and posting to their boards. American Family Insurance, for instance, has a wide range of practical boards for its audience, including Keep Your Family Safe, A Healthy & Fit Lifestyle, and Dreams in Motion (all about cars).

Pinterest is really no different from any other social media site or any other attempt to encourage others to share your information. It's just that, in this case, it is visual images you are sharing, and pictures often trump words!

You should also make an effort to connect with people through the site. When you like a board, comment on it. When you repin a pin, explain why, and tell what you like about it. While it is not a word-heavy environment, there are still conversations going on through Pinterest, and you should make an effort to become a part of them.

Sharing Images

Pinterest is built on sharing. The more you like and repin what others have to offer, the more they'll like and repin what you're offering (assuming, of course, that your content is good and aligned with their interests). To prime the pump, don't be afraid to encourage a call-to-action in your pins to increase engagement.

ALERT

There are some great photographic images floating around on Pinterest and on the Internet at large. But if you didn't snap the shot yourself, you must do two things before you post it: first, make sure you aren't violating any copyright protections related to the image; second, clearly identify the source. Include a link back to the image, along with the name of the photographer or website that owns the rights to the image.

While in the Pinterest environment, in most cases it's fine to share an image—especially if that image is from a retailer whose presence on Pinterest is to expand the reach and awareness of their products and services—it would not be okay to attempt to "sell" that image or to capitalize on its use in a monetary way. It's a gray area, though, so when in doubt, it's always a good idea to seek permission directly from the copyright holder.

Just be careful when you pin. Copyright infringement has emerged as a significant issue. While many businesses are delighted to have images of their products and services shared, because it helps them to market these offerings, others are not so delighted. Make sure you know the source of the pin you are posting, or even repinning, to ensure that you are not infringing on someone else's property. Pinterest offers details on its site both about how to avoid this infringement and what to do if it happens to you.

Best Practices for Pinterest Engagement

As with everything, remember your target audience. Pin and repin relevant content. Craft your campaigns around seasons and holidays. Pinterest is all about images. The more attractive, attention-getting, and high quality the images on your website, the greater the odds that visitors will pin those images to their Pinterest boards.

If your business is one that is likely to lend itself to visitors pinning images from your website, make sure to add the Pin It button to your site to remind them and make it easy for them to do so. The button, which appears as an icon, can be placed next to any image that you want to encourage visitors to pin.

Make sure that your own boards are interesting and relevant and that they do a good job of supporting and showcasing your brand and the products and services you offer. Use Pinterest's analytics to determine which pins are most popular among users and which are most effective in driving traffic to your website.

Think outside the box! Pinterest thrives on creativity. Create colorful pins and graphics, such as infographics, with facts about your product or service. Each pin can be linked to an outside website, so pinning your own products and services will drive more traffic to your website.

Other Emerging Visual Platforms

Pinterest's popularity has quickly spawned a number of other social media applications that leverage the use of visual imagery to drive engagement. Most popular are Instagram, Vine, and Flickr, but new options are emerging and gaining traction continually.

Instagram

According to eBizMBA, an online business guide to the web's best resources for small businesses, Pinterest has taken the number four spot in terms of the most popular social media network, with more than 150 million monthly visitors. It has spawned an interest in, and competition among, other visually oriented social media tools, like Instagram.

Launched in 2010, the platform was created by Kevin Systrom and Mike Krieger and has quickly grown to over 100 million active users. Facebook acquired Instagram in 2012. Instagram allows users to share photos and videos that they have augmented through various filters to create unique and interesting visuals that they can then share on other social networking services. Videos can be up to fifteen seconds long.

ESSENTIAL

When posting an image on Pinterest take advantage of the opportunity to provide a description, both to help inform your audience and to boost SEO. The better your descriptions, the more likely they are to attract attention and generate likes and repins. Although the descriptions themselves should be factually accurate, you might want to consider adding a brief, yet creative, summary of why you posted the image.

Each user can create a profile, which may include personal information as well as recently shared images. A new feature introduced in late 2013—Instagram Direct—lets users send images to just selected individuals or to members of a group (similar to another service, Snapchat).

Vine

Vine is an online photo management and sharing tool that was introduced by Twitter. Similar to Twitter tweets, Vine videos are short—six seconds or less. Vine was initially made available on iPhone and iPod platforms and expanded to Android in 2013.

Users simply create short looping videos and upload them to readily share with others.

Snapchat

Snapchat is a short photo and video messaging application. The whole idea behind Snapchat was to allow users to share images that would "disappear" in a few seconds—initially in one to ten seconds. This appealed primarily to a younger audience segment whose provocative images on sites like Facebook have left some embarrassed as they entered the workforce.

So, what's the allure for businesses? The fast-moving nature of Snapchat lends itself to quick promotions and calls to action that can create interest and drive activity. For instance, some retailers use the tool to offer coupons.

Taco Bell used the app to reintroduce its Beefy Crunchy Burrito. The New Orleans Saints use it to release photos and sneak peeks of the season. Snapchat is making its way up the ladder and is being used by brands around the world. It can be used for coupons, promotional announcements, and more. A version made specifically for businesses, called Confide, may become more and more popular in the next few months.

By the time you read this, it's likely that some of these tools may have declined in popularity and others have emerged. Such is the nature of social media. For marketers whose audiences are increasingly online it pays to stay on top of what's happening in the social environment and to learn from the successes, and failures, of others.

CHAPTER 17

Using Online Communities for Customer Engagement

The Internet makes it easier than ever before to network with others from around the country—and even around the world! One great way to do this is by participating in, or launching, online communities. If you have something you want to talk about, you can find a community online with like-minded people who have shared interests. Whether representing social networks (like Twitter, Facebook, and LinkedIn), proprietary sites made available by organizations and individuals, or large Internet sites like BuddyPic or Something Awful, there's something for everyone.

Establishing Your Objectives

Before becoming involved in online communities, and just as with any communication effort, you need to identify your specific, measurable objectives. Then you need to define, in excruciating detail, your target audience. Identifying whether your audience is "out there" is the next step in terms of joining or attempting to create a community. If they are, determine what value you can provide (based on what *that potential audience* values, not simply on what you wish to communicate). What will cause them to choose to engage with you in a meaningful way via online communities?

Being able to do this well really depends on how ultra-specific you are about your target audience and how much you know about them. Effective online communities are those where:

- The audience is well defined and well maintained; only members who share certain attributes and interests are allowed to join the group. That helps to ensure that conversations will be on topic and relevant.
- Posts are monitored to ensure a focus on useful information, rather than promotional items. Promotional items are promptly removed (and those who continue to post them are removed as well).
- Group owners don't monopolize the conversation, but chime in every now and then to engage the audience, pose provocative questions, or provide support, encouragement, and feedback to others. Regular participation is critical.
- Information conveyed is meaningful and has value for participants. Based on the unique focus of the group, it's important to ensure that the audience gets relevant information that interests and engages them.
- The environment is professional and welcoming. One important role of the group manager is to establish and reinforce group guidelines. The more you can do to make it safe for people to share their thoughts, the more thoughts they'll share!

There are a variety of audiences and inputs that can be monitored via online groups. For example, you might want to connect with a certain segment of customers, a group of prospects, a group of business leaders in your community, or a group of like-minded enthusiasts about some hobby or vocation. While your customers represent one key audience that you want to engage with online, there are other audiences that you might also want to engage with or monitor, including prospects, professionals with shared interests, and even competitors. There is much to learn in these forums, and they can serve as an important input for small businesses. Participation in these communities, whether you are active or simply monitoring the conversations, can reveal interests, help identify trends, and provide insights into the common sentiment of various groups around specific topics.

Proprietary vs. Public Communities

At one time proprietary communities, housed and managed on companies' own websites, were most prevalent on online forums. But open communities like LinkedIn groups and Google+ Communities have become more popular. Consequently, many businesses have migrated their own communities to these public forums, but not all. Some continue to find proprietary sites valuable, particularly for very specialized, niche audiences.

There is another consideration as well. Despite the prevalence and popularity of online communities like Facebook, Twitter, and LinkedIn, these communities are not owned by you. That means they are subject to the rules and whims of the organizations and individuals who do own them. And, as hard as it may be to believe today, some of these platforms may eventually go away. If and when they do, your community goes with them.

QUESTION

Whatever happened to AOL?
AOL, or America Online, was a big deal for its time. It was launched in 1985 and was the first ever widely used online community. Its proprietary software was available only to registered users and allowed them access to a wide range of communities on the site. In 2000 AOL was purchased by Time Warner. AOL still exists, but now refers to itself as a "broadband company."

While that may not be an immediate risk, it is a risk that should be considered. Your vital, vibrant, and growing LinkedIn group, for instance, could be lost if LinkedIn ever falls out of favor. Think it won't ever happen? So did AOL and MySpace.

On the other hand, proprietary communities have the benefit of ownership. Your group on your site is controlled entirely by you. What's lacking, though, is the power of scale that heavily trafficked sites like Facebook, LinkedIn, and others can bring. It's a balancing act and one that should be carefully considered.

Owning vs. Participating in Communities

Another consideration about involvement in online communities is whether you want to be a participant or a group owner. Being a group owner is a commitment and responsibility. Of the millions of groups that are online, many have fallen inactive and have been so for months, or even years.

If you decide to own and manage a group, you must be committed to monitoring the group, engaging in conversations with group members, and continually "priming the pump" with interesting and relevant content.

Vibrant Online Communities

It is absolutely possible to have a vibrant online community.

For example, Kristin Baird, RN, is the owner of Baird Group, a consulting group specializing in customer service improvement and mystery shopping for healthcare organizations. She formed her LinkedIn group, Patient Experience Champions, in 2009, and it has been active ever since. It boasted more than 2,700 members in 2014 with about ten new members joining each week.

ESSENTIAL

If your community is very large, it may make sense to segment it into smaller sub-categories to ensure that the conversations taking place are relevant and of interest. While it can be time-consuming to manage multiple online discussions, the time you need to spend can pay off.

Inclusion is a Business Strategy is another active, individually owned and managed LinkedIn group. Started in 2010, the group is owned by Shirley

Engelmeier with InclusionINC, a global consulting and learning organization. With about 700 members, the group serves as a hub for HR practitioners and diversity and inclusion experts on issues related to the business impacts of building inclusive business environments.

Your goal is to target very specific groups of individuals whose interests you understand well and whom you can engage on an ongoing basis. As those who have attempted to create online groups know, it's not a simple task. It can take time to build a following, engage followers, and get them to contribute to the discussion.

Participating in Other Communities

Another alternative for those who don't feel they have the time or energy to go this route is to participate in existing communities. In fact, even though you may want to create your own online communities, don't overlook the benefit that participation in others' communities may bring you.

ALERT

Be careful out there! There's a risk of being defamed—or defaming someone else—online. Defamation involves false statements about others that could cause them harm. When defamation relates to a company's products or services it's known as libel. Importantly, just because an individual or company isn't identified by name doesn't mean that defamation hasn't occurred.

Sanguine BioSciences is a biomedical research company that engages in online communities to source noninvasive biospecimens like blood, urine, and saliva for use in its research. Not exactly the type of thing that you would think could resonate online, yet the organization has been successful in engaging with various groups to generate the donations it is looking for. Sanguine uses support group pages on sites like Facebook to educate and engage patients. "Support group online communities are by far the most successful campaigns," says Jarone Ashkenazi, with Bob Gold & Associates, Sanguine's PR firm.

Sanguine takes advantage of outside social media sites and the benefits of peer-to-peer sharing, says Ashkenazi. The company is most active on

Facebook, but also takes part in support group pages of other organizations that are focused on specific diseases.

"Support group online communities are by far the most successful campaigns," says Ashkenazi. "Patients are already engaged and conversations naturally flow among the members. The conversion rate from sign-up to blood donation is significantly higher when compared to other social media channels."

What groups might represent benefits for your company? It will obviously depend on your goals and your audience. A good starting point to find these groups is through a simple online search using phrases such as "online groups for . . . " or "forums for . . . " Once you've found groups that seem to represent some potential value, spend some time "lurking" to get the lay of the land and understand the stated, or unstated, rules of engagement among group members. Then consider ways you might join the conversation and draw attention to your business and its products and services.

Keep in mind, though, that any of these activities should be more focused on providing useful information and engaging in relevant conversation than on blatantly attempting to sell your goods and services.

Blogs as Communities

Blogs can also serve as a way to create community. "CustomerThink" is a concept that is used by Roberts Communications—an idea that allows Roberts employees to gain insight into the behaviors of a client's target audience and what causes them to react positively to an advertising or marketing campaign. The company's *Carrot Stick* blog (*www.behaviorchange.net*) focuses on behavior change in the health, money, business, and considered-retail decisions arenas and allows the Roberts team to communicate with and offer advice to clients and other marketers through the information it provides.

Internal Communities

Don't overlook the opportunity to use internal communities as a powerful customer engagement tool. Internal communities of employees sharing best practices, challenges, and advice can be a good way to create conversation around customer engagement.

Consider ways that you might segment your employee audience into special interest groups that reflect either their professional or personal interests. For example, you might have communities built around roles in the company (a community for accounting staff, for instance) or communities built around personal hobbies (a community for bowlers). You may even choose to engage with employees who are no longer with you (a community for retirees, for instance). Think creatively about ways that you might engage your employee audience by identifying specific areas of interest or needs that these types of communities might serve.

The Benefits of Online Engagement

There are many benefits to online engagement with customers. One big benefit is the ability to "listen in" on customers and potential customers to learn about what interests them, what concerns they may have, and what unidentified needs may exist that you might be able to fill. For example, Nailah Blades is the co-founder of Donna + Nailah, a digital marketing agency specializing in social media marketing for lifestyle brands. "We are big proponents of monitoring and engaging with customers online through social media platforms," says Nailah. "Some call it customer service. We prefer to call it customer listening." These days, she says, "the power of your brand lies in the hands of your consumers." Consequently, social media platforms can have a significant impact in terms of how your brand is viewed, online and off.

QUESTION

What's the largest online community?
Gaia Online, according to TopTenz.net. It has about 2 billion posts and about 40,000 users engaged in the community at any point in time. What are they talking about? Video games and anime, and most of them are teenagers. The site is a virtual gold mine for various sellers who offer anything from gaming systems to free collectibles and contests.

Blades uses tools like Hootsuite to easily monitor online discussions. "We set up streams so that we can get a good overview of who is talking about us and what they are saying," she says. Streams are set up for their handle, competitors, hashtags, and important keywords. "Then, if anyone is talking to or about us, we can jump in with the appropriate response," she says.

Their efforts have paid off, she says. "We've seen a dramatic increase in customer engagement from using these tools and best practices. We've seen happy customers purchase more products, unhappy customers change their tune, and lots and lots of referrals."

Your customers are already talking about you online. All you need to do is jump in and join the conversation!

Priming the Pump

For every brave soul who posts a comment on a public website or blog, there are likely hundreds of others simply "lurking" in the background. Content providers crave interaction and want to encourage discussion, yet many find themselves faced with a dearth of comments, save for perhaps those spammy postings that pop up every once in a while. What can they do?

ESSENTIAL

Your words speak volumes in online forums. That means not only the words you choose, but also how you link them together, whether you've spelled them correctly, used proper grammar, etc. In an online forum it's not just about maintaining professionalism, which you, of course, must do, but also about monitoring the impressions you convey through your language choices and communication prowess.

LinkedIn groups are a good example of this, notes Wayne Breitbarth, a social media trainer and consultant and the author of *The Power Formula for LinkedIn Success* (Greenleaf Book Group, 2011). The results of an annual survey he conducts about LinkedIn are consistent from year to year: "LinkedIn groups are always either the first top-rated or the second-rated feature every time." Since this feature is one that is popular with LinkedIn users, it pays for marketers to become engaged either through joining and participating in groups, or starting groups of their own.

So it's not that the audience doesn't exist. The people are out there. The challenge for business owners hoping to engage customers in conversations is to make things interesting. But that is often easier said than done. The key is to pay attention to what your customers are telling you through your personal interactions and online. What needs do they have? What concerns or issues do they face in their lives that you could help to address, simplify, or minimize? The more helpful you can be in providing information to those you serve, the better and more long-lasting relationships you will form. In the online environment, making these connections is far more about telling than about selling.

Best Practices in Online Community Engagement

Growing an audience through online forums takes a combination of emotional and technical efforts. Navin Nagiah is CEO of DNN, a content management system that serves as the foundation for more than 800,000 websites worldwide. The first challenge most community owners face, says Nagiah, is a classic "chicken and egg" scenario. "You can't have engagement if you don't have active users. But how do you attract users into an empty community?"

Online communities, he says, are much like start-up businesses. He recommends focusing on finding the "right" set of early adopters to get the community off to a strong start. A good starting point may be your own employees or your own loyal customers. Invite them to participate and fuel the flames of conversation through active participation yourself.

Once that foundation is built, the next challenge is maintaining sustained engagement. "There's always a lot of excitement when a new community is launched," he says. "But, after the first three, six or twelve months, has the initial burst of activity continued?" Sustain engagement by monitoring activity in the group, posting items that are of interest to the community based on the conversations that are taking place, and, above all, by maintaining a focus on sharing valuable information rather than blatantly marketing your products and services.

Best Practice Tips

Nagiah offers some best practices that can help community owners and managers build and foster an active community:

- Identify and assign a community manager, because very few online communities thrive without one. The community manager helps direct the flow of information and activity. In addition, he or she keeps members interested and engaged. Imagine a four-way intersection without a traffic light or traffic cop. That's your community without a community manager.
- Understand the difference between extrinsic and intrinsic motivation, and use both of them accordingly. Extrinsic rewards relate to tangible items, such as points or gift cards. Users will fight hard to attain them, but their impact may not be sustainable over the long term. Intrinsic rewards relate to the jobs (or activities) themselves. In a community, an intrinsic reward might be as simple as a "like." A deeper intrinsic reward may be an elevation in reputation among trusted peers. Take advantage of intrinsic rewards for long-term engagement from members.
- Make members feel appreciated for their activities and efforts. They'll like to know that "community management" is watching and that you appreciate them. In fact, this is an excellent form of intrinsic reward.

The best way to become adept at building online communities is to build some! Here are some additional tips that can help you get started:

- Define your audience in advance, and be specific. Address the specific issues that might be plaguing them and effectively draw them into the conversation.
- Embrace controversy. Speak up for, or against, a key industry issue. But make sure to do this in a way that is consistent with your brand image.
- Use celebrity references, if relevant. The world loves celebrities, and these types of posts tend to generate interest.
- Ask someone you know to be the first to comment. It can help to have someone be a conversation-starter.

- Watch your tone. A blog, post, or article that is written in a tone that is too authoritative may discourage comments.
- Share information about your community through social media channels. Point to new topics, articles, and other links.

As you're attempting to form and grow a community, and even after that community has achieved critical mass, it's important to be actively engaged in the conversations. Make sure someone from your business is monitoring the conversations. If you look at other successful groups, you'll see that this is exactly what their group leaders do.

ALERT

It pays to moderate. While the Internet was initially embraced as a democratized system where free speech would reign, most business-people quickly found that it made sense to moderate the discussions taking place in their forums. Whether guarding against spam, profanity, or illegal activity, you should have steps in place to both manage and moderate what's happening in your communities.

Success in generating productive online conversation is really much like traditional relationship-building. It's about understanding what's important to your audience, being engaged and engaging, and providing positive feedback and support along the way.

Popular Online Communities

There is much to be learned from communities that are active, engaged, and thriving. Navin Nagiah points to a couple of these active communities that small businesses may want to check out.

Quora was launched in 2010. It's an online community that revolves around questions and answers. A Quora user posts a question (e.g., "How do entrepreneurs and start-ups deal with the risk of getting their ideas stolen when pitching to angels and venture capitalists, pre-launch?") and Quora users submit answers. Users can up-vote or down-vote individual answers to indicate whether the answers were useful (or not). Quora is home to a number of celebrities and authorities. If you ask a question about Jimmy Wales (cofounder of Wikipedia), you're likely to get a response from Mr. Wales himself.

SchoolDude, Navin Nagiah says, is a provider of software applications that help educational institutions better manage their facilities and IT operations. SchoolDude manages a thriving online community directly on its website. Community participants include SchoolDude customers and partners, along with prospects who are considering the purchase of SchoolDude solutions. SchoolDude is using its online community to provide "crowdsourced" customer support, educate customers about new product features, and solicit product innovation ideas from customers. As a result of the user-generated content created by the community, SchoolDude saw a 54 percent increase in website page views in the first few months that its community went live.

Finally, Nagiah says: "Hand-in-hand with sustained engagement is the challenge of building a long-term relationship with community members. When you get married, you expect a life-long relationship: you're not expecting to file for a divorce a year later. With online communities, you'll need to figure out ways to make members stay with you (and stay active) over the long term."

Whether you're participating in a public or private group, or managing one of your own, there are a myriad of opportunities that can be gained from this type of interaction. Never before, in fact, have small businesses had such a ready-made opportunity to connect with and learn from key audiences.

CHAPTER 18

Using Public Relations for Customer Engagement

Public relations can be defined as managing public perceptions through communication designed to influence people's opinions and perspectives. This is typically done through the use of intermediaries who carry the message. Unlike advertising, in which you are talking about yourself, public relations involves getting messages to your audience through other channels, most typically the news media.

The Role of the Media

News media play an important role in carrying messages to their audiences. While that role has changed over the past several years as more and more people communicate online, and the traditional role of the media has become somewhat blurred, the media still represents an important tool for businesses to use for engaging with their audiences, including their customers.

FACT

With the ability for literally anyone to share messages with the masses via the Internet, the concept of citizen journalists has emerged. These are just everyday people who, because they have built an audience, have the ability to influence others through their online messages, whether through blogs, social media posts, or comments in online communities. This can be both a benefit and a downfall for small business owners.

Think about your own interactions with the businesses that offer the products and services you use, and how you are most influenced. Your own personal experiences are probably the most significant way in which you form impressions of the businesses you frequent. Next most influential is likely to be the recommendations of others, or word of mouth. What comes after this? Advertising? No—public relations: the things we hear about businesses and their products or services from others, generally the media. Because these are third-party perspectives they are viewed as more credible than the things businesses say about themselves through their own advertising, on their websites, or through social media.

The media serves as the conduit for businesses to get their messages in front of their target audiences.

Gaining exposure through the media continues to be a great way for organizations to reach and influence various audiences. And, of course, today the "media" has vastly expanded to include not only traditional media (print and broadcast), but also blogs and other online venues. Successful media exposure requires both proactive and reactive efforts. At the outset you should:

- **Identify your overall goals and objectives.** What are you hoping to achieve through your media efforts?
- **Clarify the audiences you are hoping to influence.** While some may think of media coverage as "free" exposure, the truth is that your time also represents a cost to your organization. And, importantly, your time is finite. If you're spending time pursuing coverage in venues that don't really reflect your core audiences, you're wasting your time.
- **Identify the media outlets that reach your target audiences most effectively.** That may not always mean the most obvious. Sometimes a smaller audience of key influencers is more valuable than a broad audience that doesn't contain a significant percentage of your desired market.
- **Identify key, general messages that you wish to embed in all of your communications.** What are the most important points that you wish people to take away from all of your communications?

An important part of this process is identifying, and prioritizing, the media you wish to cover you, your business, and its products and services.

ESSENTIAL

What are the media interested in? News! One of the big missteps that many individuals and organizations make as they're attempting to generate media exposure for their businesses is to take an approach that is too marketing oriented or promotional in nature. The goal is to find a way to create a "news hook" with your story.

Identifying Target Media Outlets

Not all media will be equally important to your business. In fact, while it may be very prestigious to gain coverage in an outlet like the *Wall Street Journal*, for instance, if your market is local, it is probably more effective for your messages to be shared through local communication channels. But, again, it depends. The first step in considering how to most effectively reach out to the media is identifying target media outlets that reach the audiences you wish to engage. There are a variety of tools to help you do this.

Subscription-based services like Cision, PR Newswire's Agility, and Vocus offer searchable databases of thousands of media outlets that can be accessed to build media contact lists and reach out to relevant media professionals, including editors, writers, freelancers, producers, etc. For some businesses, however, the cost of these services can be prohibitive. Fortunately, a simple online search can yield information about media outlets that are local, regional, or national, making it possible for you to develop your own lists of outlets and contact information at low, or no, cost.

ALERT

While in pre-Internet days it was common for organizations to send out mass mailings to various media outlets, in the online environment that is considered to be spam and can alienate reporters, editors, and journalists. It's important to take the time to understand each of the media outlets you'd like to engage.

As you are identifying the target media that you would like to use to share information about your products or services, you need to think about the audiences for those media outlets. Your goal is to match your target audiences to their target audiences. For example, if you're attempting to connect with local college students, the college newspaper might be a great media outlet for you to build a relationship with. If you're attempting to connect with moms around the country, mommy bloggers may be able to effectively, and credibly, carry your message forward.

Your list of target outlets should include contact information for editors (print) or producers (broadcast) as well as journalists and freelancers who may regularly contribute to these outlets. Today that contact information should include phone, e-mail, and social media (e.g., Twitter or LinkedIn) addresses. Once your list is developed you will want to prioritize it in terms of your top, mid-, and low-level targets. Since reporters, editors, and producers often want to cover issues exclusively, or first, it can be a good idea to start with your top-tier targets and then move down the list.

Effective Pitches

It often comes as a surprise to business owners that the media is not out there actively pounding the pavement looking for "news." While that may occur in rare instances, today's busy media professionals rely heavily on the input and insights they receive from PR agencies, publicists—and you!

FACT

While some people may refer to a news release as a press release, the former term is preferred. Why? Because "press release" suggests that the release is specific to print (or press) publications. The term "news release" is broader and encompasses broadcast media as well as online media outlets.

In the past, news releases served as the primary way for businesses to share information and news with the media in the hope that the media would cover them and their stories. While news releases are still widely used, today's pitches also are often less formal. It is very common for pitches to be sent through a brief e-mail, which makes it very easy, inexpensive, and quick for you to get your news in front of your target media outlets. Whether you are using a news release or an e-mail pitch (or a combination of both), some basic principles apply.

Pitching effectively to the media is a combination of both science and art—and is, ultimately, based on solid relationships. Once you establish a reputation as a trusted and reliable source it is not unusual for media contacts to reach out to *you* when they are working on a story.

Keep a Good Media Relationship

Gaining traction with the media is not as difficult as it may seem, but it does require a different way of thinking—a shift from "me, me, me" to "you, you, you." Following are some tips to get you started:

- **Become familiar with your desired media outlets.** What types of material or information do they cover? Who are their reporters and editors? Your goal is to pitch them material that will meet their needs, which means it pays to know as much as you can about them so as not to "miss the mark."
- **Make connections.** Remember the "R" in public relations—this is a relationship business. You need to get to know the media "gatekeepers" who can put your name in the news. Follow them on Twitter. Connect with them on LinkedIn. Reach out via e-mail or phone. But do so with a purpose. These are busy people, and unless you have something relevant to offer them you are wasting their time—and yours!
- **Find a news angle for your pitches.** The media is not in the business of promoting you, or your business. They are in the business of providing newsworthy information to their audiences. To be successful in pitching to them you need to deliver on the news angle. Blatant marketing or self-promotion is a huge turnoff!
- **Be accessible and helpful.** It's a competitive world out there, and many people are clamoring for coverage. If you want to be picked, you need to be available; have relevant, on-point, and accurate information; and be as helpful as possible. This means providing a lot of background information and detail and sometimes even pointing out other sources of information.

What You Might Be Doing Wrong

Business owners often complain that the media doesn't cover their news or that their news releases and pitches go unnoticed. There may be good reason for this. For example:

- You're pitching to the wrong outlet, or the wrong individual. There are many e-mail news release services today, and they can be great to get your message out quickly, inexpensively, and broadly. It's the "broadly" that can create problems. The less "dialed in" your message is to a particular media outlet, the less likely it is to be picked up. Media gatekeepers are very good at spotting generic pitches, and they don't like them.

- You don't know how to pitch. Whether crafting a news release, sending a quick e-mail pitch, or simply picking up the phone to contact a journalist, your focus needs to be on their needs, not yours. It's no different from creating advertising messages, or any communication messages for that matter. Always ask yourself, "What's in it for them?"
- You're too pushy or demanding. Pitching means suggesting a story, not requesting or demanding one. There is a subtle, but very important distinction. Being too pushy also involves attempting to exercise too much of what's called "editorial control." Don't say, "Here's what you need to include." Don't ask to review what the journalist plans to use before it runs.
- Your timing is off. Sometimes, while you may have a great idea for a story, it's just not the right time. Maybe it is because some other "bigger news" makes your information less timely or relevant. Maybe it is because another similar piece was recently run.

Today more than ever, companies and individuals are hoping to get media exposure. After all, they figure (and not unreasonably) that media exposure is "free" and that this coverage tends to be more favorably perceived than are the advertising messages you share about yourself.

ESSENTIAL

Gaining a reputation as a go-to source can help ensure that you receive consistent and positive coverage in the media outlets you are targeting. Being a go-to source requires you to be focused on the needs of not only the media contact, but, most important, the audience for that media outlet.

Many novice "pitch people" make these same kinds of seemingly minor errors as they try to get their story covered. Unfortunately, many of these errors aren't minor at all. Tick off a reporter once and the chances of connecting again in the future are slim. Building strong relationships with reporters is the best way to see your name in print. Offer on-subject, useful information that is high on content and low on sales-speak. That's the best way to ensure that you get your messages out there and that reporters remember you for future stories.

Proactive Versus Reactive Pitches

The world of pitching to the media has changed significantly thanks to online communications. In the past, businesses would create and send news releases to a list of outlets that they hoped might be interested in what they had to offer. And, of course, this still happens today. But today there are also some great online services that provide businesses with the opportunity to review queries from journalists and reporters about the stories they're working on. These reporters are inviting pitches that can provide them with relevant information and quotable sources for their stories.

Two of the most popular and widely used online tools for this purpose are ProfNet (*www.prnewswire.com*) and Help a Reporter Out, also known as HARO (*www.helpareporter.com*). On these sites journalists and reporters basically advertise their needs for input for stories they're working on. For instance:

Valentine's Day is all about sharing the love. I'm looking for examples of businesses (preferably small or locally owned) that have joined up for a Valentine's Day special. Tell me what you're doing with another company!

Requirements: I'm interested in hearing directly from business owners who have tried this in the past or are trying it this year. Open to all sorts of unique ideas, but you must actually have done it or be doing it. Please give me a description of your special [promotion] in your response.

This query represents a great opportunity for spas and bistros to get their name in front of a market of potential customers.

The posts and requests found on these sites run the gamut from appeals from bloggers to major news outlets. The ability to effectively connect and receive coverage through these tools requires much the same approach as when pitching proactively. Most important, make sure you can offer what the journalist is looking for and that your approach is informational rather than promotional in nature.

ALERT

When you respond to pitches that have been posted in forums like HARO and ProfNet, keep in mind that your e-mail may be one of literally hundreds. If your e-mail subject line includes the forum where you saw the query and repeats the query's title, you will have a better chance of breaking through the clutter and getting noticed.

Getting the Attention You Deserve

The use of these sites is free to journalists; those interested in media coverage pay a small fee to receive access to the posts. If your target audience is regional, or national, the cost can be well worth it. Then it becomes a matter of effectively engaging with reporters to get picked as a potential source. Some key things to remember to boost your odds of success:

- Give the reporter the information requested. This isn't the time to pitch a different story, or to ignore the specifics of the request. So, for instance, if someone is looking for sources on the West Coast, don't respond if you're in the Midwest simply because you think you have something really interesting to offer.
- Follow directions. This includes paying attention to the deadline included in the listing as well as any pertinent details within. If the reporter asks you to include three tips, make sure to include (at least) three tips.
- Provide a detailed response. A response like "I would be a great source!" does not provide any information to allow the reporter to consider you in relation to the literally dozens of other responses that may come in. Recognize that it is very likely that the reporter may simply quote from your response rather than reaching out to request an interview. For this reason it is a good idea to include a detailed response that includes information about your background and credentials, an equally detailed response to questions, and, as appropriate, links to

additional information that you may have available on your website, blog, or through other sources.

- Understand that you are competing with others (often *many* others) for attention. Try to offer a unique perspective rather than information that could be shared by anyone.
- Finally, as when drafting news releases or proactive pitches, recognize that your focus should be on meeting the needs and interests of the ultimate audience and providing valuable and useful information.

When you are proactively sending pitches, you will need to be a bit more creative. Keep in mind that reporters' e-mail boxes are often very full. Your subject line should be succinct and offer an immediate, newsworthy benefit to their target audience. Don't try to be clever thinking that you will pique the journalists' attention. Err on the side of literal, rather than figurative, language. For instance: "Local business introduces new product to meet the needs of returning veterans," or "Female business leader appointed to chair board of *Fortune* 100 company in a male-dominated industry."

Responding to Media Inquiries

Sometimes you are reaching out to the media and sometimes they may reach out to you. The latter may be prompted by a news release you have generated, coverage you've received through some other media outlet, or interest that may have been prompted through your website or other online activities. (In some cases, this interest may also be prompted by a crisis or negative situation; more about these special situations later.)

ESSENTIAL

Never attempt to avoid the media, regardless of how negative or controversial the potential story may be. Consider this: if you don't take the opportunity to share your side of the story, who will? The media will get their story whether or not you choose to participate. Don't try to hide; be quick, be clear, and be forthcoming.

Whether the media is responding to a news release or pitch that you have generated or reaching out to you based on their own interest in and awareness of you or your organization, there are some general practices that you should follow.

First, recognize that you need to be available and responsive. If you're not, the journalist will move on to another potential source. The media will not wait for you. They are generally working under tight deadlines, so the coverage goes to the person who responds first—and best!

In order to best prepare for the interview, you should ask the reporter these questions:

- Can you tell me about the story you're working on? Is there a particular perspective you hope to cover?
- Who else will you be interviewing?
- What will you need from me? How much time will this take? Is there any background information we could provide?
- Who will be doing the interview?
- Are there any questions you could send me ahead of time so I can make sure to be prepared?
- When will this piece publish/air?

Keep in mind that the reporter is under no obligation to answer any of these questions, but it doesn't hurt to ask!

QUESTION

Should my name go on the news release as the contact person?
It depends. It should if you are the person most likely to be available when the media calls or e-mails you for information. If that isn't the case, the contact person should be someone in your organization who will be available to respond most of the time, whether by phone or by e-mail.

Sometimes the responses that you receive to these questions might indicate that you are not the best person in your organization to do the interview. It is always helpful to offer a spokesperson who is knowledgeable about the issue or topic. Just because you're the owner of the business doesn't mean that you should always be the spokesperson!

When the media call, make sure that you take the time to prepare for the interview. Never "wing it," regardless of how often you may have talked about this particular topic. As you prepare you will want to think both about your key messages and the target audience—those who will be reading or viewing the information. Your goal is to convey your key messages in a way that will resonate with the target audience and leave a lasting impact.

While hopefully most of your interactions with the media will be positive and pleasant, there may be occasions when the media call about some issue or concern that you would rather not have covered for the world to see.

Handling Crisis Situations

When a crisis situation occurs, you need to respond, regardless of how big, ugly, and scary it seems. It is far, far, far better to say *something* than to say *nothing,* for several reasons. First, you look bad when you say nothing. "Company XYZ was unavailable for comment," or "Company XYZ would not comment" are statements that only convey to the audience that you are trying to hide something or that you are afraid to talk. Both of those things may be true, but that's not the impression you should leave with your audience.

Besides, someone else will always fill in the blanks. The media are not just going to give up if they can't get comments from you. They will simply get comments from other people. And that is all they will have to go on when they tell the story. It's not that they are intentionally conveying inaccurate information—it's that *you* did not provide them with any information, so they cannot possibly be expected to convey your side of the story.

By not responding, you may potentially prolong the pain. Depending on the story and the interest it generates, you may decide at some point in time that you really should comment. That just keeps the story out there. Had you commented at the outset, you would have had a far better chance of watching it die a natural death, which *all* stories, regardless of how sensational, eventually do.

Don't wait until a crisis situation occurs to determine your strategy. In today's lightning-fast social media environment, you literally don't have time to devise a strategy once something has already "hit the fan," as they say. Take time now to think about the issues that might impact you, to develop policies and responsibilities for responding if something does, to establish relationships with outside resources if necessary, and to prepare your potential spokespeople to do a good job of representing your organization even in big, bad, and ugly situations.

One More Way to Get Media Exposure

Over the past few years, as you probably know, the economy has had a marked impact on the media industry, particularly for print journalists. Entire organizations have closed or been acquired and many have laid off staffers, leaving those left standing busier than ever before (and journalists have always been very, very busy and working under tight deadlines). This unfortunate situation for media representatives represents a possible opportunity for you. Why? Because media outlets are more and more open to considering "contributed pieces," or content that is written and submitted by a source rather than a journalist.

FACT

Content marketing is a term that has emerged in the twenty-first century to refer to the increasingly widespread use of quality content to engage with customers and other audiences while boosting traffic to websites. The content you generate can be used in multiple forums including your website, blogs, social media, and other channels.

This is an option you might propose along with your e-mail pitch to editors or producers: "I'm available for an interview, or if you prefer, I would be glad to provide you with a contributed (or bylined) piece on this topic." You may be pleasantly surprised at how many editors take you up on this offer. (Note: this is not something to offer writers or freelance journalists; they will be doing the writing themselves and may be offended by such an offer.)

Contributing a Piece

If you receive an opportunity to contribute content, keep these key points in mind:

- Go light on the blatant self-promotion. Yes, this is an opportunity to promote yourself and your business, but it should be presented as news, not advertising.
- Write with the audience in mind. What is it about what you have to say that will resonate with the audience and provide them with value?
- Don't be afraid to "give away your secrets." These days information is widely available, free of charge. This is an opportunity to get your name out there, boost your credibility, and, hopefully, keep your phones ringing and the revenue coming in!
- Follow up and seek feedback. Thank the publication after your piece has been published or aired and ask for feedback about anything you could do better/differently next time.
- Explore opportunities for regularly contributed pieces. Even the top publications are open to this; many business consultants contribute columns regularly to such publications as *Forbes* and *Fast Company*, for instance.
- Make sure your writing skills are at least "good." Remember that the goal is to make the editor's or producer's job easier, not more difficult. If too much editing needs to be done on your piece, you won't have an opportunity to submit again.
- Don't be surprised or annoyed if the media outlet edits what you submit. It is, after all, editorial content, not advertising.

Best Practices in Media Relations

While the media may seem intimidating, it may help you to recognize that they need you as much as you need them! Media outlets are always interested in finding useful, interesting information to share with their audiences. That's where you come in. It's important, though, to focus on providing news, not promotional information. The media is not interested in providing you with "free advertising." Following some best practices can help ensure that you form strong relationships with the media to help get your messages out to your mutual audiences.

- Develop good relationships with the media long before you "need" them. You don't want your first interaction with the media to be when you're not prepared, or when the coverage results from a crisis situation. If you've developed a solid relationship with the media outlets that matter to you, you'll be in a much better position to respond to requests that may not show you, or your business, in the best light. There will be a foundation of trust established that will serve you well. Establishing a solid relationship means being available when the media call; responding promptly and respecting media deadlines; being forthright and honest. If you develop a reputation for being someone the media can rely on to be truthful and helpful, you will be much more likely to be perceived credibly during sensitive situations.
- Know the media that's likely to target you and the media that you'd like to target. Be proactive in your dealings with the media. Develop a list of the media in which you'd like to receive coverage as well as a list of media that are likely to be interested in your business and its activities. Your local media outlets are likely to be your best bets.
- Create and focus on key messages. You should have both general key messages about your business and its products/services that you use for every interview and specific key messages that you develop for each media interaction. Very often, at the end of an interview, the reporter will say something like, "Do you have anything else to add?" or "Are there any additional points you would like to make?" That's your opportunity to say, "Yes!" This is your chance to make sure that your key points have been conveyed.
- Be a "broken record." While you can never anticipate with 100 percent accuracy what questions a reporter is going to ask you, you do know with 100 percent certainty what *your* key messages are. You should refer to those key messages again and again throughout the interview. Don't be afraid to be repetitive. Keep in mind that interviews are made up of "sound bites," and you can never know which comments the reporter will decide to use. If you make the same key

points again and again, albeit in slightly different ways, you can be more confident that *your* messages will reach the audience.

- Maintain control. Don't be intimidated by the media. They need you and your cooperation as much as you need their unbiased and professional handling of whatever issue it is that you're being interviewed about. So, while you should be aware of media deadlines and attempt to honor them whenever possible, never feel pressured to respond to a media inquiry. Always take the time to make sure that you've gathered the background information and facts that you need and that you've developed your key messages.

- Take advantage of live interviews. Most people dread the live interview. But, in fact, the live interview can be your best opportunity to ensure that the points you want to make are made and received by the audience. Why? Because what you say is received *verbatim* by the television or radio audience, and that provides you with total control. Your comments are not edited, because you are speaking live! Take advantage of that control by maintaining focus on your key messages.

- Make the reporter's job easy. Provide background information and additional materials, especially if your message is complex and you're concerned about the reporter "getting it right." The added benefit of providing background information, though, is that reporters are busy people and if you've provided good information, that's well prepared and not too self-promotional, it's likely to be used.

CHAPTER 19

Creating an Engagement Plan

Effectively engaging with your key audiences doesn't happen by chance. To be successful in creating long-lasting relationships with customers you need to have a plan. That plan should be focused on meeting some clearly identified goals and objectives by effectively meeting the needs of your various audiences. Remember, it's always all about them, not about you!

Integrated Marketing Communications

Over the past few years, there has been a growing realization that companies need to do more than just market to customers to engage them—they need to communicate with them. You may have heard the catch phrase "integrated marketing communications" recently. The American Marketing Association defines integrated marketing communications like this: "A planning process designed to assure that all brand contacts received by a customer or prospect for a product, service, or organization are relevant to that person and consistent over time."

Making the Most of Your Message

All communications that are produced by an organization need to be integrated and consistent for maximum impact. In many organizations today, as in the past, the marketing communications function exists and operates separately from, for instance, the public relations function, the shareholder communication function, and the employee communication function. That's good news for small businesses! In fact, with a smaller staff, it can be much easier to ensure that messages are integrated and consistent.

The concept of integrated marketing communications points to the fact that every message that emanates from an organization impacts marketing. By integrating all of those messages, the communication value to the organization can increase exponentially.

FACT

While many people think of marketing as consisting only of advertising, the truth is that marketing encompasses a broad range of functions—product, price, place, and promotion. The promotion element, often called the "promotion mix," includes advertising, but also includes public relations (PR), direct sales, and events. Advertising is just one element of the marketing mix.

To better understand the concept of integrated marketing communications, consider a recent purchase you made. What influenced that purchase? Was it a television ad? An ad in a print publication? A news item in a print publication or in a televised news report? Something you saw online in a forum or on a social media site? A word-of-mouth recommendation from a friend? As you contemplate these options you'll probably realize that your decision was impacted by a variety of factors and messages that came from multiple places. While there are certainly times when a single message can influence a purchase decision, it is most often the total impact of a series of communications that positively influences a consumer's decision to act.

Integrated marketing communications can maximize messages from an organization through repetition and reinforcement across multiple channels. Those channels might include the more obvious advertising media (television, radio, newspaper). They should also include messages sent through public relations efforts (news media, individual interviews). And, of course, in the twenty-first century, they must also include online messages that can reach audiences through any variety of channels including website, social media platforms, online review sites, and more.

Importantly, these messages should also be effectively coordinated through employees—from salespeople, to call center staff, to receptionists, and back office staff. Everybody in your business has an opportunity to contribute, positively or negatively, to the customer experience. Because of this it is also very important that your integrated marketing efforts include internal messages to your employees; they are a key audience that is often overlooked.

ALERT

Be aware that it's not just your business's formal messages that impact how customers perceive you. Every interaction they have with a member or representative of your organization has an impact. For this reason, it's important that you provide employees with the information they need to be effective in their customer interactions.

Creating an "engagement plan" can help ensure that you are effectively leveraging all of the communication tools and tactics available to you to connect with, engage, and compel your audiences to some desired action. The steps in creating this plan are very much the same as the steps in creating any sort of strategic plan. They involve establishing goals and objectives, conducing a SWOT analysis (this will be discussed in greater detail later), creating strategies and tactics, determining how to measure success, and creating a plan for evaluation and continuous improvement.

Establishing Your Goals and Objectives

The children's book *Alice in Wonderland* can give you some insight into the purpose of goals. When Alice asks the Cheshire cat for some help in deciding which route to take, the cat asks where she would like to go. Not an unreasonable question. Alice says she doesn't know, to which the cat responds: "So, it doesn't matter which way you go . . ."

ESSENTIAL

Contrary to popular opinion, goals are not specific; objectives are! This confusion may arise because outside of the business arena, goals generally relate to personal desires such as New Year's resolutions: "I'd like to lose ten pounds by the end of the year." From a business planning perspective, goals are broad; objectives are specific.

Creating Goals

And so it goes with strategic planning. Without a goal, how can you possibly determine how to get where you'd like to go? And that, in essence, defines what a goal is—it is simply a statement of where you'd like to go, the end point that will be your measure of success. A goal can be thought of as a desired end state. In terms of customer engagement some possible goals might be:

- Reduce customer turnover
- Increase customer retention
- Increase customer satisfaction
- Reduce number of complaints
- Increase positive word of mouth
- Increase referrals

Note that all of these are broad statements. While they indicate a sense of general direction ("increase . . ." or "reduce . . ."), they are not specifically measurable. That's where objectives come into play.

Create Your Objectives

Your objectives should support your goals and provide a specific indication of what you wish to accomplish. A commonly used acronym can help here: your objectives should be SMART.

While there is some variation, depending on the source, SMART generally stands for Specific, Measurable, Attainable, Relevant, and Time bound. *All* of these elements must be present for an objective to be an objective.

QUESTION

How can I be sure that my objectives are SMART?
Test them. Creating a simple checklist can help. As you finalize objectives, take a critical look at them to ensure that they are aligned with your mission, vision, and desired direction. The bottom line: objectives must be so specific that there will be no doubt about whether or not you have achieved them once your planning period is over.

"Specific" means that it is very clear what you are hoping to achieve. "Measurable" means that you can literally determine whether or not you have achieved the objective. "Attainable" means that it is realistic. "Relevant" means that the objective is related to your mission, vision, values, and goals. "Time bound" means that you have indicated a time frame within which you will achieve the objective. Here are some examples of objectives:

- Increase customer satisfaction by 25 percent by the end of the year.
- Generate 100 new customer referrals during the third quarter.
- Decrease the number of lost customers by 10 percent over the next six months.

You should focus on creating objectives that are outcome oriented, rather than process oriented. In other words, you are looking for results, not action. So, for instance, a statement like, "Become involved in two new social media channels by the end of the year" could arguably be considered an objective but does meet the SMART criteria; it doesn't lead to a measurement that will help you to determine outcomes. Your focus should be on results!

Conducting a SWOT Analysis

A SWOT analysis is a prioritized list of strengths, weaknesses, opportunities, and threats that have an impact on the success of your plan. In this case, it would be the elements that impact your ability to effectively engage with your target audiences.

While some many consider the SWOT analysis process to be simply a "silly exercise," in fact the process is extremely important and can help ensure that you are focused on the right things, not overlooking important factors and not making assumptions that can lead to missteps when it comes to the creation and implementation of your strategies and tactics.

ALERT

There is danger in approaching the SWOT analysis without the benefit of solid information. If you don't have the information you need now, make a commitment to obtain it for your next planning cycle. Too often the assumptions made may not reflect reality. It pays to hold up all assumptions to the acid test of good data.

Conducting a SWOT analysis involves a brainstorming activity in which a group of people familiar with the issue and desired outcome come together and brainstorm strengths and weaknesses (internal to the organization) and opportunities and threats (external to the organization). The list generated is based on a combination of data that has been gathered from internal and external sources (for instance, customer satisfaction data, information about the competitive environment) as well as personal knowledge and experience.

There are no "right" or "wrong" answers when conducting a SWOT analysis, and the person leading the activity should make sure to stay on task and not let the group devolve into a discussion of the merits of each point raised. The relative value of the items on the lists generated will emerge through the process.

ESSENTIAL

SWOT analyses, like any brainstorming activity, can easily get out of control. This is where a skilled facilitator comes in. The facilitator should help guide, but not participate in, the process and ensure that the session allows input from all without evolving into discussion on the points raised.

A flip chart and marker can be used to capture these inputs, starting with strengths and moving on to weaknesses, opportunities, and threats. Each list should be considered individually and items added until the group has run out of ideas. If ideas come up later, they can be added to previous lists.

Once lists are completed, they are reviewed, evaluated, and prioritized, often using a "voting" process whereby each participant has a certain number of votes to "spend" among each list as the person sees fit, indicating which items for each category are most important. The collective "votes" are tallied and a "Top 5" (or some other agreed-upon number) is created. The group should then consider whether those items that bubble to the top seem to truly represent the most important impacts in each of these areas.

SWOT analyses should be based on "real" data, not guesswork. If the SWOT is grounded in reality, the strategies that are developed from it will be realistic and will appropriately direct the efforts of the business. For instance, if an organization says that its strength is customer service—despite not having data to substantiate that opinion—and then creates a strategy designed to leverage that supposedly great reputation, the strategy is destined to fail. By the same token, opportunities may be missed if important data is not used or considered during the SWOT process.

When you do a SWOT analysis, include broad input. Small organizations, in particular, may find it useful to gather input from their employees and perhaps some key customers to make sure they have not missed any key points. Gathering broad input can provide an important "reality check" for the work done by the project team and can generate support and buy-in for the plan from key audiences, like employees and customers.

Once the analysis is done, focus on the "big rocks." Prioritize the list in some manner to provide focus on the few critical factors that are most likely to influence success.

The SWOT you come up with to help you develop a customer engagement plan will be specifically related to issues that impact engagement. If you were, for instance, creating a plan to help improve employee recruitment, you would be focused on things that impact employee recruitment. If you were creating a plan to start a new business, your SWOT would take a broad look at all of the organizational elements and environmental factors impacting the potential success of that business.

Should employees be included in the SWOT analysis process?
Absolutely! The more input you can gather, the better. Remember, the success of your planning process relies to a large degree on the accuracy of the SWOT analysis. By gathering broad input—from employees, customers, vendors, and others—you can ensure that this will be the case.

Once the original lists are created, prioritized, and reviewed, the resulting list of key factors in each category provides the basis for strategy development.

Creating Strategies

Strategies are approaches taken by an organization to achieve its goals and objectives by leveraging strengths and opportunities and overcoming weaknesses and threats. That's why the SWOT analysis is so important and also why it is so important that the SWOT be based on "real data" rather than opinion or conjecture. After all, it does you no good to leverage a strength or overcome a threat that doesn't exist!

FACT

The Art of War is a classic book on military strategy written by Sun Tzu, a Chinese military general. Despite the fact that it was written around 500 B.C. and focused on military strategy, it has become a go-to book for business strategists who have found the wisdom contained in the book to apply to the business issues they face.

Make a Chart

Here's a simple example of how the SWOT might be used to suggest some potential strategies for effectively engaging customers. Suppose you are operating a pizza restaurant. You have completed a SWOT analysis, prioritized it, and have come up with a table that looks like this:

Strengths	Weaknesses
Very high Net Promoter scores	Lack of clear processes for engaging with customers
High traffic to website	No consistent method for prospecting for sales leads
Employees supportive of brand	Salespeople often working at cross-purposes
Strong bottom line	Losing some long-term customers to competition
Opportunities	**Threats**
To better engage with customers through proprietary social media channel	Increasing competition
To leverage high number of LinkedIn followers in online discussion	Internet "trolls"
To proactively solicit word of mouth and recommendations through a referral program	Major competitor has created an exclusive sponsorship with primary local media outlet
To use employees more formally as brand ambassadors	

In considering this list, your group should think creatively about how it might capitalize on your company's internal strengths and take advantage of opportunities, while minimizing internal weaknesses and avoiding external threats. Categories may be considered alone, or in combination. For instance, using the SWOT presented in the table, some of your strategies might be:

- Take advantage of high traffic websites that engage visitors and high Net Promoter scores to offset the growing number of Internet "trolls" posting comments on public sites.
- Create a closed group on LinkedIn to leverage high number of followers and engage them in discussions that lead to insights about improving processes.
- Leverage employee ambassadors and online engagement to offset threat from competitor's new relationship with local media outlet.

As when developing the SWOT, the development of strategies should occur through brainstorming, without evaluating, commenting on, or dismissing the potential strategies raised. Participants should be encouraged to be creative and to think in innovative ways about how they might, for instance, turn a weakness into an opportunity by effectively leveraging strengths or opportunities.

ESSENTIAL

The development of the SWOT doesn't have to take place in person. Today's technology means that brainstorming can take place online. Input can be gathered from a wide range of sources, reviewed and synthesized, and then "voted on" using one of the many types of online polling or surveying programs now widely available.

Creating strategies involves forward-looking thinking. Strategy development involves thinking broadly about the approach that you will take. Your strategies are, in essence, a description of how you will accomplish your objectives. Strategies describe a general approach, rather than specific actions or tactics, which will be developed next.

Identifying Tactics

Tactics tend to be the place where most people like to start when creating a "plan." But tactics really represent the *last* step in the planning process because they should emerge from all of the steps that have already been taken. Tactics are the "to do" part of your plan—the specific things that you will do to communicate with and engage your audience. While strategies give a general indication of how you will approach the accomplishment of an identified objective, tactics outline specifically what you will do. For instance, these are the customer engagement tactics of one small business:

- Create a customer newsletter
- Develop a contest to crowdsource new product name ideas from customers
- Start an Instagram account
- Test a traditional direct mailer with XYZ market segment

The possibilities are endless, but must be aligned with your goals, objectives, and strategies to ensure effectiveness.

Tips for Effectively Implementing Your Plan

Here are some additional tips to help ensure that your tactics drive the implementation of your plan:

- Brainstorm and then prioritize your list of tactics. The goal should be to achieve the most with the least. What elements are most likely to help you achieve your objectives?
- Make sure you have the resources available (time and money) to put the tactic in place.
- Involve those who will actually be doing the work in the process of creating the tactics. This will generate buy-in.
- Consider the consistency and appropriateness of the tactics to your business mission, vision, and goals.

In creating tactics you will also consider questions related to who will be assigned to accomplish the task, by when it should be accomplished, and at what cost. These elements will not necessarily be included in your statement of the tactic, but will be key items to include in the plan to make sure that you have the resources to make it happen.

ALERT

Don't start with tactics first! That is the downfall of many a planning effort. Unfortunately, tactics are where most people like to begin. It's easy to come up with good ideas. It's harder to make sure that those good ideas are aligned with solid information and that strategy development is based on a formal planning process.

The goal when developing tactics is not to simply develop a laundry list of things that you could do, but a list of those things that would be best to do given your stated strategies, objectives, and goals. "Best" can be further defined as those things that would cost the least (in terms of time and effort) to achieve the most (consistent with your objectives). Overkill represents wasted resources. Underkill represents lost opportunity.

How to Measure Success

The measurement of your engagement plan is very important. You need to determine what success will look like. These measures should come directly from your goals and objectives. Measurability is key. Objectives should be stated in such a way that, at the end of the planning period, two independent observers could look at the objective and the results and agree on whether or not the objective has been achieved. That is the acid test.

For instance, if your goal is to reduce customer turnover, you would want to measure the number of lost customers over some particular period of time. If your goal is to increase customer satisfaction, you would need to devise an assessment to measure the current level of satisfaction and then measure satisfaction levels at particular points in time by means of the same assessment.

It is important to not only indicate *what* the measure is, but also *how* you will attain the measure. This is an important consideration for any business, but particularly so for small businesses. Sometimes it is simply too difficult and too costly to attain a measure. If that is the case you will want to find equally relevant but more easily attainable ways of measuring success.

It also is important that the collection and reporting of your measures doesn't consume the majority of your time. You want the majority of your time to be spent focusing on the implementation of your plan! Communicating performance is best done simply, and there are some commonly used reporting formats that can help you do just that.

Evaluation and Improvement

As you identify the measures that you will monitor, it will be important to assign responsibility for monitoring and reporting on progress. Some of these activities may occur at the individual or department level; others may occur at the planning-team level as individual measures are aggregated. It doesn't really matter where the reporting occurs, or who does the reporting, although it makes sense for reporting to occur as close as possible to where the information is attained.

What matters most, though, is that you know who is going to be held accountable to track the measures that let you know how you're doing.

Tracking Your Measurements

There are various ways that companies track and report progress on measures related to their strategic plans. Two common methods of reporting are dashboards and scorecards.

A dashboard is a very simple method of communicating progress on measures. It uses a color-coded approach based on the familiar traffic-light signals: green, yellow, and red. Green indicates that targets are being met; red that targets are not being met; and yellow that targets are at risk of not being met.

Another commonly used approach to measurement is a scorecard format, popularized by Robert S. Kaplan and David P. Norton in their now classic book *The Balanced Scorecard*. The concept of the balanced scorecard is that all of an organization's activities need to be balanced to effectively achieve its goals. By visualizing goals in a scorecard format, businesses can more readily see areas that may be working at cross-purposes, or identify opportunities to leverage certain activities for greater success. For instance, an organization focused on cutting costs may have a policy in place to limit the amount of time that call center staff spends on the phone, but this policy may have a negative impact on customer satisfaction.

Using either of these methods, and tracking performance over time, can give you an early indication of when some course correction or adjustment may be needed and also help you identify areas that are performing above expectations and that you might want to ramp up.

While it's important to establish and use measures to monitor performance, don't just measure and report—do something about the results! Areas of exceptional performance can signal the opportunity to document best practices or to share best practices with other parts of your company. For instance, suppose you have five restaurant locations and each is tracking customer satisfaction on a dashboard. One of the five locations is consistently "in the green." That reflects an opportunity to find out what that location is doing differently and then to share those best practices with the other locations.

CHAPTER 20

When Things Go Wrong

It used to be that consumers shared opinions about products and services at the water cooler or over the backyard fence. While word of mouth was (and is) valuable, the reach it could achieve in the "old days" was minimal. That's not the case anymore. Although there is still plenty of old-fashioned word of mouth taking place in break rooms and backyards, the power of technology has amped up the ability to spread messages.

The Voice of the Consumer

Today consumers have the ability to share their comments on products and services more broadly than in the past. That is one of the primary differences between social and more traditional media. Consumers today can post their comments directly on advertisers' sites, on their own websites or social media pages, or on consumer rating sites designed specifically to generate feedback, both good and bad.

FACT

Research conducted by NewVoiceMedia indicates that a startling $41 billion is lost by U.S. companies every year following bad customer experiences. Unfortunately for small business owners, customer expectations are continually on the rise. Today's customers expect that they will receive personal and engaging services every time they interact with you. That means you must deliver!

Small businesses must realize that, if they are communicating online, they're involved in a conversation—many conversations actually. That can be a very good thing; after all, marketers today can spread their messages far more broadly and at far less cost than they could ever do in the past. But that also can sometimes be a bad thing. Tick someone off in cyberspace and the conversation can quickly go viral.

It's important for all business owners to understand the significant value that their customers hold. Existing customers are worth more than prospective customers. Yet, too often, businesses spend more time, effort, and energy on courting new customers than they do in seeking to satisfy, and even delight, their existing customers. A lost customer represents both lost revenue and lost brand equity, especially if those lost customers feel as if they have been mistreated, misled, or otherwise negatively impacted.

Don't fall into this trap! Make sure that you are spending ample time, energy, and effort engaging with and delighting your current customers.

Monitoring Customer Satisfaction

How can you monitor customer satisfaction? In a number of ways that are both proactive and reactive. Proactively, you should be asking your customers on a regular basis how your business is doing. This can be done in person, through comment cards, or through online feedback forms. Doing this regularly with all, or a percentage of, your customers can give you an ongoing sense of how you're doing—and where there may be emerging issues.

You must also be in a position to effectively respond to comments and complaints that could be received in any variety of forums, many online.

Consumer review sites are common these days, from Amazon book reviews to Angie's List and Yelp! While some of the sites, and the posts they contain, have come under fire based on their veracity (or lack thereof), their power to influence still remains. Arguably more important than these managed review sites, though, are the grassroots comments being shared 24/7 by consumers through e-mail, social media sites, and communication channels like Google Hangouts and Skype.

ALERT

The Internet is rife with negative customer commentary these days. Even if you don't have active social media accounts for your business, you should be scanning the online sites to determine whether your business is being mentioned. Consider that, according to research by NewVoiceMedia, 27 percent of those in Gen Y say they prefer to air their customer grievances through social media.

There's ample opportunity these days for consumers to hear about the latest and greatest new technology, new toy, or new vacation destination spot. This serves marketers well, and they should not hesitate to suggest to their satisfied customers that they "spread the word" (just as they might have done in days gone by). And, when they see positive comments, it's certainly okay to point them out by thanking the person who shared and even sharing the comments through their own social media channels.

There's a flip side, of course: Not all comments shared are positive.

Sometimes consumers are not satisfied. While common wisdom suggests that dissatisfied consumers have always shared their dissatisfaction with others—to a larger degree, even, than their satisfaction—those numbers have grown significantly in the digital age. Research conducted in 1999 by CX Act (formerly TARP Worldwide) suggested that dissatisfied customers would tell ten people about their bad experiences, and that those ten would each tell another five, resulting in a total of fifty people getting this message. Consider that, today, each of those ten people might have several hundred connections across various social media channels, and each of those might also have hundreds . . . and, exponentially, you can see where this is going.

ESSENTIAL

If you're proclaiming "customer service is our top priority" in your communication materials, on your website, and in your on-hold messages (as ironic as that may be!), you'd better be sure you're taking steps to deliver. It's bad enough to not provide great service; consumers feel that it's even worse when the companies they deal with promise high levels of service but fail to deliver.

The sad truth is that we are far more likely to share the bad than the good. Consider your own interactions with merchants and marketers. What's the last great experience you had? How many people did you tell about it (if any)? What's the last bad experience you had? Did you share? Chances are the answer is "yes."

For marketers this very viral nature of consumer word of mouth (or word of mouse) doesn't really mean anything fundamentally different than it ever did. You should still be focused on:

- Delivering a positive experience
- Following up effectively if the situation wasn't positive, and making things right
- Monitoring and responding to feedback, whether positive or negative

The actions are the same; it's just the scope that's different. And it's that change in scope that can be either a good thing or a bad thing. The question is, what are you doing about it?

The Role of Service Recovery

CX Act, formerly TARP Worldwide, is a company that specializes in researching the customer experience. Their research has suggested that companies that fail to meet customer expectations, but perform service recovery effectively, can achieve higher satisfaction levels than companies that never failed to meet expectations in the first place.

QUESTION

What's the best way to turn loyal customers into brand ambassadors? Ask them! Your loyal customers can represent a great opportunity to spread the good word about your products, services, and service. But don't expect that they will just automatically do that. It can help to ask, or suggest, that they do so. Those who are already loyal and highly engaged customers are often glad to spread these words of praise, but they might need a little reminding now and then.

This is known as the service recovery paradox, and there is plenty of evidence to suggest that not only is it a real phenomenon, but also is an important consideration for companies of any size. Still skeptical? Think of your own interactions as a customer. Have you ever had a poor service situation that was handled expertly? How was your impression of the company impacted by this situation?

It can be interesting and instructive to learn from the apologies of others. For example, in 2011, when Netflix attempted to shift customers from receiving movies in the mail to receiving them online through pricing changes, the backlash was swift and vicious. Netflix attempted to recover through multiple mea culpas, including on its blog. Unfortunately, their actions had hit a nerve, resulting in more than 27,000 follow-up comments to CEO and cofounder Reed Hastings's posting. One might say that "hell hath no fury like a customer scorned."

Here is another example. After almost casually announcing plans to institute a $5 per month debit card fee, Bank of America backed off on its plans in the face of a massive consumer revolt. Despite apologies, and even though they had never actually implemented the fee, Bank of America took a big PR hit. Credit unions around the country took advantage of the brouhaha by sponsoring a "Bank Transfer Day," and many consumers did just that, moving en masse from banks to credit unions during the melee.

Even not-for-profits can be at risk, as Susan G. Komen Foundation's very public problems pointed out. When the Foundation announced that it was defunding Planned Parenthood, hackles were raised around the country. Like Bank of America, the Komen Foundation also backed off on its decision, and a top official resigned in the aftermath of the public outcry. But, also like Bank of America, the public drubbing was damaging.

What can you learn from these situations? Perhaps that the service recovery paradox isn't such a paradox after all.

It may be true that "in the old days," when bad behaviors and subsequent apologies could be delivered one-on-one, effective service recovery could result in higher levels of loyalty and word of mouth than existed before the offending incident took place. But in today's rapid-paced communication environment, fueled by ready access to social media tools that can broadcast consumer concerns before companies even know they exist, it seems that the safest route would be not to offend in the first place.

A tall order, no doubt, but if the worst should happen through some misstep on the part of you or one of your employees, the best that you can do is respond quickly and sincerely, stay above the fray, and most important, learn from the experience.

Turning Negatives Into Positives

Even negative experiences can result in positive outcomes and create strong brand advocates for your company and its products and services. CX Act's research illustrates this, and your own consumer experiences are likely to support this data.

Think about it. Have there been instances when you have been unhappy with a product or service, or the service you have received from a company? Now think of a time when you were dissatisfied, expressed your dissatisfaction, and received an exceptional response from the company. Chances are that, in those instances, you became a very strong supporter or advocate for the company.

FACT

It is six to seven times more expensive to gain a new customer than it is to keep an existing one, according to the White House Office of Consumer Affairs. This means you should not only focus on attracting new customers, but also take steps to ensure that you understand your existing customers and regularly deliver what they value so they will stay with you through the long haul.

That's the way it goes. Even when a bad situation occurs, turning that situation around in a responsive and positive way can lead to positive results.

Jay Skowron, founder of Hospitality Defender, a company that helps other companies in the hospitality industry manage their online presence, says that he monitors complaints via social media and, when he spots one, "we respond within minutes, asking for details and offering a resolution for problems." Of his company's work with one particular client over the period of a year and a half, he says, "we've been able to increase their Yelp! ratings and overall reputation online to maintain them at a 4+ star rating and keep their social media presence fresh and interactive."

What Employees Need to Know

The larger your business grows, the less control you have over day-to-day interactions with customers and the more you will rely on employees to effectively manage those interactions. That can be a bit frightening, but it's a fact of business life for successful businesses.

As you grow, it's important that you ensure that employees are informed, knowledgeable, and committed to your service philosophies; that they understand the policies that guide their interactions with customers in positive and not-so-positive situations; and, most important, that they feel empowered on occasion to step outside the bounds of these policies as appropriate.

That's right; sometimes you want your employees to not follow your policies. You don't want employees to be automatons. You want them to be advocates on behalf of both your company and your customers and to know when it's right to "bend the rules" a bit to retain a customer (remember, it costs far more to gain a new customer than it does to retain an existing one).

ALERT

When customers leave you, they often take others with them. If you don't already have a mechanism in place to quickly determine when a customer is "lost," you should place this item high on your to-do list. Not only can you gain valuable information from these departing customers, but you can also potentially avoid additional damage generated through negative word of mouth.

Nordstrom is a good example of a company that is often held up as one that allows its employees the freedom and flexibility to make on-the-spot decisions to serve customer needs. The Ritz-Carlton is another. There are certainly many more.

What these companies have in common is the realization that as employees interact with customers, no two situations will be the same. Policies are important to provide guidance, but rigidly adhering to policies that can't possibly be drafted to cover every possible scenario can be a major detriment to successful customer engagement.

Still, of course, your company must comply with any rules, regulations, or laws that apply in your industry. Finding that balance can be challenging but involves, above all, ongoing communication, education, and training so that employees understand the regulations that apply and also recognize when they are empowered to step outside the bounds of policy to delight a customer.

Holding up examples of situations in which employees have done this well—and talking about situations in which it would not be appropriate to meet a customer demand—can go a long way.

Although customer satisfaction is important, the old saying that "the customer is always right" is not necessarily true. You need to ensure that your employees understand when the customer is not right and that they know how to address those situations, while also being able to recognize opportunities to meet customers' needs as appropriate.

QUESTION

Do automated phone systems lead to poor service perceptions? It's not so much whether you have one of these systems; it's how you use it that really matters. Research conducted by Liel Leibovitz, while New York University Assistant Professor of Communications, indicated that almost 80 percent of those responding felt that they would either probably or definitely avoid giving future business to a company that had a poor automated telephone service system.

Simple? No. It's an ongoing challenge for businesses of any size, but the effort and energy you apply here will pay off significantly in terms of satisfied and loyal customers who spread positive word of mouth and help you to keep a constant flow of new customers coming into your door or to your website.

Best Practices in Service Recovery

There is one thing you can be certain of: you *are* going to disappoint a customer at some point in time. When you do, follow these tips from Lydia Ramsey, business etiquette expert and the author of *Manners That Sell*:

- Avoid any delay in setting things right by giving your employees the authority to correct the situation immediately. Any delay will only make matters worse.
- Offer your customer an additional free product or service. You are guaranteed to get your investment back.
- Take responsibility and offer a sincere apology regardless of who made the mistake.
- Never become defensive or argumentative.

If you handle these situations effectively, you may create a very loyal customer. Doing so, though, requires a team effort among all members of your organization. It's important that every member of your staff, and, in fact, anyone who has interactions with your customers on your behalf, has the information they need to ensure that they are serving your interests effectively.

Importantly, it pays to be alert to the potential for customer dissatisfaction rather than waiting for customers to come to you to point out that something is wrong.

One woman tells of a phenomenal service experience she recently had while on a trip with her mother. They had stopped at a McDonald's where this woman, who prefers Coke products, found that Coke was temporarily unavailable. So, she decided to walk across the parking lot to a nearby gas station, Road Ranger.

She got her Diet Coke and took her place at the end of one of the long lines at the counter. A woman behind the counter caught her eye and asked, "Are you just buying the soda?"

"Yes," she answered.

"Go ahead, there's no need to pay," the clerk said. Surprised, and not sure she understood, the customer responded: "Oh no, I need to pay for this."

But the clerk again said, "No, no need to pay. Go ahead."

ESSENTIAL

Sometimes all it takes is a sincere apology and a promise to make things right! All businesses make missteps from time to time. What's more important than the fact that you made a misstep is how you recover from it. Work with your staff to develop policies and processes designed to delight customers after you've disappointed them. It may seem counterintuitive, but it works.

That's a great example of being proactive and, in the process, turning what could have become a negative situation into a very positive outcome. How many people do you think this customer tells about her experience with Road Ranger?

A lot of organizations spend a lot of money on advertising to raise awareness and preference for their products and services. Advertising certainly has its place. But, as this example illustrates, it is often the simple "random acts of service" that can have the most impact on an organization's reputation.

Service Tips

Here are some additional tips to ensure that your service and service recovery efforts are paying off:

- Be proactive. Consider and develop a process, up front, to be prepared to respond to instances when consumers post negative or critical information online.
- Make sure your policies indicate who will respond, how, and within what time frame.
- Develop and approve key messages in advance to respond to the most likely types of comments and complaints (your own customer feedback history can provide you with some clues here).
- Make sure that someone is assigned to monitor online activity on a regular basis, and that there is backup when that person is unavailable. Tools like Radian6, an online analytics tool, can help to automate this process.
- Ensure that responses to comments are prompt.
- Have an open mind; recognize that you may not have all the right answers or know all there is to know about your customers' needs. Be open to perspectives/opinions that may be different from your own, particularly if those perspectives are critical of what you have to offer.
- Provide numerous opportunities and options for customers to interact with you. These might include communicating in person, via phone/hotline, e-mail, social media, suggestion boxes, surveys/polls, etc.
- Develop processes for gathering, synthesizing, analyzing, and sharing the information you receive. This can help you identify trends and areas of common concerns or delight among customers.
- Create two-way conversations; be responsive. Don't ignore or overlook input that you receive. Respond to or engage in conversations

even when you receive negative feedback or input. Again, be open-minded and willing to listen nondefensively.

- Be conversational rather than corporate in your approach/tone. People establish rapport with people, not companies. This is particularly pertinent for those hoping to connect with consumers via social media. Would you rather "friend" a person or an organization?
- Listen and learn. It is relatively easy and inexpensive to gain market insights through conversations and connections with customers, potential customers, and consumers at large. The keys, though, are to be open-minded and to take steps to capture, assess, and act on the information you receive.
- With highly charged situations or comments, attempt to move the discussion "offline" through a general response in the public forum that includes an invitation for a one-on-one conversation with the poster, who may also be contacted via other channels if possible (e.g., by private message, e-mail, or phone).

Keep in mind that consumers do know that even good organizations may sometimes make mistakes. Making the mistake is often not what matters most. What matters most is how you respond.

Customer Engagement Case Studies and Success Stories

Vonage Business Solutions: B2B Customer Service Recovery

Jared Morling is director of Customer Success for Vonage Business Solutions. He offers some tips for B2B companies on how to effectively turn potentially negative situations around.

Be Present

Simply being available to your customers goes a long way, particularly if they're confident they can locate you if an issue arises. Customers want to reach you in the method of their choosing. Explore multiple channels of support, beyond traditional phone support, that also make sense for your business (e.g., e-mail, website, chat, and social media). If customers cannot reach you, how will you resolve their concerns?

Set Expectations for Resolution

When a customer reaches out with an issue, be sure to state a reasonable expectation for a resolution, ideally within a specific time frame. Customer issues will not go away if ignored, and if a customer has no expectation of when a response will be received, you are essentially creating a second concern. Even if the problem cannot be solved right away, or at all, stay proactive and responsive throughout. While this may be a basic standard of service, it has a lasting impact when expectations are missed.

Empower Your Support Team

Whenever possible, give your support team the authority to make it easy to make things right. Establish a support budget or "Just Say Yes" fund, for example, with the sole purpose of correcting mistakes or keeping a customer via a credit, cost reduction, or service/product addition. By reducing required interactions with management before decisions are made, or before money is spent, the support team is empowered to resolve issues and satisfy the customer much more quickly.

Learn to Listen

Great resolutions begin by carefully listening and understanding the problem the customer is experiencing, allowing a recovery tailored to the specific problem. "When one of our customers experiences a technical problem, immediately offering a credit for service certainly doesn't demonstrate our ability and willingness to solve it. Our first task is to listen and evaluate. When the situation warrants, we authorize our team to bring in an elevated level of support—one that a customer may not traditionally have access to—in order to address their concern. This process of listening and then taking all necessary steps for resolution often serves to develop customer confidence and long-term loyalty," says Morling.

Invite Feedback

Survey your customers about their experience with your support service, and develop processes to follow up periodically to ensure their satisfaction with the resolution you provided. Demonstrating that their feedback is acknowledged and can actually contribute to improved service confirms that you're listening and value what they have to say. For example, Vonage Business Solutions allows its support team to submit product-enhancement requests following its interactions with customers. It's a customer recovery and retention mechanism that doesn't require a monetary offer to resolve.

Reward Your Customers

Don't wait until your customers ask for something newer, cheaper, or different from your current offering. Develop ongoing occasions to engage customers and show your appreciation for their business. "One of our more popular programs over the years included a reward for all customers who shared their positive experiences with our product and support teams. It's an unexpected customer perk that reminds us that it's always more expensive to acquire a new customer than to cultivate an existing relationship," says Morling.

Roto-Rooter: Addressing Service Calls Gone Wrong (B2C)

Paul Abrams, Director of Public Relations for Roto-Rooter, a plumbing and drain service organization that has been in business for more than seventy-five years, says that the biggest challenge organizations face when met with a crisis is the lack of a crisis communication plan. Regardless of the nature of a business, a plan for handling negative situations should be laid out fully for every employee, practiced, rehearsed, and learned. Learning the plan and understanding when and how it applies should be part of every new-hire training program, as well as ongoing training for any group dealing with customers. He offers the following advice:

Dealing with Unhappy Customers

If you don't already have a crisis plan, begin by determining the ten "worst case scenarios" for your business—that is, what are the most likely really bad things that "could" happen? Determine who exactly would or could be affected by these scenarios, and which of your company's publics will need to be assuaged, convinced, protected, or calmed and exactly who will be doing the communications.

When an in-person interaction between company and client goes wrong, which in any service business is inevitable, the most important step is to gather all the facts. Understand both sides of the story, and perhaps most important, let the customer share everything. Let them vent, let them yell, let them "get it out of their system"—as long as, obviously, it doesn't cross a line beyond professional courtesy. In most cases, the customer just wants to be heard, and feel that they are being listened to. Remember, the last thing you want is for this to escalate into larger circles of correspondence. You must manage the situation. Do not yell. Do not "be right." It's not the time for that. Step one is gathering information in an objective and professional fashion.

Once you have the information, share back the customer's assertions, and then assure the customer that you will take the necessary steps to resolve the situation. Get it in writing, save the date and time, and if at all possible, record the incident. Do not promise and do not offer delivery at this point—just that you will take the necessary steps to resolve the situation, understand exactly what they are expecting that will satisfy them, and give them a time frame when they can expect a return correspondence.

Avoid Escalation

The overarching goal of managing crisis situations is to manage perception: how the client will view you, your team, and your company, how the public at large will view you, and even how your employees will view you. Resolving a customer conflict is not about ignoring the conflict; it is all about the response and the conflict resolution. Speak with the team involved, and find out exactly what happened and what they believe caused this type of reaction with the customer. Once you have spoken with your service team and understand the issue, now is the time to determine fault. If it is indeed on the part of your team, address that, correct it, and move forward. Contact the client, do not admit fault, but explain professionally that something was not done per training and standards and that you will do x to make it right. If this is satisfactory to the customer, you'll likely be amazed at how pleased this makes them.

If it is, however, determined to be a customer issue, you then must decide if you wish to take any further steps to correct what you have determined to be a customer issue, not a business issue. Remember, while the customer is always right, there are indeed those times that no amount of work or service will satisfy certain folks. Again, in this situation, communication is key. "Sir/Ma'am, I understand how you feel, here's what I can do, is this acceptable?" If yes, do it. If not, then simply reiterate that you're sorry but this is not in the bounds of what can be done. Offer to refund any dollars and refer them to another professional.

Never escalate. Always maintain control. Always be the professional.

Sheri Fink, Children's Author

Alex Dominguez represents Sheri Fink, a bestselling and award-winning children's author. She speaks all over the world. Her business is all about engagement with fans. Dominguez helps Fink engage with fans online through Facebook. At events, Dominguez says, he makes time to connect directly with fans to inspire and encourage them, while exposing fans to Fink's brand. He also responds to all fan mail, whether electronic or traditional.

Dominguez measures results by using simple, personal tools. His measures also include how much fun he's having and how much of a connection he is feeling to his company's fans.

The amount of fan mail and online engagement has grown immensely in the past six months, with Facebook fans rising to about 13,000. He shares three tips for effective social engagement:

- Be authentic. When you share (online or in person) from the heart, it resonates with fans and uplifts everyone. It's all about empowering others to see and feel the greatness within themselves.
- Playfully interact with fans. Make it fun. Don't outsource your Facebook fan page . . . it's one of the best ways to connect directly with fans. Fun for everyone!
- Make live experiences memorable. People will always remember the way you made them feel. Treat each fan like they're the most important person in your world (with dignity, respect, and love), because they are in that moment.

Hospitality Defender

Hospitality Defender is a San Francisco–based company that specializes in reputation management, social media, and secret shopping for the hospitality industry, helping restaurants and hotels with their online brand and reputation. Twitter and Yelp! are the primary tools used for customer engagement.

On Twitter, says founder and principal Jay Skowron, every tweet in which Hospitality Defender is mentioned is responded to with a personal thank-you and an individual response. Twitter is also used as a form of marketing research. The company searches Twitter to monitor what people are talking about to help define their target audience's desires.

Skowron says that similarly, on Yelp! (a site that connects customers with local businesses through suggestions and reviews), they respond to each review, whether positive or negative. If the review is negative, they offer their apologies along with an incentive to return, such as a gift card.

Hospitality Defender uses a proprietary database to track reviews and update them as time progresses. They also track Twitter using monthly reports for each client, showing engagement, trends, and more.

Skowron says the best advice he has to offer others is to *engage* fans through every platform possible. People love to be talked about by businesses because it shows a human aspect online, he says. "If there's a problem that's being aired on social media, address it right out in the open," he suggests. "Businesses can no longer afford to ignore the power of social media."

Scottevest

Scottevest is a technology-enabled clothing company based in the Boise, Idaho, area. The company was founded by Scott Jordan, who serves as CEO. Although Jordan faced many adversities in his career while starting a business, the lessons learned attribute to his current success.

Scottevest creates customer engagement through personal relationships with customers. The company is active on Twitter, Facebook, YouTube, Pinterest, and LinkedIn. One of the key social tactics leveraged across these sites is personalized video messages to answer questions customers might have. Customers are also connected directly via Skype. The company prides itself on using these tools to create personal relationships with many of its customers.

Scottevest responds to all questions, e-mails, and phone calls within an hour of the contact, and uses online technology to create long-lasting relationships with customers.

The amount of success Scottevest has gained through its engagement activities is measured through Google Documents and Google Analytics.

One unique element of the company's website is an image of Jordan that appears on the bottom right-hand side of every page, inviting visitors to "Ask me anything right now." It's a visible indication of Scottevest's desire for engagement. Linger on any page long enough and a pop-up box will appear, proclaiming "Pocket Consultant to the Rescue," with a support agent identified by first name saying "Welcome to SCOTTEVEST! If you have any questions about our products, please don't hesitate to ask—we're standing by to help you."

APPENDIX B

Additional Resources

Useful Online Tools

HOOTSUITE

www.hootsuite.com

This social media dashboard allows you to manage multiple social networks, schedule messages and tweets, track brand mentions, analyze social media traffic, and more. Some brands using Hootsuite include PepsiCo, Sony Music, CBS, and Virgin Mobile.

TWEETDECK

https://tweetdeck.twitter.com

Similar to Hootsuite, TweetDeck gives you the ability to monitor and schedule tweets, get alerts to keep up with emerging information, build custom timelines, filter searches, and more.

SOCIALBRO

www.socialbro.com

Beyond other sites, SocialBro shows you how to most effectively interact with your customers by analyzing your audience. It can show you the best time to tweet, how to identify your influencers and supporters, and how to understand your Twitter community. This site also shows insights and data on your Twitter account and gives you efficient follow/unfollow tools and campaign creation tools.

CISION

http://us.cision.com

Communicators look to sites like Cision to find media information. Cision is a great place to find leads for writing, but it also allows you to connect with people and audiences around the world, understand public perception, respond to crisis, and analyze media results and coverage from a global media community.

AGILITY BY PR NEWSWIRE
https://agility.prnewswire.com
Agility is a program by PR Newswire that allows users to monitor trending topics on the web, target the media, distribute news to large audiences, and report on activity.

VOCUS
www.vocus.com
Vocus is marketing software that enables companies to acquire and retain customers. The PR Suite gives you the ability to connect with journalists and bloggers, send news releases, monitor news, reach influencers, and measure results. The Marketing Suite lets you create online marketing campaigns, lead customers to landing pages, and measure results through analytics reports.

Customer Engagement Resources

BUSINESS 2 COMMUNITY
www.business2community.com
Business 2 Community is an online community focused on sharing the latest news surrounding marketing, branding, social engagement, and more. Bloggers provide a view of the business landscape based on industry news, trends, and real-life experiences.

ENGAGE CUSTOMER
www.engagecustomer.com
This site shows how customer and employee engagement can drive performance and profitability through articles on social media, customer interaction, engagement, and more.

KLOUT
www.klout.com
This site lets you identify your audience with insights and engage influencers with perks and ads. It also allows you to measure your influence and share and create content.

INDEX

We Have
EVERYTHING®
on Anything!

With more than 19 million copies sold, the Everything® series has become one of America's favorite resources for solving problems, learning new skills, and organizing lives. Our brand is not only recognizable—it's also welcomed.

The series is a hand-in-hand partner for people who are ready to tackle new subjects—like you!

For more information on the Everything® series, please visit *www.adamsmedia.com*.

The Everything® list spans a wide range of subjects, with more than 500 titles covering 25 different categories:

Business	History	Reference
Careers	Home Improvement	Religion
Children's Storybooks	Everything Kids	Self-Help
Computers	Languages	Sports & Fitness
Cooking	Music	Travel
Crafts and Hobbies	New Age	Wedding
Education/Schools	Parenting	Writing
Games and Puzzles	Personal Finance	
Health	Pets	